# ETHICAL NATURALISM AND THE MODERN WORLD-VIEW

# ETHICAL NATURALISM
# AND THE
# MODERN WORLD-VIEW

BY

E. M. ADAMS

GREENWOOD PRESS, PUBLISHERS
WESTPORT, CONNECTICUT

*The Library of Congress has catalogued this publication as follows:*

**Library of Congress Cataloging in Publication Data**

Adams, Elie Maynard, 1919-
   Ethical naturalism and the modern world-view.

   Reprint of the ed. published by the University of
North Carolina Press, Chapel Hill.
   Bibliography: p.
   1. Ethics. 2. Naturalism. I. Title.
[BJ37.A3 1973]       170       73-3019
ISBN 0-8371-6820-1

Originally published in 1960
by The University of North Carolina Press, Chapel Hill

Reprinted with the permission
of The University of North Carolina Press

First Greenwood Reprinting 1973

Library of Congress Catalogue Card Number 73-3019

ISBN 0-8371-6820-1

Printed in the United States of America

To my mother and father

B. C. A.—W. H. A.

# PREFACE

Ethical discourse is a species of value-talk, and many of its problems are shared by the genus. This is true of the problem of naturalism, which occurs not only in the philosophy of ethics but in the philosophy of value in general. Then why not deal with it in terms of value-language as such? In the first place, I am interested in ethics itself; but even if my concern were simply the problem without regard to where it appears, ethics would be of primary interest since the problem is most acute there. Naturalists find ethics the most recalcitrant value-field, and it provides them their severest test. Some who hold to naturalism in other value-areas are nonnaturalists in ethics. Some who profess or are usually believed to be naturalistic all the way unwittingly smuggle in nonnaturalism here. Also, it may well be that ethics in a way embraces all values of whatever description. Since the problem of naturalism is both general and specific, it will do no harm to talk about value- and ethical concepts interchangeably in some contexts. But there is no intent to say anything in this book about aesthetic and other kinds of nonmoral value-concepts other than what may be true of them generically as value-concepts. This is primarily a study in the philosophy of ethics but with a concern for general value-theory.

I use the term 'ethical naturalism' in a much broader sense than that usually found in the literature. As it is used in this study, it embraces not only that which is usually so designated, which is here referred to as *classical ethical naturalism,* but also the emotive theory and certain versions of the "good-reasons" position, which I call 'logical naturalism.' The justification of this extension of the term, as I argue in Chapter I, lies in a fuller and deeper understanding of classical ethical naturalism which reveals its relationship to metaphysical naturalism. Much of philosophy is done, especially in our own age, in a somewhat piecemeal fashion without much self-understanding and self-criticism of its own basic commitments. Consequently, conclusions are often reached about limited problems without an awareness of a larger framework that is assumed or taken for granted. Yet the assumed framework shapes and determines the specific conclusions. I contend that this has been true of much recent ethical theory. On fundamental issues—at the level at which classical ethical naturalism is related to metaphysical naturalism and the term acquires significance—the classical naturalist, the emotivist, and the good-reasons ethicist are in fundamental agreement. They are engaged, although somewhat unconsciously, I believe, in showing that value-language and the experience it expresses have no unique ontological significance distinct from that of the language of modern science or its common-sense counterpart. This is part, I contend, of the general program of metaphysical naturalism, which argues that reality as experienced by man is as it is shown to be by the categorial structure of the language of science. These several ethical theories differ only in the ways in which they attempt to carry out the program. The classical naturalist attempts to show that value-language is of no unique ontological significance by showing that whatever is sayable in value-language is sayable in the language of science. This he attempts to do by "naturalistic" definition of value-terms. The emotivist attempts to show the same thing by arguing that value-sentences as such actually say nothing and thus cannot have any ontological significance whatever. Their uniqueness lies in their pragmatic function of expressing and evoking feelings and attitudes. The good-reasons or logical ethicist contends that the only thing unique about ethical discourse is not in what is said but in a peculiar kind of argument or logical relation, which, however, is of no ontological significance. Since all three seem to be engaged in what is basically the same enterprise, I feel justified in considering all of them ethical naturalists. Their differences amount to only a family squabble.

One contribution I hope that this work makes is just this deeper and fuller understanding of the nature and significance of these several forms of ethical naturalism. This alone, I think, would justify my labors. But I hope for more. The plan of the book is to try each of these forms of ethical naturalism to see if any can withstand the fire of criticism. Although I began the study with the conviction that some form or other of ethical naturalism could be made tenable, after ten years of struggle with the problems involved I have become convinced that the basic program itself, not merely certain ways of carrying it out, is untenable. This I hope is a second contribution. But I like to think that the most important thing I have achieved is a somewhat novel but yet tenable theory of value, according to which value-requiredness is a unique categorial feature of reality known to us through our affective-conative experiences, which I contend are cognitive in nature. If we are to formulate an adequate philosophy of reality, we must take account of its categorial features as revealed in all dimensions of human experience. Metaphysical naturalism (and thus ethical naturalism as well) is wrong, I argue, precisely because it counts only our sensory experiences and thought confirmable in terms of them as cognitive. So, lastly, I hope this study has made some contribution to a more adequate general epistemological and metaphysical view.

The extent of my intellectual indebtedness is unmeasurable. My ideas have taken shape under the impact of the writings of philosophers of the present and the past and the discussions of my teachers, colleagues, and students. Among these there are two I am indebted to above all others: my former teacher, Ralph Barton Perry, and my present colleague, Everett W. Hall.

I am obligated to several who have made a rather special contribution to this work. L. O. Kattsoff and W. H. Poteat, by assuming extra teaching responsibilities, made it possible for me to have a reduced teaching load in the fall of 1956 and, therefore, to concentrate on this work. Everett W. Hall, William G. Toland, and Maurice Natanson have read the manuscript, either in whole or in part, and have made many valuable criticisms. Mrs. Doris Calhoun, Mrs. Martha Crevar, and Mrs. Shelley Howard have provided expert secretarial assistance.

Also, I wish to acknowledge my debt to *Mind, The Philosophical Quarterly, Philosophical Studies, Journal of Philosophy,* and *Philosophy and Phenomenological Research* for permission to use material that first appeared in these journals in article form and to the publishers and authors who have kindly given permission to quote from their materials.

Publication of this book has been made possible by a grant from the University of North Carolina Research Council and by a grant of the Ford Foundation under its program for assisting American university presses in the publication of works in the humanities and the social sciences.

E. M. Adams

Chapel Hill, N.C.

# CONTENTS

# ETHICAL NATURALISM AND THE MODERN WORLD-VIEW

# CHAPTER I

# THE PROBLEM OF ETHICAL
# NATURALISM

1.1 *Morality, ethics, philosophy of ethics*

The clear delineation of what constitutes a philosophical problem and how it differs from those of other disciplines has been a tortuous and uncertain process. However it seems fairly well settled, to some at least, that this much can be said: philosophical problems are meta-problems. They are about our thought and talk about other problems. The philosophy of science, for example, is not about the physical world in the way in which science is. It does not do science. It is about science. In like manner, philosophy of ethics is about ethics but it is not itself ethics. Just as the philosophy of science does not formulate and does not verify scientific statements, philosophy of ethics does not formulate and does not attempt to substantiate any ethical judgments.

This seems simple enough. However, in the postwar period, although it has been readily allowed (in some quarters at least) that moral philosophy is a meta-discipline, there is disagreement concerning what it is about. Hampshire, in an article that heralded a new approach, charges much of moral philosophy with mistakenly studying the problems of the moral critic rather than those of the moral agent. "If one reads the Nichomachean Ethics after reading the works of (for example) Professor G. E. Moore or Sir David Ross or Professor Stevenson," he writes, "one has the impression of confronting a wholly different subject. The first point of difference can be tentatively expressed by saying that Aristotle is almost entirely concerned to analyze the problems of the moral *agent,* while most contemporary moral philosophers seem to be primarily concerned to analyze the problems of the moral *judge* or critic. . . . The difference between these two approaches to the problems of moral philosophy emerges most clearly from the analogy between aesthetics and ethics. . . . For Aristotle (as for Plato) the aesthetic analogy which illuminates the problem of moral philosophy is the analogy between the artist or craftsman's characteristic procedures in designing and executing his work and the similar, but also different, procedures which we all use in designing and executing practical policies in ordinary life. For contemporary moral philosophers, largely preoccupied with elucidating sentences which express moral praise or blame (moral 'judgments' in the sense in which a judge gives judgments), the relevant analogy is between sentences expressing moral praise or condemnation and sentences expressing aesthetic praise or condemnation. . . . Leaving aside the analogy, the issue is—Is the answer to the question 'what are the distinguishing characteristics of sentences expressing moral praise or blame?' necessarily the same as the answer to the question 'what are the distinguishing characteristics of moral problems as they present themselves to us as practical agents?'? . . . My thesis," he continues, "is that the answer to the second question must contain the answer to the first, but that, if one tries to answer the first question without approaching it as part of the second, the answer will tend to be, not only incomplete, but positively misleading; and that the now most widely accepted philosophical interpretations of moral judgments, their logical status and peculiarities, are radically misleading for this reason. They purport to be logical characterizations of moral judgments and of the distinguishing features of moral arguments, but in these characterizations the *primary* use of moral judgments (= decisions) is largely or even entirely ignored."[1] And so he says, "An informative treatise on ethics—or on the ethics of a particular society or person—would contain an accumulation of examples selected to illustrate the kind of decisions which are said to be right in various circumstances, and the reasons given and the arguments used in concluding that they are right. An uninformative treatise on ethics consists of specimens of moral sentences, separated from actual or imaginable contexts of arguments about particular practical problems, and treated as texts for the definition of moral terms." He says also, "The type of analysis which consists in defining, or finding synonyms for the moral terms of a particular language cannot illuminate the nature of moral decisions or practical problems; it is no more than local dictionary-making, or the elimination of redundant terms, which is useful only as preliminary to the study of typical moral arguments."[2]

I find little, if any, real difference between the agent's and the critic's use of moral language in a practical situation. The agent is himself a critic. He proposes to himself a possible course of action and then appraises it morally. He asks himself such questions as "if I should do so-and-so, would it be right; would it be what I ought to do in this situation?" Also, the critic of another in a practical situation is attempting directly to influence behavior by his moral judgment. The important distinction, it seems to me, lies between the use of moral language in a practical situation, whether by the critic or agent (for the agent is a critic and the critic is an agent if the situation is practical), and its use in a somewhat detached, academic atmosphere to appraise particular actions (such as, was it right for Brutus to stab Caesar?) or general kinds of doings (such as, is racial segregation of a certain type wrong?). One might be in a quandary about the latter kind of thing and be moved to reflect upon it in an attempt to reach a settled opinion on the matter when com-

1. Stuart Hampshire, "Fallacies in Moral Philosophy," *Mind*, N.S., LVIII, No. 232 (Oct., 1949), 466-69.
2. *Ibid.*, p. 481.

pletely divorced from a practical situation. It seems quite possible for one to have curiosity about such a matter in the same manner in which one has scientific curiosity about something, without being moved by some immediate practical concern. Reflection of this kind might be called 'ethics' to distinguish it from moral inquiry in a practical situation, which we might call 'morality.'

The assumption is that there is a three-way distinction between morality, ethics, and the philosophy of ethics in a way somewhat parallel to the distinction between engineering, science, and the philosophy of science. The engineer is the person who primarily takes descriptive-explanatory knowledge, whether it is from what we call common-sense knowledge (that acquired in the general process of staying alive by reflective problem-solving) or from the most advanced sciences, and puts it to work in the process of using and controlling the environment for human purposes. Science as a systematic discipline was preceded by the hit-or-miss, trial-and-error method of common sense that produced a certain amount of understanding of things. This may be thought of as the early stages of science itself in that it produces a descriptive-explanatory account of things, however inadequate and restricted it may be. The rudimentary engineering that put this bit to work in man's behalf produced more understanding. So science, as a systematic discipline, had a working basis when it appeared on the scene. And in this area the old adage that nothing succeeds like success is certainly true. When science works hand in hand with technology, each in turn advancing the other, knowledge seems to make great strides forward. But the relationship to be pointed up between science and engineering is that the engineer takes the findings of science and puts them to use in man's practical endeavor of adjusting to and controlling his environment. The philosophy of science (the term 'science' is used to include its commonsensical childhood) is a study of science itself, not its subject-matter. It is meta-science, a study of the scientific conceptual scheme. The specific nature of this will be discussed in some detail later (1.4).

The parallel intended is that morality is like engineering in that it is the use of moral wisdom or precepts, whether acquired at the common-sense or a more systematic level of ethical inquiry, in the process of deliberating, deciding, counselling, appraising, criticizing, and the like. Although there is moral "knowledge" or wisdom to be used, it is largely commonsensical. Man has not developed a systematic discipline for furthering wisdom in the manner of science. There is no recognized area of formal study that investigates such phenomena as the acts of persons and institutions in terms of an ethical conceptual scheme and expresses its findings in ethical propositions ('ought'-sentences and sentences with ethical predicates like 'right,' 'wrong,' 'good,' 'bad'). This would be ethics proper, as the term is here used. It would be the analogue of science. It may be that no such discipline is needed or possible. But there is some reflective thought in this area that goes beyond the common-sense method. In a broad sense we may use 'ethics' to indicate both the common-sense process and this reflective procedure, whether fully systematic or not, that yields moral wisdom. Ethics, then, serves morality in the way in which science serves engineering. But of course there has not been the separation of the two as in the case of advanced science and engineering. And it may be that the divorce is not possible. Science can operate separately from engineering because it is experimental. It does not have to wait for the engineer to put its theories to the test. In the area of morals, the ethicist has to wait for the most part upon morality for any "empirical" testing. Nonetheless the distinction can be made. And there is a body of moral precepts produced by common sense and somewhat systematic reflective observation of the human situation, which may be thought of as in a way parallel with the body of scientific knowledge that is available to the engineer, there to be used by the moral agent or critic in dealing with particular situations.

The problem is whether moral philosophy is meta-ethics or meta-morality. We might interpret Hampshire's indictment of

modern moral philosophy as charging it with having been largely philosophy of ethics rather than philosophy of morality. I
wish to defend the more traditional view that moral philosophy
is justified in looking primarily to the use of moral language by
the ethicist. Hampshire and others of his persuasion are against
this kind of moral philosophy because they think of it as uninformative, trivial, local dictionary-making which ignores the primary use of moral discourse. This judgment, I submit, is a
consequence of their having a different conception of the objective of moral philosophy. They are concerned with elucidating
the logical characteristics of moral judgments and the distinguishing features of moral arguments; or, as Toulmin would say, their
purpose in doing philosophy is to make a language map, showing
the different kinds of words and sentences according to their uses.
What is needed in moral philosophy, according to him, is a "descriptive account of our ethical concepts—some device for bringing out the relation between the manner in which ethical sentences are used and the manners in which others are used—so as
to give their place on the language-map."[3] The contemporary
linguistic analyst often seems to think of his language map-mak-
ing as the objective of doing philosophy, but Hampshire thinks
of it as a means of elucidating the "distinguishing characteristics
of moral problems as they present themselves to us as practical
agents" and Toulmin says "It will be from such a description,
or 'language-map', . . . that we shall obtain the understanding
that we seek—whether of the generality of ethical judgments,
their expressive and theoretical force, the function and importance
of moral principles, the place of the moralist, or the principles
of the open 'society'; or, most important, what it is that makes
an ethical argument a valid argument, and what things are *good
reasons* for ethical judgments."[4]

    In terms of their objective, the semantic approach of much of

---

3. S. E. Toulmin, *An Examination of the Place of Reason in Ethics* (Cambridge, Eng.: University Press, 1950), pp. 194-95.
    4. *Ibid.*, p. 195.

the philosophy of ethics seems misguided and unfruitful. The whole school of contemporary linguistic analysis attacks traditional philosophy in general for its one-sided view of language, for its primary concern with declarative sentences and terms with semantic significance. This, I think, is due to the fact that traditional philosophers have been concerned with language only insofar as it is related to their purpose of understanding reality as experienced by us, whereas many contemporary analysts are concerned with understanding language as such without regard to its ontological significance. If the ultimate objective of philosophical analysis of moral discourse is to disclose its ontological significance, it may be that the traditional semantic approach is the proper and most fruitful way of going about it. Much of the descriptive detail of the use of moral terms by the moral agent or engineer may be superfluous and may get in the way. Our concern should be to get at the semantic dimension of moral discourse and insofar as possible consider it in abstraction from its pragmatic aspects. The nonsemantic dimensions, including both the syntactical and pragmatic (in Charles Morris' sense), should be considered only as they have a bearing upon what moral discourse says or shows about the categorial features of reality. And it is moral language as employed by the ethicist rather than by the moralist that may best be studied for this purpose, for the use that he makes of it is more restricted to the use that is relevant for disclosing its ontological significance; just as the philosopher can ignore the engineer's use of descriptive-explanatory language because it appears in a purer form (with fewer extraneous uses mixed in) in the talk of the scientist. But insofar as ethics and morality are not as distinct as science and engineering, we cannot ignore the moralist's use of ethical language to the same extent that we can ignore the engineer's use in analyzing the language of science. Nevertheless, it is the philosophy of ethics rather than the philosophy of morality, to the extent that the two can be distinguished, that is more likely to be fruitful in getting at the ontological significance of moral language. The nature of philosophy in general and of philosophy of ethics in particular will be discussed in more detail later (1.3) and also the views of Hampshire, Toulmin, and others like them (4.1-4). Our concern here is simply to mark the distinction between morality, ethics, and philosophy of ethics.

The problem of naturalism is a problem for neither morality nor ethics but for philosophy of ethics.

## 1.2 *Ethical naturalism*

The term 'naturalism,' as it is used in philosophical discourse about ethics, is not so univocal and clear that we can proceed without first specifying how it shall be used. There are at least three distinct meanings of it to be found in the literature.

1. There is G. E. Moore's use, according to which naturalism consists of defining 'good' or other value-concepts in terms of natural concepts or, as he would put it, identifying *good* with some *natural* object or property.[5] Moore has struggled to get at just what he means by 'natural' when applied to properties. When speaking of objects he says it means "something of which the existence is admittedly an object of experience."[6] Again, he says, "If we consider whether any object is of such a nature that it may be said to exist now, to have existed, or to be about to exist, then we may know that that object is a natural object, and that nothing of which this is not true, is a natural object."[7] But natural properties are not simply the properties of natural objects, according to his use, for he wants to say that some natural objects are good, that is, according to his theory, that they have a nonnatural property. In *Principia Ethica* his test of whether a property was natural or not also concerned its existence in time. "Can we imagine 'good' as existing *by itself* in time," he asks, "and not merely as a property of some natural object? For myself, I cannot so imagine it, whereas with the greater number of properties of objects—those which I call the natural properties—

5. *Principia Ethica* (Cambridge, Eng.: University Press, 1903), pp. 38-39.
6. *Ibid.*, p. 38.
7. *Ibid.*, p. 40.

their existence does seem to me to be independent of the existence of those objects. They are, in fact, rather parts of which the object is made up than mere predicates which attach to it. If they were all taken away, no object would be left, not even a bare substance: for they are in themselves substantial and give to the object all the substance that it has. But this is not so with good."[8] Later he says, "This suggestion which I made in *Principia* seems to me now to be utterly silly and preposterous."[9] He then goes on to say that there are two accounts of the distinction between natural and nonnatural properties which may be true: (1) the one which he gave in *Philosophical Studies* (p. 274), according to which a property is natural if and only if, in ascribing it to a natural object, one describes (in one particular sense) that object to some extent; it is nonnatural if and only if, in ascribing it to an object, one does not describe (in this one particular sense) it at all. However, he says that he is unable to specify just what that "one particular sense" of 'describe' is. (2) C. D. Broad's criterion to the effect that a natural property is one "which (a) we become aware of by inspecting our sense-data or introspecting our experiences, or (b) is definable wholly in terms of the former kind together with the notions of cause and substance."[10] And a nonnatural property is said to be one of which this is not true.

I think that what Moore is getting at is that a natural property is one that would or might be taken note of or have a role in a scientific (a descriptive-explanatory) account of things. A. C. Ewing takes this position. He says that a naturalistic view in ethics is "one which, while admitting that ethical propositions are sometimes true, analyses ethical concepts solely in terms of the concepts of a natural science."[11] C. D. Broad says that "if natu-

8. *Ibid.*, p. 41.

9. "A Reply to My Critics," in *The Philosophy of G. E. Moore,* ed. Paul Arthur Schilpp (New York: Tudor Publishing Co., 1942), pp. 581-82.

10. "Moore's Ethical Doctrines," *ibid.*, p. 62.

11. *The Definition of the Good* (New York: The Macmillan Company, 1947), p. 36.

ralism be true, ethics is not an autonomous science [discipline]; it is a department or an application of one or more of the natural or historical sciences."[12] Indeed Moore himself says that, according to naturalism, "ethics is an empirical or positive science: its conclusions could be all established by means of empirical observation and induction."[13] Again, he says, "I have appropriated the name Naturalism to a particular method of approaching ethics—a method which, strictly understood, is inconsistent with the possibility of any ethics whatsoever. This method consists in substituting for 'good' some one property of a natural object or of a collection of natural objects; and in thus replacing ethics by some one of the natural sciences."[14]

What Moore, Broad, and Ewing are getting at, I think, is that ethical naturalism is part of the general naturalistic view that the empirical, descriptive-explanatory conceptual scheme of common sense and science is fully adequate to categorize all dimensions of human experience and when fully understood gives us the "correct" view of the nature of reality (or at least as it is experienced by man). The program of naturalism in ethics, then, is to show that the language of ethics has no distinctive ontological significance by expressing the semantic meaning of ethical words in terms of the concepts of the scientific framework of thought. In this way what is perhaps the most formidable hurdle for the naturalistic world-view (the picture of reality embedded in the language of science) is overcome. Moral experience is shown to reveal no entities or traits of reality not included in or shown by an empirical descriptive-explanatory account.

2. There is the use that identifies naturalism in ethics with those theories that commit what G. E. Moore called 'the naturalistic fallacy.'[15] Although it is not too clear just what the fal-

12. "Some of the Main Problems of Ethics," *Philosophy*, XXI, No. 79 (July, 1946), 103.
13. *Principia Ethica*, p. 39.
14. *Ibid.*, p. 40.
15. See R. M. Hare, *The Language of Morals* (Oxford: Clarendon Press, 1951), pp. 81-82.

laciousness consists of, a point whose discussion will be deferred to the next chapter, the process concerned is clearly that of defining value-concepts in terms of nonvalue-concepts, whether scientific, metaphysical, or what have you. He himself recognized two types of theories that commit it, namely, "naturalistic" theories in the sense of (1) above and what he called 'metaphysical' theories (he includes here the views of the Stoics, Spinoza, Kant, and the Hegelians), which identify value with "an object which is only inferred to exist in a supersensible real world."[16] The matter would have been clearer if he had not called the alleged fallacy 'naturalistic,' for some have come to conceive of naturalism in ethics in terms of it, because of its unfortunate name.

3. There is the use of 'naturalism' to designate those theories that deny that there are values in the world in an irreducible or unexplainable-away sense.[17] This might seem to be simply a restatement of (2) in the material made of speech, but this is not quite so. The difference lies in the phrase 'unexplainable-away.' Naturalism in the sense of (2) denies that there are values in an irreducible sense. Reductionism in the form of *definition* of value-concepts in terms of nonvalue-concepts is essential to it. Consequently emotive and commendatory (e.g., R. M. Hare's) theories are not "naturalistic," but in the sense under consideration, namely (3), they are clearly naturalistic because they deny that there are values *in an unexplainable-away* sense. However, (3) does embrace under "naturalism" alternative theories similar to (2). Within the framework of (3), one might hold either (a) that there are no values in the world that are not reducible or explainable-away in terms of the naturalistic (the empirical, descriptive-explanatory) conceptual scheme of things; or (b) one might hold that even if there are values which are not reducible or explainable-away in the manner of (a), there are no

16. *Principia Ethica*, pp. 38-39.
17. See Everett W. Hall, "Practical Reason(s) and the Deadlock in Ethics," *Mind*, N.S., LXIV, No. 255 (July, 1955), 319 ff.

values in the world that are not reducible or explainable-away in terms of some nonnaturalistic conceptual scheme, e.g., theological or "metaphysical" in Moore's sense. These alternatives coincide with the "naturalistic" and "metaphysical" theories that Moore recognized as committing his naturalistic fallacy, except for the fact that they are broad enough to embrace the noncognitive (the emotive and commendatory) theories as well and that therefore they need not commit the fallacy as he formulated it.

It seems inappropriate and also confusing to use 'naturalism' in the sense of either (2) or (3). Both pervert a term with a well-established use in philosophy and are likely to muddy the issues to the point that we lose sight of some important matters, especially the relation of ethical to ontological naturalism. Sense (1) was formulated at the beginning of the century. There have been unforeseen developments since then, especially the appearance of the emotive and commendatory theories, which render it obsolete in terms of its own intent. I think that it will be allowed on almost all sides that theories were called 'naturalistic' by Moore not so much because they *defined* value-concepts in terms of naturalistic concepts but because they denied that there are values as such, in a *sui generis* sense, over and above natural objects. It was only by naturalistic definition that he thought, in 1903, that this denial could be made at all plausible. But now we know of other ways, e.g., the emotive, commendatory, and perhaps other theories. Therefore, the concept of naturalistic ethics needs reformulation.

4. The sense in which I shall use it is simply (1) amended to account for later developments, and we find it so amended as alternative (a) under (3). A naturalistic ethical theory, as the term is used in this work, is one that holds that there are no values in the world that are not reducible to or explainable away in terms of the naturalistic conceptual scheme of things. If one should be forced to reject naturalism in this sense, there would still be the problem of whether there were values in an irreducible or unexplainable-away sense, provided that one recognized some

nonvalue, nonnaturalistic conceptual scheme as a possibility. Otherwise one would have to recognize values as entities in the world.

The problem of naturalism in ethics, then, as I conceive it, is whether there are values in the world in a sense that renders inadequate the naturalistic world-view, the picture of reality embodied in our scientific framework of thought. Naturalistic ethics claims that there are not; it attempts to show that there are not by defining value-concepts in terms of descriptive-explanatory concepts or by accounting for the use of value-words in such a way that they do not commit us to there being values in the world in the sense that the nonnaturalist claims.

### 1.3 The problem of what there is

The problem of naturalism in ethics then is part of the central philosophical problem of *what there is in the world*. Although recently many philosophers seem to have forsaken this problem for a descriptive account of how language functions or is used, I agree with G. E. Moore that "the most important and interesting thing which philosophers have tried to do is no less than—to give a general description of the *whole* of the Universe, mentioning all the most important kinds of things which we know to be in it, considering how far it is likely that there are in it important kinds of things which we do not absolutely *know* to be in it, and also considering the most important ways in which these various kinds of things are related to one another."[18]  The study of language can be immensely helpful and linguistic analysis a powerful technique in this enterprise, but when "philosophy" becomes the study of language as an end in itself, it has become something different from what it has been traditionally.

The general description of the whole of the universe which Moore speaks of is likely to be misleading. If we are to understand the problem of naturalism in ethics, we must first under-

18. *Some Main Problems of Philosophy* (New York: The Macmillan Company, 1953), p. 1.

stand the kind of picture of reality with which philosophy is concerned and especially the philosophical problem about what there is and how it is to be approached. It is not my intent to say what the "real" nature of philosophy is. I am willing to admit that there may be quite different things that bear the name. Yet I do think that the conception of it which I shall expound conforms fairly well with much of what philosophers have been doing through the centuries, if not with what they have said they were doing. But I shall not argue for the view here expressed. My primary concern is to let the reader know what I am doing. If he does not share, or at least understand, the problem in the manner in which I conceive it, what I have to say will not be intelligible. While I am concerned with one problem, he will be thinking of another, which is highly likely in philosophical discussion even when every precaution is taken.

The word 'philosophy,' as I shall use it, has two distinct meanings, which, when the occasion demands, I shall distinguish by subscripts. In ordinary usage, we speak of the philosophy of this or that—the philosophy of big business, the president's philosophy of the presidency, the philosophy of the communists, and so on. Although in this sense the term is not very precise, it has a meaning which is fairly obvious. It refers to the general framework of ideas and attitudes in terms of which problems are formulated, debated, and solved. Such a framework, for the most part, is simply taken for granted and used. It provides the conceptual equipment and the commitments necessary to get started on intellectual and practical problems. It makes possible the identification of a subject-matter or problem-area, the formulation of the problem, the framing of possible solutions, and the selection of the one deemed satisfactory. In other words, one's framework in this sense consists of what one brings to a problem and is not itself subject to being called into question or held in suspect in thinking about the matter and trying to solve it. In this sense, everyone has a philosophy, whether or not one is aware of the fact. I shall indicate this sense of the term by 'philosophy₁.'

We often find two people or groups trying to work on the same problem but unable to reach an agreement, whether intellectual or practical, because they are operating with different philosophies. Consider a naturalistic scientist and a Christian thinker of the 1880's investigating the question of biological evolution, or a communist and an American capitalist trying to reach an agreement about some political or economic issue. Their differences could not be resolved by any amount of investigation and consideration of the "facts" of the case, for their differences would lie in their frameworks of thought and attitude.

Philosophy as a discipline, which I shall designate by 'philosophy₂' (when it is necessary to distinguish it from philosophy₁), takes a philosophy₁ as its subject-matter and attempts to formulate, clarify, criticize, evaluate, and often reconstruct it. Philosophical theories are the product of doing philosophy in this sense. Of course philosophy₂, as a formal discipline, does not concern itself with all philosophies₁. No professional philosopher as such would be likely to concern himself with the philosophy₁ of an individual like the president, of General Motors, or of the New Deal. But a biographer or historian might. It is not uncommon to find articles on "The American Philosophy," "The Philosophy of Big Business," and so forth. Often philosophies₁ of this kind are largely a set of general beliefs or attitudes that may differ from less general ones only in their greater generality and their privileged position as functionally a priori (as part of the unquestioned framework). It may be that they can be subjected to testing in a perfectly straightforward manner like ordinary beliefs and attitudes in terms of a still more basic framework. The professional philosopher is usually after bigger game. He may be concerned with the philosophy₁ of Christianity, of democratic liberalism, of communism, of natural science, of mathematics, and the like. But even here he is restricted. The most general and all inclusive framework or philosophy₁ that one operates with is embedded in one's natural language, in its categorial terms and its basic structure. It consists of the most general kinds of entities the language provides one with the linguistic means of talking about (physical objects, minds, classes, properties, relations, events, facts, values, meanings, truths, etc.) and the most general kinds of things it provides a means of saying about them (that they exist, are possible, contingent, necessary, or ought to-be; that they are related in certain general ways —temporally, spatially, causally, quantitatively, logically, semantically, and so forth; and that they can be known and evaluated in certain general ways).

The categorial features of a natural language consist of the basic distinctions that the people of one's culture and their ancestors have noted and found important in their long struggle to come to grips with and to adjust to reality. They consist of the basic ways in which people have come to delineate the primitive, uncategorized stuff of experience (virgin reality) to give us the world-order of our mature experience. "The primitive, uncategorized stuff of experience" is not to be thought of as a given. We are never aware of it as such. The stuff that is categorized in our experience is only logically primitive. Becoming aware of it involves noting distinctions and thereby categorizing in terms of them. Even James's "buzzing confusion" of the infant involves making distinctions, for there can be no confusion where no distinctions are noted. Awareness, by its very nature, is of something; and the something, in order to be *something,* has to be delineated.

The first task of philosophy₂ is an analytic one, regardless of the level of the philosophy₁ with which it is' concerned. The philosopher, by analysis of what is said or decided about particular issues, must unearth and explore what is taken for granted and must give it formulation in as clear and precise a manner as possible; or, if it is so basic that it defies formulation, he must throw what light is possible upon the matter by whatever means available. It is from what is unearthed at the basic level of our framework of thought that we form a general "description" of the world as experienced by us.

There are several ways in which language reveals our categorial system. Since Aristotle recognized only two ways in which something could be introduced into language, namely, by an expression that can replace the 'S' or by one that can replace the 'P' in 'S is P' to yield a significant sentence, he and his scholastic disciples derived their list of categories of being from a classification of the linguistic expressions that could be values of the variables 'S' or 'P' in 'S is P.' It was recognized that some things, in fact many things, could be introduced into language by values of either 'S' or 'P,' but that some things could occur in language only as what was meant by a value of 'S.' The latter were given a privileged position. They are the primary substances that *are* or exist in their own right, and everything else *is* only in a secondary sense, as some kind of a feature or modification of a primary substance. Kant looked to another feature of language, the logical structure of statements, in deriving his set of categories. The fact that statements are universal, particular, or singular, affirmative, negative, or what he called 'infinite,' categorical, hypothetical, or disjunctive, and problematic, assertoric, or apodeictic is what is significant about them for his categorial analysis. Although his specific classification of statements according to logical structure and the somewhat mysterious ways in which he derived categories cannot be justified, his recognition of the significance of this feature of language for categorical analysis is an important step in the history of philosophy. However, his classification is not a replacement for the Aristotelian technique but a supplement. In an attempt to unearth the picture of reality embedded in a language, we must look to the ways in which entities may be introduced into language (after the Aristotelian manner), namely, as logical subject and predicate and also to the complex logical structure of language itself with regard to what it says or shows about experienced reality.

We cannot use either of these approaches uncritically. It has been argued powerfully by some that much of the logical structure of language is not of ontological significance. The contention of Russell's and Wittgenstein's doctrine of logical atomism is that only the logical structure of atomic propositions is of ontological importance, all the other being purely linguistic. All I wish to point up here is that logical structure is not to be taken uncritically as a guide to the structure of reality but that it may prove to be important in some respects.

Also, what is apparently introduced into language as something meant by a logical subject or predicate is not to be taken naïvely as part of the furniture of the world. There are a number of linguistic means by which things are introduced as something meant by logical subjects and predicates, namely the whole battery of denoting or referring techniques—names, pronouns, definite and indefinite descriptions, etc. Of course the most common device for introducing something by means of a predicate is by naming. When we say, 'The ball is red,' the color quality or attribute is named by 'red.' (The difference between 'red' and 'redness' is syntactical rather than semantic. The former is a predicate, the other a logical subject.) But we might introduce redness by a predicate in other ways. We might say, 'The ball is the color of the book,' 'The ball is a short-wave frequency color,' or 'The ball is some color or other.' But things are more frequently introduced into language in nonnaming ways by logical subjects. This is simply because there is not the need for naming as many of the things that occur in language most frequently as meant by a logical subject as there is for those that appear most frequently as meant by a logical predicate. All these devices for introducing entities into language are only apparent ontological indicators, for (1) we can seemingly talk about nonexistent or even imposible things, such as round squares, golden mountains, the kings of the United States, Pegasus, and ghosts; and (2) we can talk about nations, minds, gods, physical objects, and the like. But these facts do not settle the philosophical question about the existence of such entities.

The former is the problem of whether or not a term occurs designatively in a given context, whether or not it is used to designate something. Quine has proposed a test for determining the matter, namely, whether or not the sentence in which the term in question occurs may be existentially generalized.[19] For example, from the sentence 'Socrates is mortal' we may justifiably infer 'Something is mortal' or, in the idiom of the logician, '( x) x is mortal.' But from 'Pegasus can fly' we are not justified in inferring '(∃ x) x can fly,' for, as Quine says, "The idea behind such inference is that whatever is true of the object designated by a given substantive is true of something; and clearly the inference loses its justification when the substantive in question does not happen to designate."[20]

Although Quine arrived at his existential generalization device from a consideration of problems of type (1), that is, he formulated it to distinguish between apparent and genuine designative occurrences of terms, he generalizes it so that it applies to problems of type (2) or else he sees no problem in regard to (2) other than that of (1). He says, "The ontology to which one's use of language commits him comprises simply the objects that he treats as falling within the subject matter of his quantifiers, within the range of values of his variables."[21] Applying this formula to problems of type (2), he says, "There is certainly commitment to entities through discourse; for we are quite capable of saying in so many words that *there are* black swans, that *there is* a mountain more than 9,000 meters high, and that *there are* prime numbers above a hundred. Saying these things, we also say by implication that there are physical objects and abstract entities; for all black swans are physical objects and all

19. Willard V. Quine, "Notes on Existence and Necessity," *Journal of Philosophy*, XL, No. 5 (March 4, 1943), 113 ff.
20. *Ibid.*, p. 116.
21. *Ibid.*, p. 118.

the prime numbers above a hundred are abstract entities."[22] It was on a somewhat similar basis that Moore attempted to prove that there are physical objects with his famous hand-argument.[23] His point was that the statement 'This is a hand' (indicating his own raised hand) is true, and also 'All hands are physical objects' is true. Therefore 'this is a physical object' is true. And from this, Quine's existential generalization follows. So there are physical objects.

But this does not seem to be a way of settling the philosophical problem about what there is. When a philosopher asks, 'Are there physical objects? minds? abstract entities? values? and the like?' he already knows that our natural language provides us with the means of talking about such entities. He demonstrates that fact in formulating his question. He is not asking whether the terms that mean or refer to such entities may be values of quantified variables. This would be to ask whether the classes concerned have members. If his questions were of this type, he would find his answers by seeing a chair here and a table there; by encountering the mind of another, if not of himself, in such a way that provides him with ample grounds for saying truthfully sometimes, 'He has a keen mind' or 'His was the best mind I ever encountered'; by finding out that there is a prime number greater than 100; by discovering the values of matrimony; and the like. Philosophers who ask these questions must have something else in mind.

Carnap has attempted to distinguish two kinds of question of existence,[24] what he calls 'internal' and 'external' questions. The former concerns the existence of entities of a specified kind, a simple matter of whether a class has any members. This is what the philosophical question of existence was said not to be

22. "On Carnap's Views on Ontology," *Philosophical Studies*, II, No 5. (1951), 67.

23. "Proof of an External World," *British Academy Proceedings*, XXV (1939), 273-300.

24. Rudolf Carnap, "Empiricism, Semantics, and Ontology," *Revue internationale de philosophie*, IV, No. 11 (Jan., 1950), 20 ff.

in the preceding paragraph. An "external" question, according to Carnap, concerns "the existence or reality of the framework itself." This, he says, is not a theoretical question but one concerning the advisability of adopting the category or, as he says, the framework.

First of all, we must not think that an external question is simply a matter of whether a basic category like physical objects has members, whereas an internal question concerns a subclass like hands. There are both internal and external questions about both categories and subclasses. It so happens that philosophers are concerned with the external questions about categories. A scientist might very well raise an external existential question about a class of objects, which would take the form of whether it served the purposes of science to continue classifying things in terms of the class in question. Maybe a new way of classifying, a regrouping of things in terms of different features, would be more fruitful. A librarian might raise the external question about his own classificatory system and end by adopting an entirely new one. This kind of question is entirely different from the internal one, whether or not there are, for instance, books in certain classifications within a given classificatory system.

It seems to me, however, that where philosophy is concerned, there are at least two different kinds of question embraced under Carnap's external questions, or else a third kind that he has not considered. It makes no difference which way we interpret it. One, it seems to me, is central to analytic philosophy (philosophy as analysis of a given framework of thought); the other, to speculative philosophy (the construction or proposal of a new or modified categorial system). The first concerns whether a given category is basic. This is not a matter of whether it is a category or a subclass of a category but rather of whether it is reducible to some other in the sense that whatever is sayable in terms of it can be said in terms of another.

Quine's ontological indicator derived from his existential generalization-test of the designative occurrence of a term does not touch this problem. The formula was, it will be recalled, "The ontology to which one's use of language commits him comprises simply the *objects that he treats* as falling within the subject-matter of his quantifiers—within the range of values of his variables." One might very well treat minds, gods, physical objects, abstract entities, values, and the like as falling within the subject-matter of one's quantifiers, and yet these categories would be eliminatable in favor of others without restriction on sayable truths. Quine later presents a modification of his earlier formula that covers this matter, contrary to the version already quoted. He says, "We are convicted of a particular ontological presupposition if, and only if, the alleged presupposition *has to be reckoned* among the entities over which our variables range in order to render one of our affirmations true."[25] This is a matter of whether the apparent reference to such entities can be avoided by some form of paraphrase or translation. It is far removed from the existential generalization-test for the designative occurrence of a term. The latter shows that our language commits us to there being physical objects because we say that there are black swans and there are hands. But the former does not show any such thing from these facts. It might be possible, as the sense-datum philosophers have argued, that all statements about physical objects are translatable into sentences that are not about physical objects but about sense-data. If so, then my using language in a manner that treats physical objects as falling within the range of my quantifiers does not commit me to there being such entities.

The problem here is whether the category marks some distinction in reality that is fundamental or basic to the framework or whether it is a luxury or convenience that can be eliminated without altering experienced reality categorized in terms of the framework. Such criticism of categories has abounded in modern philosophy. Consider the attempts to show that the cate-

25. *From a Logical Point of View* (Cambridge, Mass.: Harvard University Press, 1953), p. 13; italics added here and above.

gories of physical objects, minds, nations, values, and the like are reducible to some other. It is a paring-down and tidying-up operation within the framework in order to see the basic structure of reality as delineated by it.

The second external question concerns evaluation and reconstruction of a basic categorial framework. This is the job of what has traditionally been called 'speculative philosophy.' The problem here is not whether the categories of a given framework mark distinctions that are in reality to be noted. That is a matter for analytic philosophy in determining whether the categories are basic. The present problem is whether categorizing in terms of the particular distinctions that are admittedly in reality is better than categorizing in terms of some others; whether the given categorial framework is the most fruitful possible for human purposes; and whether it is the best available for man in his attempts to come to grips with reality and to adjust to it in all dimensions of human experience.

The picture assumed in this discussion is that there is an ocean of reality with a structure of its own. Man experiences it in a number of ways: through his ordinary senses, feelings, and emotions, rational insight, religious experiences, and perhaps other ways. These experiences involve taking note of certain distinctions in the virgin reality and delineating it in terms of them. In this way our experience of reality and the conceptual framework embodied in our natural language grow together so that the categorial structure of our language reflects the categorial structure of experienced reality. Thus there is no question whether the categorial system unearthed by analytic philosophy is true of reality as experienced by us, except insofar as it is a question whether analytic philosophy$_2$ has correctly formulated the categorial framework embodied in our natural language or, what amounts to the same thing, the categorial framework of common-sense experience. Formulation of this categorial system gives us a general picture of reality as experienced by us, but it is quite different from the kind of information provided by a scientific theory. Science attempts to discover new truths about experienceable things, and therefore its theories are subject to control by what turns up in experience. Analytic philosophy is concerned with explicating and formulating what is built into experience itself. Aristotle thought of philosophy$_2$ as a discipline concerned with abstracting from experienced reality its basic structure. This we do, I think, but he was not aware of how it happens to be built into experienced reality. He made no distinction between experienced reality and reality. Kant thought that the categorial structure built into the world of experienced objects was grounded in the structure of the human mind as such. The view that I am suggesting is this: the categorial structure is a priori in regard to experienced reality, but its source is not simply the structure of the mind; it consists of distinctions in the ocean of reality itself that have been selected by the mind (no doubt largely because of its own peculiar structure and limitations) for delineating the real.

Although a correctly formulated categorial system of a natural language (or of common sense) is necessarily true of experienced reality for those operating within the framework, there is the problem of its evaluation in terms of its fruitfulness for man. This is a vague matter, and any evaluating attempt is likely to beg the question at issue. It is meaningless to say that such a framework is true of the ocean of reality itself, although the distinctions that it notes are there. It seems quite plausible to think that it might well be categorized in terms of other distinctions which might be noted by ourselves and especially by creatures quite different from us. If we were immensely smaller than we are or immensely larger, or had senses other than those we have, or lacked some we have, no doubt we would have noted distinctions differently and might well have chosen different ones for the basic categorizing ones. It seems reasonable to think that taking any of a variety of sets of distinctions as basic or categorial, we could have categorized the reality we have contact with in such a way that it would be intelligible. However, all such possibilities might not serve us equally well. We do find changes in this regard in philosophies₁, but usually they occur very gradually. Sometimes there are revolutions, however. Such a revolution occurred in the early modern period with the rise of modern science. Speculative philosophers attempt to do it deliberately, but usually in piecemeal fashion. They propose a change here and a change there. They necessarily have to repair the ship of common sense while at sea; they must have something to support them while they work.

If we think of the problem of ethical naturalism in terms of whether there are values in the world, especially ethical values, in a sense that makes the naturalistic conceptual scheme inadequate, we are likely to think of it as a speculative philosophical problem. But the problem is more correctly stated in this manner: have we in our common-sense experience noted a feature of reality and taken it up in our common-sense categorial system which the naturalistic categorial system ignores? Or is the alleged category of values not really basic (in the sense that whatever is sayable in terms of it is sayable in terms of naturalistic concepts)? Or is there no such category at all, and have we been misled in thinking that there is by misunderstanding the function of value-language? In short, is there a category of values in our common-sense conceptual scheme and, if so, is it basic or reducible? In this sense, the problem is primarily one for analytic philosophy, and it must be settled before the speculative aspect of it can be properly raised.

## 1.4 *Metaphysical naturalism*

It is important to consider the conceptual scheme which naturalism in the broader sense holds to be fully adequate for reality as it is experienced by man. Modern naturalism is by and large scientific naturalism. It looks to science, or its common-sense counterpart, for all genuine knowledge of reality. Hume expresses this temper of the modern mind in a dramatic manner when he says, "When we run over libraries, persuaded of these principles [his empiricism], what havoc must we make? If we take in our hand any volume of divinity or school metaphysics, for instance; let us ask, *Does it contain any abstract reasoning concerning quantity or number?* No. *Does it contain any experimental reasoning concerning matters of fact and existence?* No. Commit it then to the flames: for it can contain nothing but sophistry and illusion." So scientific inquiry is held to be the only reliable and fruitful form of discovering the truth about reality; and its categorial framework is assumed to cut reality at the joints and thereby to reflect its nature and structure. It is to the language of science and its common-sense counterpart, then, that philosophers must turn, according to the naturalist, in order to find the true categorial picture of reality as experienced by man.

We must not be misled, however, by the role of mathematics in science. To the naturalist it is only a tool or instrument to be used in science and is not itself a part of the study of reality. "Empiricism" (in the modern restricted sense) is one of the chief tenets of the naturalist's position. All knowledge of reality is via the external senses or introspection. What is not verifiable by data obtainable in either of these ways is not knowable; indeed, as the extremists would insist, it is not even thinkable. Meaning, or cognitive claims in general, not merely knowledge, is restricted to the empirical.

This is of considerable ontological significance. It leads to the conclusion that the *kinds* of "things" there are and the kinds of qualities and relations they have are restricted to the kinds of things mentionable and sayable in "empirically" (I use quotes to indicate the restricted sense in which it is used by modern naturalists) verifiable language. It takes only a little reflection to see that this makes for a rather austere and puritanical ontology. But of those things and features of them that it does allow, it holds, as Ernest Nagel says, that their "manifest plurality and variety . . . are an irreducible feature of the cosmos, not a deceptive appearance cloaking some more homogeneous 'ultimate reality' or transempirical substance, and that the sequential orders in which events occur or the manifold relations of dependence in which things exist are *contingent* connections, not the embodiments of a fixed and unified pattern of logically necessary links."[26]

Science is concerned not merely with description but also with explanation. Modern science is an empirical, descriptive-explanatory account of things. It attempts not only to say what a thing is and to describe it in detail but to account for its being as it is and not otherwise. The extent to which a "scientific" discipline is thought to have matured or to have developed into a full-fledged science is appraised in terms of the extent to which it is still merely descriptive or the extent to which it has become explanatory.

Modern science not only is different from its Greek and medieval predecessor in that it is "empirical" in a thoroughgoing way, but it also has a different conception of what constitutes an explanation. No doubt its empirical character has had a lot to do with this change. In fact, it may have required it. But regardless of the reason for the shift in what is considered an explanation, it is an important fact that bears upon our enterprise. One way of stating the difference is to say that Greek and medieval scientific explanations involved value-considerations, whereas modern science is value-free. In explaining why something was as it was and not otherwise, the Greek and medieval scientists attempted to show that it was best that way or that that was how it ought to be. But the good and the bad, the right and the wrong, the "ought" and the "ought-not" of things, are ignored by the modern scientist in giving a descriptive-explanatory account of an occurrence or state of affairs, whether it concerns the orbit of a planet, social change, or the behavior of a person. Of course modern science takes account of the valuations (the likes and dislikes, the approvals and disapprovals) of people

26. "Naturalism Reconsidered," *Proceedings and Addresses of the American Philosophical Association*, XXVIII (1954-55), 9.

in its account of individual or social behavior, but these are psychological occurrences, not values in the sense with which we are concerned.

Some of the Greek thinkers, especially some of the pre-Socratics, seemed to operate with something like a modern conception of what constitutes an explanation. With them in mind, Socrates contrasted the views that I am trying to distinguish this way:

"When I was young, Cebes, I had a prodigious desire to know that department of philosophy which is called the investigation of nature; to know the causes of things. . . . I was always agitating myself with the consideration of questions such as these: —Is the growth of animals the result of some decay which the hot and cold principle contracts, as some have said? Is the blood the element with which we think, or the air, or the fire? Or perhaps nothing of the kind—but the brain may be the originating power of the perceptions of hearing and sight and smell, and memory and opinion may come from them, and science may be based on memory and opinion when they have attained fixity. And then I went on to examine the corruption of them, and then to the things of heaven and earth. . . . Nor am I any longer satisfied that I understand the reason why one or anything else is either generated or destroyed or is at all, but I have in mind some confused notion of a new method. . . .

"Then I heard some one reading, as he said, from a book of Anaxagoras, that mind was the disposer and cause of all, and I was delighted at this notion, . . . and I said to myself: If Mind is the disposer, Mind will dispose all for the best, and put each particular in the best place; and I argued that if any one desired to find out the cause of the generation or destruction or existence of anything, he must find out what state of being or doing or suffering was best for that thing . . . and I rejoiced to think that I had found in Anaxagoras a teacher of the causes of existence such as I desired, and I imagined that he would tell me first whether the earth is flat or round; and whichever was true, he would proceed to explain the cause and the necessity of this being so, that this was best; and if he said the earth was in the centre, he would explain further that this position was the best, and I should be satisfied with the explanation given, and not want any other sort of cause."[27]

The kind of explanation that Socrates favored was teleological. It accounted for things in terms of "ends" or "goals" which were such not because they were aimed at or sought but because they were what ought to-be. I think it is fairly safe to say, without laboring the point, that modern science explains an event in terms of antecedent conditions and general laws or regularities which are "empirically" established. The naturalist and the scientist himself often think of this in terms of the common-sense category of causation. The explanatory antecedent conditions connected by general laws with the event to be explained are thought of as causal conditions.

What is accepted as an explanation of an occurrence or state of affairs presupposes or reflects a philosophical theory of change, for the explanation is framed in terms of what is thought to have a bearing or influence upon change. If one believes that gods control the changes that occur, one frames one's explanation of the event accordingly; if one believes that values or "ought to-be's" exercise control over change, one offers a teleological explanation; if one believes that "mechanical causes" or causal antecedent conditions alone influence or "determine" what happens, then one is satisfied with a modern scientific explanation of anything.

The thoroughgoing naturalist accepts what counts as an explanation in modern science as the only acceptable mode of explanation of events, whether an ordinary natural occurrence, a human action, or even a thought or desire. Furthermore, he fully accepts the theory of change presupposed by it. Nagel, in the address already cited, offers this as one of the two central

27. Plato, *Phaedo*, 96–97; trans. B. Jowett (New York: Random House, 1937), I, 480–82.

theses of naturalism. (The other was the plurality and contingency of things mentioned earlier.) He speaks of it as belief in "the existential and causal primacy of organized matter in the executive order of nature," which he says is "the assumption that the occurrence of events, qualities and processes, and the characteristic behaviors of various individuals, are contingent on the organization of spatiotemporally located bodies, whose internal structures and external relations determine and limit the appearance and disappearance of everything that happens. . . . Naturalism," he continues, "does not maintain that only what is material exists, since many things noted in experience, for example, modes of action, relations of meaning, dreams, joys, plans, aspirations, are not as such material bodies or organizations of material bodies. What naturalism does assert as a truth about nature is that though *forms* of behavior or *functions* of material systems are indefeasibly parts of nature, forms and functions are not themselves agents in their own realization or in the realization of anything else. In the conception of nature's processes which naturalism affirms, there is no place for the operation of disembodied forces. No place for an immaterial spirit directing the course of events, no place for the survival of personality after the corruption of the body which exhibits it."

The more recent naturalists have not often felt seriously challenged from the theological quarter and for the most part have refused to enter into debate over religious matters. But they have accepted three challenges. The language of mathematics, talk about the mental, and moral discourse (or value-language in general) seem to indicate something about reality other than that reflected in empirical, descriptive-explanatory language. Although individual philosophers may not have thought of themselves as working on such a grand program, it seems to make sense of much modern (especially recent) philosophy to interpret it as trying to make good the ontological claims of naturalism. The whole development of modern extensional logic seems to be part of this program. Witness its claims that logical connectives are truth-functional, that all logical truths are linguistic, and that mathematics is reducible to logic or at least that mathematical truths are analytic. It is specifically an attempt to make out the case for empiricism and the contingency thesis of naturalism. To admit any nonempirical knowledge of reality or to admit any necessary truths about reality would be to give up naturalism. There have been many attempts to show that concepts of the mental are not radically different from concepts of other natural processes and that therefore mental phenomena are natural and quite amenable to scientific study. And of course much of modern philosophy of ethics has been concerned to make out a case for ethical naturalism, to show that ethical discourse has no unique ontological significance that would prove naturalistic metaphysics to be untenable.

Notable examples of this kind of naturalism are Hume's *Treatise*, Russell's *Logical Atomism*, Wittgenstein's *Tractatus*, the whole program of the logical positivists, and a considerable part of the work of contemporary informal analysts. John Dewey no doubt is one of the first philosophers thought of in some quarters when naturalism is mentioned. However, his philosophy is not as clear-cut a case of naturalism (as I am conceiving it) as the above examples. At least it is not so on first thought. In the first place, something can be said for the view that he interprets the language of science in terms of the language of value, instead of the other way around. He seems especially to reduce epistemic terms to value-concepts. In the second place, although he is an empiricist of a kind, he broadens the concept of experience to include the affective, the emotional, the abnormal, and everything else, as well as introspective and sensory experience, as revelatory of traits of reality. Nonetheless, when we get at what all of this amounts to in the end, it may be said that he is a "rough-cut" naturalist not too far removed from our conception, for all of this has its setting and meaning within the framework of on-going processes of activity and their obstructions and nothing more.

A full-fledged critical appraisal of naturalism would involve an examination of how well its case can be made out against the apparent unique ontological significance of mathematics and logic, mental, moral, and religious language, and the like. But such a comprehensive task is too much for one book or person. In this work, I am concerned with the case for naturalism only insofar as it bears upon the realm of moral experience.

# CHAPTER II

# CLASSICAL ETHICAL NATURALISM

2.1 *Three kinds of ethical naturalism*

That there is value- (and, in particular, ethical) language is an undisputed fact. No one denies that our language provides us with the means of saying that some things are *good,* some *bad;* that some acts are *right,* some *wrong;* that some things *ought to-be* or *ought to have* certain features, some *ought not to-be* or *ought not to have* some characteristic or other; that some things are *virtues* and some *vices;* that people have *duties* and *rights;* and the like. It would seem that whenever language has developed to any considerable extent—and this embraces all natural human languages—it contains ethical components. Our use of ethical language seems to commit us to there being values in the world in a way that is not recognized or shown in our modern scientific[1] linguistic framework. Naturalism in value-theory contends that it does not, and it must assume the burden of proof.

It is convenient to distinguish three kinds of naturalists: (1) classical naturalists, who hold that ethical sentences have cognitive meaning and truth-values but are translatable into the

1. For the sake of convenience, instead of saying 'descriptive-explanatory language' I shall say either 'the language of science' or 'scientific language.' However, it is to be kept in mind that the descriptive-explanatory language embraces both an aspect of common-sense language and the language of science (in the ordinary sense). But since the language of science is descriptive-explanatory it will do no harm to extend the term to cover the descriptive-explanatory part of common-sense language.

language of science; (2) emotive naturalists, who hold that ethical sentences are not cognitively meaningful, at least not in a distinctively ethical sense; and (3) "good-reasons" or logical naturalists, who hold that ethical sentences are meaningful—although not true or false—but justified or not in terms of good reasons or the lack of them.

## 2.2 Classical naturalism

Classical naturalists, assuming that ethical sentences are cognitively (semantically) meaningful and have truth-values, claim that they have no special ontological significance which invalidates metaphysical naturalism. They attempt to make their case by showing that the use of value-language which seems to commit us to values in some unique sense is an avoidable way of talking—that what is sayable in terms of value-language can be said in a nonvalue paraphrase in terms of the language of science. The device by which they attempt to show this is naturalistic definition of the distinctively value-concepts like 'good,' 'right,' and 'ought,'—definition of them in terms of the concepts of science. Their enterprise is not simply to point up a similarity between value and ordinary descriptive sentences as Toulmin indicates,[2] nor merely a bit of sterile, local dictionary-making as Hampshire charges.[3] Although some may have engaged in the defining process without fully appreciating the significance of their labors, classical naturalists are not only concerned with understanding moral discourse, the perplexities of moral experience, or even the moral enterprise itself; they are also making a case for an important theory of reality.

Classical naturalists have, for the most part, concentrated their analytic powers on 'good' and 'evil,' both in their generic and in their moral senses, with a relative neglect of 'right' and 'wrong,' and especially 'ought' and 'ought not.' Apparently they have thought that the other value-concepts could be defined in terms

2. *The Place of Reason in Ethics,* pp. 193-94.
3. "Fallacies in Moral Philosophy," *Mind,* N.S., LVIII, No. 232 (Oct., 1949), 481.

of 'good' and that the naturalist's case turned upon the success or failure of a naturalistic definition of it.

There is no point in attempting to approximate an exhaustive list of naturalistic definitions that have been proposed. The following are among the ones that have been most discussed.

(1.1) 'x is good' means *I, the speaker, like or desire x* (Hobbes).

(1.2) 'x is morally good' means *The one who is the agreed upon judge or ruler likes or desires x* (Hobbes).

(2.1) 'x is good in itself' means *x is pleasant* (Hume).

(2.2) 'x is morally good' means *A typical, disinterested person, well informed of the facts, would under ordinary circumstances have that feeling or attitude toward x which we call 'approval'* (Hume).

(3.1) 'x is good in itself' means *x is desirable for its own sake* (x is such that it would be desired by any "normal" person with knowledge and experience of it) (Mill and perhaps Bentham).

(3.2) 'x is morally good in itself' means *x is desirable by society* (x is such that in general the means of attaining it are looked upon with favor by the people of the society when they are well informed about it, and obstacles or hindrances to its attainment are looked upon with disfavor) (Mill).

(4.1) 'x is good' means *Someone has a positive interest in x* (Perry).

(4.2) 'x is morally good' means *x is the object of the inclusive, integrated set of relevant interests* (Perry).

(5.1) 'x is good' means *x is truthfully judged to be such that it would promote, further, or assist a course of activity* (Dewey).

(5.2) 'x is morally good' means *x is truthfully judged to be such that it would promote, further, or assist a coordinated, unified organization of activities of the members of a society* (Dewey).

I have given only definitions of 'good,' but the correlative definitions of 'bad' or 'evil' should be obvious. And, as I have already mentioned, 'right' and 'wrong,' 'ought' and 'ought not,' would be defined in terms of what attainment of the good and avoidance of the evil requires or prohibits in a straightforward natural way.

There have been a number of arguments offered in refutation of classical naturalism. I shall first consider two that have been widely employed by the nonnaturalists as not only refuting this kind of naturalism but also lending support to nonnaturalism, namely the argument of reductionism and that of the naturalistic fallacy.

## 2.3 The argument of reductionism

Some have argued that classical naturalism reduces ethics to a branch of some one or several of the sciences and thereby explains it away. G. E. Moore puts it this way: naturalism in ethics is "a method which, strictly understood, is inconsistent with the possibility of any ethics whatsoever. This method consists in substituting for 'good' some one property of a natural object or of a collection of natural objects; and in this replacing ethics by some one of the natural sciences."[4]  And C. D. Broad says, "if naturalism be true, ethics is not an autonomous science; it is a department or an application of one or more of the natural or historical sciences."[5]

In the first place, the argument does not prove that the position is wrong but presupposes that it is, for it can be an argument against naturalism only if ethics is not a branch of science. There is nothing wrong with "reducing" ethics to science unless it is not science. If ethics is a branch of science, certainly to say that it is is not to deny that there is ethics. The point to be established is whether ethics is a branch of science. For this purpose the argument is useless.

However, the classical naturalist need not admit that his position reduces ethics to science. He does attempt to reduce the ontology of ethics to the ontology of science. No doubt Moore

4. *Principia Ethica,* p. 40.
5. "Some of the Main Problems of Ethics," *Philosophy,* XXI, No. 79 (July, 1946), 103.

and Broad would hold that this involves reduction of the kind they charge. But this is not necessarily so, or at least it has to be shown. It is not enough merely to assume it. I suppose that a naturalistic translation would be a reduction of ethics to science only if it could replace ethical language in ordinary usage. But, as I indicated earlier, classical naturalism does not require this. It is primarily, if not exclusively, concerned with the ontology of value-language. For one thing, there might be pragmatic functions of value-language devoid of ontological significance which could not be performed by scientific language. This is fundamentally the position of an emotivist like C. L. Stevenson. I shall explore this possibility in a later chapter. My only concern here is to point out that as long as this is regarded as a possibility the charge that classical naturalism reduces ethics to science (even if it would be a mistake) is not established.

For another thing, it is at least a prima facie possibility for ethics and science to enjoy a common ontology in terms of their descriptive dimension but neither to be reducible to the other by virtue of another dimension. Let me explain what I mean. Scientific sentences are descriptive, but not merely descriptive. They are descriptive-explanatory. The ultimate goal of science is not simply to give a descriptive account of things, to say what they are, but to explain things, to say why they are as they are and not otherwise. To the extent to which a scientific discipline is merely descriptive it is thought to be undeveloped as a science, whereas to the extent that it is explanatory it is considered mature. So we can say that the cognitive goal of science is descriptive-explanatory knowledge. The explanatory aspect of it has to do with the organization of descriptive statements. In a simple, first-order scientific explanation (one in which what is to be explained is a particular event or simple occurrence) we have at least two explanatory statements, one of which is a general statement or law, the other a statement of a particular fact. The statement which describes the event to be explained, which says *what* it is, is so related to the explanatory statements that it either is deducible from them or is supported by them with a high degree of probability; and it is at least highly probable that the event concerned would not have occurred if either of the explanatory statements had been false. Each statement in such an explanation is descriptive, but there is something more than description. At best a description is an answer to the questions 'what?' and 'how?' But an explanation gives an answer to 'why?' also. It gives a reason, an explanatory reason, for something's being as it is and not otherwise. This emerges out of the organization of descriptive statements. It might be missed by an analysis of single, descriptive statements of science. To think of scientific language as merely descriptive may be misleading.

Perhaps something similar is true of value-language. It is possible that although descriptive in the manner of scientific language, it has an aspect that is not identical with, but somewhat analogous to, the explanatory dimension of scientific language. Perhaps we could say that it has a justificatory dimension. Perhaps certain statements which are descriptively equivalent to their scientific counterparts can be used to *justify* (to give justifying reasons as distinct from explanatory ones) states of affairs which may be descriptively reported by other statements, just as some statements which descriptively report certain states of affairs can be used to explain another state of affairs. And perhaps the distinctive and irreducible aspect of value-language is its tie-up with this justificatory dimension, whereas scientific language has a similar tie-up with the explanatory dimension. In other words, value and scientific languages may differ with respect to the "theoretical structures" which may be built with them, while they are the same or overlap in their descriptive aspects. However, if this is the case, the naturalist must show that such a difference has no ontological significance. This is a possible way for him to explore in attempting to hold on to his position and yet to deny that it reduces ethics to science.

Even if there is no special reason, like the two just discussed, for holding that the naturalist's philosophical paraphrase is not substitutable for value-language in ordinary usage, the advocates of the position may reject the charge of reduction on general principles. Ordinary language of any description has a systematic vagueness and an open texture which befit its ordinary job in a way in which no philosophically clarified language does. But this is of no consequence, for the philosopher is not attempting to construct a language for ordinary usage. He is concerned with philosophical clarification, and to the classical naturalist this concern means making clear its ontology. His proposed translation is designed for this purpose only; this is not to reduce ethics to science. It does not propose or even claim that it is possible to replace ethical language with the language of science.

The argument, then, does not disprove classical naturalism, but it does point up the fact that the proponents of the position must account for the prima facie differences between the languages of ethics and of science and must show that they have no ontological significance.

## 2.4 *The argument of the naturalistic fallacy*

I shall now consider what is perhaps the most widely held argument against classical naturalism—what Moore called the 'naturalistic fallacy.' Prior[6] has traced the history of the argument, or somewhat similar ones, back to Cudworth and down through Shaftesbury, Hutcheson, Price, Whately, and Sidgwick. Since Moore's formulation of it in 1903, it has been championed by Ross, Ewing, Ayer, Stevenson, Hare, and many more. As it was stated in the last chapter, the alleged fallacy concerns the definition of value-concepts in terms of nonvalue-concepts, but it is not too clear just why this is supposed to be a fallacy.

Frankena has suggested that there are three fallacies involved: a generic one, which he calls the 'definist' fallacy, and then two species of it—the "naturalistic" fallacy, the fallacy allegedly committed in defining value-concepts in terms of natural or scientific

6. Arthur N. Prior, *Logic and the Basis of Ethics* (Oxford: Clarendon Press, 1949).

concepts, and the metaphysical fallacy, the one supposedly committed by theories which define value-concepts in terms of non-value, "metaphysical" concepts. The definist fallacy, acording to Frankena, is "the process of confusing or identifying two properties, of defining one property by another, or of substituting one property for another. Furthermore, the fallacy is always simply that two properties are being treated as one, and it is irrelevant, if it be the case, that one of them is natural or non-ethical and the other non-natural or ethical."[7] So the naturalistic and metaphysical fallacies would be simply different ways of committing the definist fallacy. There is, as Frankena says, only one fallacy, if it is a fallacy. Moore does seem to speak in terms of the definist fallacy. In one place he says, "If anyone were to say, for instance, that pleasure *means* the sensation of red . . . well, that would be the same fallacy which I have called the naturalistic fallacy." The motto of Moore's book, Butler's statement, "Everything is what it is, and not another thing," supports Frankena's interpretation.

If the point Frankena is making is that two distinct things must not be identified, no one will dispute it. But if one should make the mistake of counting two distinct entities as one, it is not clear how it would be a fallacy, which I presume all would consider to be a logical error of some kind. In any case, if this is the correct interpretation of the so-called fallacy, it cannot be used as an argument against classical naturalism; for the point at issue is whether there are two distinct entities, a value-entity and some natural entity more or less universally associated with it, which the classical naturalist counts as one. All the so-called fallacy proves is that if an intuitionist like Moore is right, the classical naturalist is wrong. But the intuitionist cannot establish his own position by refuting naturalism with an argument that is premised upon the correctness of his own position. When the "naturalistic fallacy" is used as an argument against classical

7. W. K. Frankena, "The Naturalistic Fallacy," *Mind*, N.S., XLVIII, No. 192 (Oct., 1939), 471.

naturalism, it itself commits the fallacy of begging the question. If Frankena's interpretation is correct, this is about what Moore has attempted to do. Perry seems to interpret Moore this way. He says, "One who upholds this view of good must be prepared to point to a distinct *quale* which appears in that region which our value terms roughly indicate, and which is different from the object's shape and size, from the interrelation of its parts, from its relation to other objects, or to a subject; and from all the other factors which belong to the same context, but are designated by words other than 'good.' The present writer, for one, finds no such residuum."[8] And there the issue must lie. Do we find a quality other than the natural qualities in the areas indicated by our value-terms? Not to find such a quality may be to overlook something, but it is not to commit a fallacy. And the argument of the naturalistic fallacy, so interpreted, is of no use whatsoever in settling the issue.

But is Frankena's interpretation of the argument correct? If it were it would be difficult to understand why so many people have thought that a simple denial of classical naturalism constituted a conclusive refutation of it. Morton White,[9] while admitting that Moore sometimes speaks of the alleged fallacy as consisting of the identification of one quality with another, contends that the argument does charge the classical naturalist with a mistake of inference, the mistake of inferring the identity of the connotation of two terms (to speak in terms of the Millian semantics) from the identity of their denotation, the mistake of inferring that F-ness is G-ness from the premise that all F's are G's and all G's are F's. This would be a fallacy somewhat akin to the fallacy of composition, even if it were true that 'F' and 'G' had identical connotations. But what evidence is there that a classical naturalist makes such an inference? It is certainly not clear that his position necessarily involves him in such a fallacy.

8. R. B. Perry, *General Theory of Value* (Cambridge, Mass.: Harvard University Press, 1954), p. 30.
9. *Toward Reunion in Philosophy* (Cambridge, Mass.: Harvard University Press, 1956), pp. 174 ff.

True, he may first discover that a value-term and some natural term are true of the same set of things. But he need not, and probably does not, infer from this fact that they have the same connotation. His procedure would probably be to search for a feature or complex of features shared in common by all the things denoted by the nonvalue-term and by none not so denoted and then to subject the feature to a reflective test to see if he recognized it as what was meant connotatively by the term and as what guided him in his application of it. If the feature should be recognized as the connotation of the nonvalue-term, he would then subject it to the reflective test to see whether he recognized it as the property that guided him in the application of the value-term also. His conclusion that the value-term had the same connotation as the nonvalue-term would be grounded in his recognition that the connotation of the one is the connotation of the other. Of course he might make a mistake. He might take the connotations to be the same when they are not. However, the mistake would not be an error of inference, but a case of mistaken identity. The question at issue between the classical naturalist and the intuition-ist like Moore would be whether the connotations were the same. All the intuitionist would be doing would be to deny the identity claimed by the clasical naturalist. Again, a denial is not an argu-ment against or a refutation of a position. If White's interpreta-tion of the fallacy is correct, the argument proves no more than it does under Frankena's interpretation. Certainly it provides no argument that is embarrassing to the classical naturalist, for it is not an argument at all.

Prior contends that Moore's argument is not a refutation of classical naturalism as such, but only of certain inconsistent naturalists. Some, he contends, say such things as 'Nothing is good but pleasure' or 'Nothing is good but what promotes bio-logical survival' and then defend these apparently significant as-sertions by saying that they are true by virtue of the fact that "that is the very meaning of the word." These are the ones, he claims, who commit the fallacy in question. In other words, the

point of the naturalistic-fallacy argument is that a naturalist cannot count a basic statement both as a definition of a value-term
and as a significant value-statement. In terms of theological
ethics, for example, one cannot define 'right' in terms of God's
will and then significantly say that what God wills is right, for
the latter statement means, on the basis of this definition, simply
that what God wills God wills.

However, there is no inconsistency as such in saying the two
things. They are simply two ways of saying the same thing: one
in the formal mode or in a meta-language and the other in the
material mode or object-language. A theological ethicist might
say that it is wrong to kill. Asked why it is wrong, he might
reply that it violates a command of God. And if asked why it
is wrong to violate a command of God, he might reply to the
effect that whatever God commands is right and, therefore, whatever is a violation of a command of his is wrong. If pushed with
the question, why is it or how does he know that whatever God
commands is right, he might reply that the word 'right' means
*commanded by God*. The fact that he would go on to answer
the last question in this manner indicates that he was not mis-
construing his answer to the preceding question. It is said that
the statement 'Whatever God commands is right' is trivial in
that, in terms of the answer to the last question, it is simply the
truism 'Whatever God wills God wills.' But we might equally
well render it (in terms of the answer to the last question) in
this manner: 'Whatever is right is right.' And if we do it this
way, we see the significance of the answer. It marks the limit
to the kind of question being asked. It shows that no more
significant questions internal to the ethical framework can be
asked and that any further skeptical questions will have to be
external—inquiries that call into question the ethical categories
in terms of which the discourse up to this point has been formulated. In other words, what is called a trivial ethical statement is
offered to show the peculiarity of the question asked. But it is
not really trivial at all. It shows the limit to a line of question-

ing and it shows and elucidates part of the framework of ethical thought. At this point the border line between ethics and the philosophy of ethics is crossed. As an ethical statement it is trivial, but as a philosophical statement showing something about ethical categories it is quite significant. An analytic statement of this kind is not language idling or gone on a holiday. Language is being put to a different use. It is no more idling or on a holiday than a worker who has been made a manager is idling or on a holiday because he is not doing what he did before. Many writers have not clearly distinguished between ethics and philosophy of ethics, and this fact has given rise to some confusion. But the difficulty is not an inconsistency between a meta-ethical statement (such as, "the word 'right' means the same as the phrase 'is commanded by God' ") and a sentence in the ethical language (e.g., 'Whatever is commanded by God is right' or 'If and only if x is commanded by God, x is right') but rather between two interpretations of the latter. In one case it is interpreted as an ethical sentence and in the other as a philosophical sentence. As a philosophical sentence, it is simply the meta-ethical sentence expressed in the material mode. It is true that philosophical sentences expressed in the material mode are likely to be misleading. But there is no fallacy involved in expressing the same statement in both modes.

Perhaps the claim is made that such naturalists do in fact count their own philosophical statement in the material mode as an ethical statement. But what evidence is there that they do? Bentham and Mill said such things as 'The only thing good is pleasure' or 'The only thing good in itself is pleasure.' There is no evidence, however, that they would have supported this statement by saying that it is so because the term 'good in itself' means pleasure. The situation that Prior is thinking of is one in which two classes are said to be coextensive (that whatever is a member of either is a member of the other) and in which this claim is supported by saying that the denotations of the two class-terms, to speak in the way of Mill's semantics again, are identical because the two terms have identical connotations. But 'pleasure' is not a class-term. It is a proper name of an abstraction. It has no connotation in Mill's sense; therefore, strictly speaking, it cannot have a denotation either. It simply names its referent. But 'good' presumably is treated as a class-term by both Bentham and Mill. What is said is that pleasure is the only thing denoted by the phrase 'good in itself.' This equates neither the denotation nor the connotation of the two terms. It simply says that only pleasure is a member of the class of things good in themselves. Although this functions as a value-statement for them, it is not defended by saying that it is true by virtue of the meaning of the word 'good.' It is not a philosophical statement at all. Bentham and Mill seem to subscribe to a philosophical position which could be formulated this way: 'good in itself' means the same as 'desirable for its own sake' (or 'is such that it would be desired for its own sake by "normal" people under "normal" conditions'). In the material mode, their position would be expressed in this manner: x is good in itself if and only if x is such that it is desirable for its own sake. Too, both of them believed that it is a psychological truth about men that they do in fact desire only pleasure for its own sake. If Bentham and Mill had explicitly formulated their grounds for saying that only pleasure is good in itself, their argument would have been this: Anything is good in itself if and only if it is desirable for its own sake. Only pleasure is desirable for its own sake. Therefore, only pleasure is good in itself.

Perhaps it would be charged that such a use of the first premise treats it as a value-judgment when in fact it is a philosophical statement. Grounds for this might be that we cannot derive a value-judgment from such a premise unless it itself is a value-judgment, since the second premise is purely factual. Bentham and Mill, it will be recalled, considered it a psychological fact that only pleasure is such that people would desire it for its own sake. It may be true that a value-judgment cannot be derived from a definitional statement and a factual truth, but if true, it is true because a value-concept cannot be defined as other concepts. It has nothing whatever to do with the fact that a philosophical statement, an analytic categorial statement in the material mode, is being put to this use. There is no inconsistency involved in using an analytic categorial statement in the material mode, together with factual truths, to derive other factual truths or value-truths and yet to state, upon being challenged, the analytic categorial statement in the formal mode to show its true colors.

Thus it is not at all clear that the naturalistic-fallacy argument, if it is interpreted as Prior does, refutes any naturalistic position. It would apply to only those positions which confuse a philosophical statement in the material mode with an ethical statement. And I know of no clear-cut case of this. Critics have thought some naturalists guilty of it because they themselves were guilty of the confusion.

So far we have not found an interpretation of the naturalistic fallacy which renders it a genuine argument against ethical naturalism. Was it that Moore just wanted to say that naturalists are wrong, and he said it in a way that made people think that he was refuting them? Although Moore's own statements about the matter are woefully confused and confusing, he did intend to charge the classical naturalist with involving himself in contradictions: "The point I have been labouring hitherto, the point that 'good is indefinable,' and that to deny this involves a fallacy, is a point capable of strict proof: for to deny it involves contradictions."[10] Now, what are the contradictions? I think he has in mind the so-called 'open question.' He says that there are only two alternatives to the position that 'good' denotes something simple and indefinable: (1) 'good' might denote a complex, analyzable property and (2) it might have no meaning at all. Alternative (1) is disposed of "by consideration of the fact that whatever definition be offered it may be always asked, with significance, of the complex, so defined, whether it is itself good."

10. *Principia Ethica*, p. 77.

This fact also eliminates (2) in that "it may be always asked, *with significance,* . . . whether it is itself good."[11]

The interpretation here being pointed up is unlike that urged by Prior. He had in mind naturalists who themselves say such things as that 'good in itself' means the same as 'pleasure' and also that the only thing good in itself is pleasure. The interpretation now under consideration has the philosopher saying 'good' means the same as 'C'; and yet it can be asked with significance in ordinary language, 'Is a Cx good?' But where is the contradiction? Perhaps it consists of these two statements: (1) the question 'Is Cx good?' cannot be asked with significance; and (2) the question 'Is Cx good?' can be asked with significance. Moore thinks that the classical naturalist would have to subscribe to (1) on the basis of his definition and to (2) by virtue of ordinary usage. Or does the alleged contradiction consist of the fact that if it can be asked with significance in ordinary language 'Is Cx good?' then it is not self-contradictory to say in ordinary language 'Cx is not good'; and yet it is self-contradictory to say it in terms of the naturalistic definition. But neither interpretation involves the naturalistic position in an internal contradiction. All the argument shows, even if one grants everything that it claims, is that no analysis of 'good' which treats it as a complex, connotative term can square with its use in ordinary language.

This may be enough to convince those who (a) hold that philosophical analyses must square with ordinary language and (b) also admit the significance in ordinary language of the recurring question 'Is Cx good?' But many philosophers do not hold that philosophical analyses of categorial terms must square completely with their use in ordinary discourse. Some regard ordinary language as too loose and therefore as permitting nonsensical questions to pose as meaningful. Some have felt it necessary to construct ideal languages, freed from the nonsense and contradictions permitted in ordinary discourse, in order to elucidate the categorial structure of reality as experienced by us.

11. *Ibid.,* p. 15.

Moore's recurrent question might be taken as indicating trouble in ordinary language which calls for the construction of an ideal language of the kind the naturalist proposes rather than as refuting his position. I am not denying that the argument gives a reason, and perhaps a good one, for rejecting classical naturalism. What I wish to point out is that it is not a "strict proof" that it is wrong. It does not show that it involves a fallacy of inference nor that it asserts or entails contradictions. Classical naturalism, as far as this interpretation of the naturalistic-fallacy argument is concerned, remains a possible position, even though there may be reasons for thinking it is wrong. Philosophers all too often think that they must prove and disprove rather than confirm and disconfirm their views; therefore they claim too much for their arguments.

There is another interpretation of the naturalistic-fallacy argument which should be discussed, but it cannot be offered as what Moore meant, for it is alien to his mode of thought. It might be contended, however, that it gets at what was really bothering him and that it formulates the difficulty with classical naturalism which he dimly saw but misformulated. I refer to Hare's interpretation, which Hare thinks is completely devastating. He says, for instance, "Naturalism in ethics, like attempts to square the circle and to 'justify induction,' will constantly recur so long as there are people who have not understood the fallacy involved."[12] He interprets the so-called fallacy this way: we cannot say that 'a good A' means the same as 'an A which is C,' where 'C' is a descriptive term, for "then it would be impossible to use the sentence 'an A which is C is good' in order to commend A's which are C; for this sentence would be analytic and equivalent to 'an A which is C is C.'"[13] He adds, "Now it seems clear that we do use sentences of the form 'an A which is C is good' in order to commend A's which are C; . . . value-terms have a special function in language, that of commending; and so they

12. *The Language of Morals*, p. 92.
13. *Ibid.*, pp. 90-91.

plainly cannot be defined in terms of other words which themselves do not perform this function; for if this is done, we are deprived of a means of performing the function."[14] Again, he says, "And clearly he [the classical naturalist] cannot say that he never wishes to commend anything for being C; for to commend things for being C is the whole object of his theory."[15]

What is this commending (and condemning) function of value-words which all classical naturalistic theories fail to accommodate? According to Hare, it is to guide choices with regard to a class of objects. "When I commend a motor-car I am guiding the choices of my hearer not only in relation to that particular motor-car but in relation to motor-cars in general. . . . The method whereby I give him this assistance is by making known to him a standard for judging motor-cars,"[16] for "whenever we commend, we have in mind something about the object commended which is the reason for our commendation."[17] "A value-judgment," Hare says, "may stand in a variety of relations to the standard to which it refers. . . . If the standard is one that is well known and generally accepted, the value-judgment may do no more than express the speaker's acceptance of or adherence to it. . . . If the hearer is someone not acquainted with the standard . . . the function of the value-judgment may be also to acquaint him with it or to teach it to him. If we do this, we are not merely informing him that the standard is of such and such a kind; we are instructing him to make his future choices on a certain principle."[18] In other words, a value-judgment commends things in terms of a standard and also commends the standard, which would, I suppose, invoke still another standard and also commend it, and so forth ad infinitum, unless somewhere a standard is simply prescribed without a

14. *Ibid.*, p. 91.
15. *Ibid.*, p. 93.
16. *Ibid.*, p. 132.
17. *Ibid.*, p. 130.
18. *Ibid.*, pp. 135-136.

reason. This makes commending (and condemning) not only a very complicated business but purely a pragmatic affair.

This interpretation of the argument is quite similar to, if not identical, with an argument given by Stevenson; but for him it is distinct from that of the naturalistic fallacy. Stevenson says that one of the requirements for the definition of 'good' is that " 'goodness' must have, so to speak, a magnetism. A person who recognizes x to be 'good' must *ipso facto* acquire a stronger tendency to act in its favor than he otherwise would have had."[19] But if one gives a definition of a value-word in terms of non-value-expressions, one can recognize the truth of a statement formulated in terms of the non-value definiens without having a stronger tendency to act in its favor. So 'good' is indefinable, he says, "for the same reasons that 'hurrah' is indefinable. . . . Although our language affords many terms that have the same descriptive meaning, it is more economical with its emotive terms. Each term bears the characteristic stamp of its emotional history."[20] For this reason value-terms have no emotive synonyms. No nonvalue–term can do the job of a value-term even if it does have the same descriptive meaning.

Stevenson and Hare agree on the reason that value-terms are indefinable in terms of nonvalue-words. Both claim that it is that such definitions do not square with their commending (and condemning) function. However, they have different theories of commending—Stevenson, a purely emotive theory; Hare, a pragmatic prescriptive theory. For Stevenson, a value-judgment commends (or condemns) by the disposition of its value-term to evoke or to influence attitudes, its emotive meaning; for Hare, a value-judgment, in the last analysis, commends (or condemns) by prescribing, by telling one to do something, in the manner of an imperative. Hare says that it instructs one to judge by a certain standard all members of the class concerned. For our

19. Charles L. Stevenson, "The Emotive Meaning of Ethical Terms," *Mind*, N.S., XLVI, No. 181 (Jan., 1937), 16.
20. *Ethics and Language* (New Haven: Yale University Press, 1944), p. 82.

purposes, the different theories of commending need not concern us at this point. Both Hare and Stevenson agree that classical naturalism is untenable because it necessarily leaves out or does not do justice to the commending (and condemning) function of value-language. Furthermore both agree that this is the real difference between value- and nonvalue-language which was behind Moore's insight into the indefinability of 'good.'

What of the argument interpreted in this manner? All that it purports to establish is that no naturalistic definition of a value-term can square with its use in ordinary language. The argument differs from what Moore was getting at in that it interprets the use with which the definition cannot be squared as pragmatic rather than semantic. There is no fallacy involved—if anything, just a mistake.

What can the classical naturalist say in reply? In the first place, he would certainly deny Hare's contention that the object of his definition of 'good' in terms of 'C' was to commend things for being C. He is not commending anything. He is trying to clarify the value-category; he wants to know what it is for something to be good. Is it something which would be reported in a scientific description of it? Or is it something unique which is reported only in value-judgments? It may be that to say 'x is good' commends x; but to say " 'x is good' means the same as 'x is C' " is not to commend x. I should think that it would not be necessary to make this elementary point. The philosopher of ethics is neither an ethicist nor a moralist. We shall shortly consider another argument against classical naturalism which consists of a charge that a proponent of the position does in fact commend things for being C by virtue of the fact that a definition of 'good' in terms of 'C' is a "persuasive definition." The naturalist is attacked both for his theory's commending and for its not commending. Certainly both cannot be legitimate charges. Regardless of whether a naturalistic definition commends, commendation is definitely not its objective.

Furthermore, the classical naturalist could easily reply that Hare and Stevenson are condemning his theory for not being something that it is not intended to be and that they, accordingly, subject it to tests which are entirely inappropriate. He is not attempting to give a full descriptive account of how value-terms are used. His whole concern is to find out what value-talk shows or indicates about reality. He is interested in only the semantics of value-language, not its pragmatics. His "definition" is intended to formulate only the semantic meaning of the value-word. Strictly speaking, it is a philosophical analysis, not a definition. The analysis is not intended to be substitutable for the value-word in ordinary discourse and to perform there the function of the value-word. It is not a dictionary synonym. It is a paraphrase for the philosophical purpose of clarifying what it is that value-sentences say or show about reality. Therefore it is not necessarily a handicap of a naturalistic definition of 'good' for the definition to be such that if it were substituted for 'good' in ordinary language, that language could not be used to commend things. It may be that the difficulty Moore was getting at in the naturalistic-fallacy argument is as Hare and Stevenson say it is. But it may also be that it is a *difficulty* for classical naturalism only if classical naturalism is interpreted to be something which it is not and thereby subjected to the inappropriate test of substitution in ordinary discourse. At any rate, the classical naturalist can put up a plausible defense of his position in this manner. Furthermore, he could contend that it is because of a fact about human nature that to say 'x is C' is to commend it. It might be a matter of fact that all people desire whatever is C, so that to tell one that an x is C is to give one information that arouses a positive interest in it. If so, the commending force of value-words might not be involved in their rules of use, not even their pragmatic rules.

However, if one should accept a nonpragmatic theory of the commending function of value-language, the classical naturalist might have more difficulty in freeing himself from Hare's version of the naturalistic-fallacy argument. It might be held that to say 'x is good' commends x, in that, as Ewing says, " 'Good' . . . carries with it the notion the good thing ought not to be wantonly sacrificed but, other things being equal, pursued"[21] and that 'ought' itself has a semantic meaning. But, as Ewing contends, no notion of 'ought' follows from 'good' conceived in any naturalistic sense. We cannot derive 'ought'-sentences from 'is'-sentences. This, he says, is fatal to all classical naturalistic definitions.[22]

Was this what Moore was getting at in terms of the naturalistic fallacy? He distinguishes between two kinds of 'ought,' as in the questions 'what ought we to do?' and 'what ought to-be?' The former, according to him, is a matter of "what things are related as *causes* to that which is good in itself";[23] the latter seems to mean the same as 'what is good in itself?' He says, "Whenever he [one] thinks of 'intrinsic value,' or 'intrinsic worth,' or says that a thing 'ought to exist,' he has before his mind the unique object—the unique property of things—which I mean by 'good.' "[24] Perhaps 'intrinsically good' carries with it the notion that what is so ought not to be wantonly sacrificed but (unless there are overriding reasons) pursued, because it means the same as, or entails, 'ought to-be.' If so, the recurring question about any naturalistic definition of the form " 'x is good' means the same as 'x is C' " can be expressed in the form of 'Ought a Cx to-be?' or 'Ought x to be C?' This way of asking the question should be permitted by Moore.

With this interpretation of the commending function of value-language, Hare's formulation of the naturalistic fallacy is seen to be not too far removed from, if not identical with, what Moore had in mind. In fact, the interpretation may reveal more clearly

21. *The Definition of the Good*, p. 56.
22. *Ibid.*, p. 57.
23. *Principia Ethica*, p. 146.
24. *Ibid.*, p. 17.

the difficulty with which he was struggling. If 'x is good' is taken to mean the same as 'x is C,' where 'C' names a natural property, the answer to the question 'Is a Cx good?' can be given, as we saw earlier, as 'A Cx is a Cx,' which shows that the limit to internal questions of this kind has been reached. The naturalist, as we have noted, can say that the question seems to be significant in a synthetic sense because of the looseness of ordinary language. Of course it remains a question of whether or not this is so. It is a point to be established. Nevertheless, the classical naturalist can explain away Moore's problem in a manner that is at least possible and can be made to seem plausible. The question before us at the moment is whether he can escape with the same plausibility if Moore's recurrent question about naturalistic definiens of 'good' is asked in terms of 'ought to-be,' which he seems to regard as synonymous with 'good' (in the sense of 'good in itself') or at least to be entailed by it. If we should give a naturalistic definition of 'good' in terms of 'C' and if 'good' entails 'ought,' what could we do with the question 'Ought Cx to-be?' or 'Ought x to be C?' Is it at all possible to translate it into the form of 'Is Cx Cx?' or 'Is Cx Dx?'

About the only possible way a naturalist could analyze 'ought to-be' to yield this result would be something like this: 'x ought to-be' means that someone, perhaps the speaker or maybe even anyone, has, or perhaps would have under certain circumstances, a certain feeling toward the existence of x (or perhaps its non-existence). I suspect that any attempt to describe the feeling concerned would be difficult without employing some such locutions as 'feels that x ought to-be,' 'feels constrained to do something about it,' or 'feeling of approval toward the existence of x' or 'feeling of disapproval toward its nonexistence.' The first suggestion of course would not do for a naturalist. The problem of 'ought' would have escaped his analysis. But I wonder if, in the last analysis, the same would not be true of the other locutions. 'Feels constrained to do something about it' in this context can only mean *feels that one ought to do something about it,* which perhaps can be accounted for only upon the premise that one feels that it ought to-be. And the feeling of approval of something involves *feeling that it is as it ought to be;* and feeling of disapproval involves *feeling that it is not as it ought to be.* (This will be developed further in Chapters III and VI.) It would seem, then, that the meaning of 'ought' eludes naturalistic analysis of this type.

Furthermore, there is at least a prima facie difficulty about 'Ought Cx to-be?' which is not present in the case of 'Is Cx good?' 'Ought' and 'C' are of different syntactical categories, whereas 'good' and 'C' are of the same. 'Ought' is either a modal term or a connective; 'good' and 'C' are predicates. But is this a difficulty between 'ought' and 'C' which does not hold between 'ought' and 'good'? It would seem not.

There are other reasons for not equating 'good' and 'ought.' 'Good' is usually predicated of what is. We do of course say such things as 'Peace is good' even when, or perhaps especially when, we are at war. But does not this mean, *It would be good to have peace* or *Peace would be good, if it were?* However, 'ought to-be' is usually said of things that are not. If we say at all 'ought to-be' of what is, we say, 'It is *as it ought to be.'* It seems wrong to equate 'good' and 'ought to-be,' but 'good' and 'as it ought to be' may mean the same; also, 'x would be good, if it were,' may mean the same as 'x ought to-be.' But this makes 'ought to-be' the basic value-term, and it is not a predicate. Thus a classical naturalistic theory would have to give a naturalistic definition of 'ought.'

As we saw above, the syntactical difference between 'x ought to-be' and 'x is C' is a prima facie reason against a naturalistic analysis of the form 'x is C.' The recurrent question in regard to any such analysis of the basic value-concept in terms of any nonvalue-expression, 'C,' in the form of 'Ought a Cx to-be?' or 'Ought x to be C?' shows up the difficulty. We cannot translate either of these into the question 'Is a Cx a Cx?' The kind of answer that the naturalist could give with 'good' considered the basic value-term is no longer open to him. He can no longer say that this "tautological" question appears to be significant in another way because of the looseness of ordinary language. If 'good' entails 'ought' in such a way that the latter is the basic value-term, it would seem that Moore's recurrent question asked in 'ought'-form would constitute a more serious problem than has been recognized in terms of the other formulation.

The classical naturalist could meet the criticism in either of two ways: (1) he could deny the meaningfulness of 'x is intrinsically good' and hold that nothing can be said to be good except as a means to something as an end; or (2) he could refuse to admit that 'x is intrinsically good (or good in itself)' entails 'x ought to-be.' The first is the position of Dewey; the second is the way of Bentham, Mill, Perry, and Lewis.

Dewey says that "Value-propositions of the distinctive sort [as distinct from propositions about valuations] exist whenever things are appraised as to their suitability and serviceability as means."[25] All value-judgments apparently are of the means-end type. He comments, "take the case of a child who has found a bright smooth stone. His sense of touch and of sight is gratified. But there is no valuation because no desire and no end-in-view, until the question arises of what shall be done with it; until the child *treasures* what he has accidentally hit upon. The moment he begins to prize and care for it he puts it to some use and thereby employs it as a *means* to some end, and, depending upon his maturity, he estimates or values it *in that relation,* or as means to end."[26]

If Dewey is right in claiming that all value-judgments are of the means-end type and that there is a continuum of means-end so that nothing is ever valued as an end in itself, then he may escape the problem of Moore's recurrent question. In the first place, the question (in the sense in which Moore was concerned)

25. John Dewey, *Theory of Valuation* (Chicago: The University of Chicago Press, 1939), p. 51.
26. *Ibid.,* p. 38.

whether an x that is C is intrinsically good or good in itself could not be asked with significance of anything. We could only ask with significance whether an x that is C is a "suitable" or serviceable means to some other end. Since there is at least an indefinite means-end continuum with each end also a means, the recurrent question, taken in this sense, is precisely what one might expect.

But Dewey's own use of value-language hardly conforms to his theory. Of course he is concerned with value-judgments only insofar as they arise in practical situations; therefore his theory does not accommodate his use of value-language in a theoretical situation. He says, "the conditions under which desires take shape and foreseen consequences are projected as ends to be reached . . . are those of need, deficit, and conflict. Apart from a condition of tension between a person and environing conditions there is . . . no occasion for evocation of desire for something else; there is nothing to induce the formation of an end, much less the formation of one end rather than any other out of the indefinite number of ends theoretically possible. Control of transformation of active tendencies into a desire in which a particular end-in-view is incorporated, is exercised by the needs or privations of an actual situation as its requirements are disclosed to observation. The 'value' of different ends that suggest themselves is estimated or measured by the capacity they exhibit to guide action in making good, *satisfying,* in its literal sense, existing lacks. Here is the factor which cuts short the process of foreseeing and weighing ends-in-view in their function as means. Sufficient unto the day is the evil thereof and sufficient also is the *good* of that which does away with the existing evil. Sufficient because it is the means of instituting a complete situation or an integrated set of conditions."[27]

This passage shows that Dewey uses value-language in a theoretical context which is not of the means-ends variety as described by him. He speaks of *deficits, needs, lacks, privations, requirements of an actual situation,* and the like. These are prior

27. *Ibid.,* pp. 45-46.

to any end-in-view and control the shaping of them. In terms of what end are the needs, lacks, privations, and requirements of a situation judged to be such, for these are value-terms? The answer is given in the passage cited: *a complete situation* or *an integrated set of conditions.*

This is the attained end or consequence if the act is successful. But this is not the end sought, the end-in-view. "The content of the end as an object *held in view,*" he says, "is intellectual or methodological; the content of the attained outcome or the end as *consequence* is existential."[28] "The attained end or consequence," he goes on to say, "is always an organization of activities . . . which enter as factors. The *end-in-view* is that particular activity which operates as a co-ordinating factor of all other subactivities involved. Recognition of the end as a co-ordination or unified organization of activities, and of the end-in-view as the special activity which is the means of effecting this co-ordination, does away with any appearance of paradox that seems to be attached to the idea of a temporal continuum of activities in which each successive stage is equally end and means. The *form* of an attained end or consequence is always the same: that of adequate co-ordination. The content or involved matter of each successive result differs from that of its predecessors; for, while it is a *reinstatement* of a unified ongoing action, after a period of interruption through conflict and need, it is also an *enactment* of a new state of affairs."[29]

Does not Dewey, then, subscribe to the view that there is an ultimate end which provides the framework for value-judgments? His idea of a universal form but different contents would be admitted by all who talk about an ultimate goal. Certainly each realization of it, regardless of how it is conceived, would be something unique with respect to content. One such realization would simply be of the same kind as others. No one, I suppose, has ever thought otherwise. Also, those who have thought in terms

28. *Ibid.,* p. 48.
29. *Ibid.,* pp. 48-49.

of an ultimate goal have not thought of it as an end-in-view, as a positively pursued goal on all fours with specific ends; rather, they have thought of it as an end which is appealed to or presupposed in value-judgments, one regulative of human decisions.

If we admit an end in itself in terms of which states of affairs are judged to have deficits, privations, and the like, and other things are judged to be good or bad, to ought to-be or ought not to-be in terms of their serviceability in removing the deficiencies, why not say that the end in itself is good in itself or intrinsically good? Is it merely because in ordinary life-situations we do not have occasion to make such value-judgments but merely to appraise situations as "troubled" and things as means? But why not in the theoretical situation do explicitly what is presupposed in the practical situation?

I think we may conclude that Dewey has not made out his case that there is no meaningful value-judgment of the form 'x is intrinsically good' or 'x is good in itself'; for this seems to be presupposed even in his account of value-judgments as of the means-end type. Furthermore, it seems reasonable to hold that any attempt of this kind would presuppose that something is good in itself. So we may conclude that this is not a possible escape for the classical naturalist.

The other way of escape mentioned is to hold that 'x is intrinsically good (or good in itself)' does not entail 'x ought to-be.' If the classical naturalist takes this way out, he can countercharge that the critic thinks that the argument of the naturalistic fallacy is valid precisely because of this mistake. So for him, the meaningfulness of the question 'Ought Cx to-be?' or 'Ought x to be C?' has no bearing upon the question whether 'x is good in itself' means the same as 'x is C.' If the naturalist replies in this way, of course he has to give a satisfactory analysis of 'ought' which will square with it. The immediate point I am concerned to make is that the question at issue may be begged by the argument of the naturalistic fallacy so that it cannot be used as an argument in settling the issue. I presume that every classical naturalist would admit the validity of the argument if he believed that 'good in itself' means the same as 'as it ought to be.' This point has to be settled before the argument can have force.

Many classical naturalists have treated 'good in itself' or 'intrinsically good' as neither synonymous with nor as entailing 'ought.' For them, to say that something is good in itself is merely to describe it, to say something factual about it. Usually it is taken to mean that all people do in fact desire it or that it is such that anyone with knowledge and experience of it would desire it; or perhaps, in the case of 'morally good in itself,' it is such that, if there were a common desire of the people of a society, it would be its object. In other words, something is said to be good in itself if it is such that people or societies naturally desire it for its own sake, not merely as a means to some other end. It is something which is desired without the benefit of deliberation and decision and provides an end, a framework, in terms of which other matters can be deliberated and decided.

Consider Bentham's position. Although he does not define 'good in itself,' he seems to presuppose that it means the same as 'desirable for its own sake' (the same as 'x is such that it would be desired by anyone with knowledge and experience of it'). Believing that pleasure is the only thing desirable in this manner, he holds that pleasure is the only thing good in itself. With respect to 'morally good in itself' he seems to hold that it means whatever is the ultimate end of human action and that this is revealed by the end which all appeal to in judging their own and the acts of others. This, he says, is the greatest happiness of all concerned. "Has the rectitude of this principle been ever formally contested?" he asks. "It should seem that it had, by those who have not known what they have been meaning [by their value-terms]. Is it susceptible of any direct proof? It should seem not: for that which is used to prove everything else, cannot itself be proved. . . . To give such a proof is as impossible as it is needless. Not that there is or ever has been that human creature breathing, however stupid or perverse, who has not on many, perhaps on most occasions of his life, deferred to it. By the natural constitution of the human frame, on most occasions of their lives men in general embrace this principle, without thinking of it: if not for the ordering of their own actions, yet for the trying of their own actions, as well as of those of other men."[30] So deliberation and decision, according to Bentham, presuppose the framework of pleasures and pains and whatever gives rise to them as things pursued and avoided, with the ultimate end in terms of which pleasures and pains are weighed and balanced and decisions made and acts appraised being the greatest possible net sum of pleasure for all concerned.

For Bentham, 'extrinsically good,' 'ought,' 'ought not,' 'right,' and 'wrong' have meaning only in terms of what is intrinsically good. "Of an action that is conformable to the principle of utility," he says, "one may always say either that it is one that ought to be done, or at least that it is not one that ought not to be done. One may say also that it is right it should be done; at least that it is not wrong it should be done; that it is a right action; at least that it is not a wrong action. When thus interpreted, the words *ought,* and *right* and *wrong,* and others of that stamp, have a meaning: when otherwise, they have none."[31]

There is some confusion that needs clearing up. If our interpretation of Bentham is correct, 'The greatest happiness of all concerned is the only thing morally intrinsically good' is a synthetic statement. It expresses a factual truth of what men ultimately desire as revealed by what they appeal to in appraising actions. It could conceivably be otherwise. So Bentham should not have defined 'ought,' 'right,' and 'wrong' in terms of the principle of utility itself but in terms of *whatever* is morally intrinsically good. 'Ought' then should have been defined to mean

30. Jeremy Bentham, *An Introduction to the Principles of Morals and Legislation* (Oxford: Clarendon Press, 1907), p. 4.
31. *Ibid.,* p. 4.

required for or a necessary condition of the existence of something which is morally intrinsically good.

Now let us return to Moore's recurrent question asked in the 'ought'-form. For Bentham 'morally good in itself' means the same as 'object of men's ultimate desire as revealed by what they appeal to in appraising actions.' The recurrent question in 'ought'-form would amount to the "tautological" question, 'Is the object of men's ultimate desire a requirement for or necessary condition of the attainment of the object of men's ultimate desire?' So the naturalist has the recurrent 'ought'-question reduced to a form he can answer in the way in which he could answer the recurrent question framed in terms of 'good'; he can say that it shows the limit to internal questions and that its apparent synthetic meaningfulness is due to the looseness of ordinary language. This is a reply to the argument which cannot be discredited by the argument itself. Thus, the question whether the presuppositions of the argument or of the reply are true must be decided on other grounds.

The issue between the classical naturalist and the critic wielding the naturalistic-fallacy argument turns upon this point: can an x that is a necessary condition of y be said to ought to-be relative to y when in no significant synthetic sense can it be said that y itself ought to-be? The classical naturalist treats 'ought' as a deliberative word. It is considered to be applicable only to that which can be deliberated about and that which is subject to decision. If commitment to our ultimate end is not subject to deliberation and decision, then 'ought' has no significant synthetic application to it. This sounds plausible within the framework of the classical naturalist. His nonnaturalist opponent contends that unless the object of man's ultimate interest ought to-be in some significant synthetic sense, then no necessary condition of it ought to-be in the sense with which he is concerned. Every argument which either uses against the other is premised upon the correctness of the arguer's own position and begs the question at issue. This is not to say that no considerations can be introduced to support one or the other position. It only means that arguments such as that of the naturalistic fallacy do not disprove a position; they only deny it.

If the classical naturalist is correct, to say that x is intrinsically good is not to commend it in the sense of implying that it ought to-be or that it ought to be pursued. To say that it is intrinsically good is the same as to say that it is such that it is desired for its own sake by those who know it and have experienced it. People by their nature are committed to it. It is not for them to make a decision about it. Yet by virtue of what 'ought' means, not by virtue of what 'intrinsically good' means, 'ought'-statements can be derived from statements of the form 'x is intrinsically good.'

It seems then that classical naturalists can defend their position against objections involved in the argument of the naturalistic fallacy only by shaping their position so that they can give an analytic answer to Moore's recurring question. If the question is asked in the form of 'Is a Cx good?' (where 'good' is defined in terms of 'C'), the answer is in the form of 'A Cx is a Cx'; if the question is asked in the form of 'Ought Cx-to-be?' it can be answered with the analytic statement 'If Cx, then Cx' or 'Cx is a necessary condition of Cx.'

Hare charges that such a position is Cartesianism in ethics,[32] which he characterizes as a position which tries "to deduce particular duties from some self-evident first principle (complete Cartesianism) or from some self-evident first principle in conjunction with factual premises (incomplete Cartesianism)." He rejects the position, whether complete or incomplete, on the ground that "a piece of genuinely evaluative moral reasoning must have as its end-product an imperative of the form 'Do so-and-so,'" where the "so-and-so" is some particular determinate act, and that we cannot deduce such particular imperatives from

32. The following discussion of Hare's charge is adapted from my article, "Cartesianism in Ethics," *Philosophy and Phenomenological Research*, XVI, No. 3 (March, 1956), 353-66.

a self-evident principle (which, for him, would have to be a general imperative) even in conjunction with factual minor premises.[33] He gives two arguments in support of this contention. Suppose, he says, that I were in doubt about whether to tell some falsehood. A moral principle that would be of any use, Hare contends, could not be self-evident, because it, perhaps in conjunction with some factual premises, would have to enjoin me not to tell (or to tell) the falsehood. But "since I am in doubt, *ex hypothesi,* whether or not to make this false statement, I must be in doubt about assenting to the command 'Do not make this statement.' But if I am in doubt about this command, I must *eo ipso* be in doubt, either about the factual premise 'the statement is false' (and this alternative is ruled out *ex hypothesi*), or else, as must be the case, about the imperative premise 'never say what is false.' "[34]

Furthermore, he contends, "It is not easier, but more difficult to assent to a very general command like 'never say what is false' than it is to assent to the particular command, 'do not say this particular thing which is false,' just as it is more difficult and dangerous to adopt the hypothesis that all mules are barren than to acknowledge the undoubted fact that this mule which has just died has had no progeny."[35]

His second argument runs like this: "No general principle can be self-evident which is to be of assistance in deciding particular questions about which we are in doubt," for if it is self-evident it is analytic, and "if it is analytic, it cannot have any content; it cannot tell me to do one thing rather than another."[36] Therefore, such a principle cannot be of any "assistance in deciding particular questions about which we are in doubt." Hence it is concluded that no general principles in ethics are self-evident.

The argument leaves the classical naturalist who gives an analytic answer to Moore's recurrent question (whether asked in

33. *The Language of Morals*, p. 39.
34. *Ibid.*, p. 41.
35. *Ibid.*, p. 40.
36. *Ibid.*, p. 41.

terms of 'good' or 'ought') unscathed. In the first place, the whole contention is based upon a misunderstanding of the nature and role of such an analytic principle in naturalism; in the second place the two arguments to show that an analytic principle would be useless do not establish their point.

Actually the first argument, if valid, proves too much; for it proves not only that no self-evident principle can be useful but that no principle whatever, whether self-evident or not, can be useful in solving the particular problem. According to it, as long as the problem exists, the principle also is in doubt. Hare tries to extricate himself from this predicament with the theory that every decision is twofold, involving a decision about the particular issue at hand and a "decision of principle."

The whole argument is based on a misformulated example, which is taken as a paradigm of all cases of evaluative moral reasoning. What is the specific problem in the example cited? Is it *"Should I make this statement?"* or *"Should I make this false statement?"* Hare vacillates back and forth between the two. He begins with the latter problem but shifts to the former when he tries to force his reasoning into a practical syllogism with a general imperative major premise and a factual minor premise. The argument he is actually employing has no factual premise. It is this:

> Never make a [known] false statement.
> Therefore, do not make this [known] false statement.

But clearly if one is in doubt about the conclusion, as is the case, then one must be in doubt about the premise. However, he applies the same reasoning to the following argument:

> Never make a [known] false statement.
> This statement is false.
> Therefore, do not make this statement.

Hare rightly contends that if one is in doubt about the conclusion, then one must be in doubt about either the imperative or the factual premise. But he fallaciously rules out, *ex hypothesi,* the possibility of doubt about the factual premise, because he considers the problem to be "Should I make this [known] *false* statement?" instead of "Should I make this statement?" One can be in doubt about whether to make *this statement* without being in doubt about whether never to make a known false statement, and the latter principle, if assented to, can be of genuine use in deciding whether to make this statement, when it is known to be false.

Of course one could not firmly accept the principle 'never make a statement known to be false' and at the same time be in doubt about whether to tell something known to be false. If the problem were whether to make a known false statement, a genuine case of reasoning about it would have to be of the form:

> Never make a known false statement *under such-and-such conditions.*
>
> To say this would be to make a known false statement *under such-and-such conditions.*
>
> Therefore, do not make this known false statement.

And there is no reason whatever why one could not be in doubt about the conclusion without having the least doubt about the imperative premise. Certainly, doubt about the factual premise cannot be ruled out *ex hypothesi.* Hare's whole argument turns upon this point, but it is valid in his case only because of his misformulation of the argument.

I certainly do not wish to contend that the principle 'never make a known false statement' or 'one ought never to make a known false statement' is self-evident. My only point is that his argument does not prove that no self-evident principle could be of use in genuine evaluative moral reasoning.

The second argument, to the effect that an analytic principle cannot have any content and therefore cannot tell us to do one thing rather than another, is also suspect. Although Hare generalizes the concept of the analytic so that it applies to imperatives as well as to statements, there is no special problem here with regard to imperatives. What he is saying would apply equally to statements. We can draw a factual conclusion from an analytic premise in conjunction with a factual premise. For example:

> All unmarried men are bachelors.
> John is an unmarried man.
> Therefore, John is a bachelor.

This is certainly logically permissible. But perhaps what he has in mind is that the conclusion follows from the factual premise alone and that therefore the analytic premise serves no function. But in the derivation of the conclusion from the factual premise the analytic premise is presupposed. True enough, there is no need for it to appear here in the material mode as a premise. But if it were not analytically true, the conclusion would not follow from the factual premise alone.

Here we have revealed the genuine status and role of the classical naturalist's analytic value-statement. It is not an ethical principle (a principle in ethics itself) to be used as an explicit premise in determining what ought to be done in particular situations. However, its formulation in the material mode has misled many in this respect, naturalists as well as their critics. As I said earlier, the naturalist's analytic answer to Moore's recurring question indicates the limit to internal questions of its kind; it marks the borderline between ethics and the philosophy of ethics. It is not an internal ethical statement at all, but a statement in the philosophy of ethics, a presupposition of ethics. It is not to be used on all fours with internal ethical principles in determining what ought to be done in a particular situation. Thus, Hare's alleged criticism of self-evident or analytic ethical principles is based upon a misconception of their nature and function. There is nothing in his argument to embarrass the classical naturalist who answers Moore's recurrent question with an analytic value-judgment.

The conclusion of this discussion, then, is that the argument of the naturalistic fallacy does not disprove classical naturalism; it does not show that the position necessarily involves a fallacy—a violation of some rule of logic, such as (as Moore charges) the assertion of contradictory statements. The "argument," as we have seen, simply presupposes that the classical naturalist is wrong. It proves nothing. It begs the real issue. But the presuppositions of the argument point up certain problems which the classical naturalist must meet. They all concern how well his position squares with the use of value-terms in ordinary language. More specifically, the argument points up the following uses which must be accommodated or explained away: (1) the apparent universal significance of the value-question 'Is x good?' where 'x' is any nonvalue-name or description and thus includes any nonvalue-term which might appear as a definiens in a naturalistic definition of a value-word; (2) the commending (and condemning) function of value-language; and (3) the apparent entailment of 'x ought to-be' by 'x is good' and yet apparently no such entailment by any purely factual statement. We have seen that the classical naturalist can handle the second use (so long as it is interpreted in a purely pragmatic way in the manner of Stevenson and Hare) by pointing out that he is not concerned with a descriptive account of how value-language functions but with what it shows about reality and that, therefore, he is interested in only the semantics of value-language. If the commending function is interpreted semantically, (2) is reduced to (3). Therefore, the problems for the classical naturalist are (1) and (3). The issue in both of these amounts to the same thing, namely, whether 'intrinsically good' or 'good in itself' means the same as or entails 'ought to-be' in a significant sense. The classical naturalist can maintain his position only by denying that it does. He must hold, it seems, that 'ought to-be' cannot be said significantly of what is said to be intrinsically good or good in itself, that 'good in itself' does not entail 'ought to-be' in any significant sense, for 'ought to-be' is defined in terms of the necessary conditions of that which is good in itself. The problem boils down to this: can 'good' in the sense of 'good in itself,' which sounds like a value-term *par excellence,* be predicated of something without implying that it ought to-be in a significant sense? Or we can put it this way: can 'ought to-be' be said of things in the sense of means or necessary conditions of something else without its being said of that of which the things in question are the means or necessary conditions? Perhaps, in the last analysis, we can only rely upon insight. The apparent universality of Moore's recurrent question is a linguistic consideration against classical naturalism. The classical naturalist, however, has his insight, based upon certain considerations, as a basis for ruling the question out and thereby marking a limit to any of its kind. The linguistic consideration, contrary to Moore and others, is not decisive, but it may be helpful in guiding our insight. Perhaps there are some further considerations bearing upon the matter. Let us move on to another argument which has been brought against the position.

## 2.5 *The argument from the nature of ethical disagreement*

The arguments considered in the last section (with the exception of Hare's version of the naturalistic fallacy) are thought by some not only to demolish classical naturalism but to lend support to an objective nonnaturalism. They never question the assumption that ethical discourse is meaningful, and for them this means that ethical terms designate properties—if not natural properties, then nonnatural ones. Therefore their attack upon classical naturalism is their most powerful defense of their own position. However, for many who accept the arguments of reductionism and of the naturalistic fallacy, nonnaturalistic objectivism is not a live option. Their epistemology and metaphysics militate against it. They are not prepared to give up naturalism so easily. Their problem is to account for the meaningfulness of moral discourse within the framework of metaphysical naturalism without accepting classical naturalism in the field of value-theory. A suggestion is found in (or at least supported by) further criticism of classical naturalism.

In his discussion of ethical agreement and disagreement, C. L. Stevenson implicitly argues against the position in this manner. Two or more people may be in ethical disagreement in regard to a matter while in complete factual agreement about it and *vice versa*. Hence the ethical aspect of the situation cannot be factual and ethical terms cannot be defined in such a manner that ethical judgments turn out to be factual. To elucidate the argument he employs an illustration in which the trustees of an estate, who have been instructed to forward any worthy charitable cause, disagree over building hospitals or endowing universities. "If the men come to agree in belief about all the factual matters they have considered, and if they continue to have divergent aims in spite of this—one still favoring the hospitals and the other the universities—they will still have an ethical issue that is unresolved. But if they come to agree, for instance, in favoring the universities, they will have brought their ethical issue to an end; and this will be so even though various beliefs, such as those about certain social effects of education, still remain debatable."[37] Toulmin makes the same point this way. "There is no reason in the world why all our words should act as names for definite and unique processes—physical or mental: only some of them, in fact, are such a kind that it makes sense to talk of such processes. And we can easily see that the class of concepts for which it does make sense cannot include ethical concepts. For, if 'goodness' or 'rightness' were something which could be definitely correlated with such a process, that would make nonsense of the crucial fact . . . that there may yet be ethical differences, even when all sources of factual disagreement have been ruled out."[38]

A somewhat similar (if not the same) point has been made, or at least suggested, by the so-called statistical argument. So far as I know it was first used by C. D. Broad as a criticism of

37. *Ethics and Language*, p. 14.
38. *The Place of Reason in Ethics*, p. 44.

Hume's naturalism. "One consequence of Hume's view . . . ," he says, "is that every dispute on questions of right and wrong is capable of being settled completely by the simple method of collecting statistics. . . . Suppose that, when all differences and confusions on these non-ethical matters have been removed, A still thinks that x is right and B still thinks that it is wrong. If Hume's theory be true, this means that A thinks that most men would feel an emotion of approval on contemplating x, whilst B thinks that most men would feel an emotion of disapproval on contemplating x. Now this is a question which can be settled by experiment, observation, collecting of statistics, and empirical generalization. This seems to me simply incredible."[39] Stevenson says that the argument applies to all traditional interest-theories. However, it is clear that he erroneously considers all of them to be reducible to Hume's position.[40] For Ewing[41] the argument becomes generalized into the form that ethical judgments simply are not statistical and cannot be verified by a statistical count of any kind, regardless of what the statistics are about. He thinks that the argument applies to all forms of psychological and biological naturalism. It is not the case, of course, that all interest-theories reduce to Broad's statistical interpretation of Hume's position; nor is it true that all psychological and biological naturalistic positions are purely or even basically statistical in character. This is not so, for example, for Dewey with his means-end judgments nor even for Perry with his complicated theory of the commensurability of interests and their threefold magnitude, involving intensive and distensive as well as extensive quantities. Perhaps the point of the argument can be generalized even further, namely, that it is absurd to think that we can settle an ethical disagreement purely and simply by empirically discovering facts of any kind, statistical or

39. *Five Types of Ethical Theory* (London: K. Paul, French, Trubner and Co., 1930), pp. 114-15.
40. "The Emotive Meaning of Ethical Terms," *Mind*, N.S., XLVI, No. 181 (Jan., 1937), 16 ff.
41. *The Definition of the Good*, p. 41.

otherwise. Interpreted in this way, the argument makes the same point as Stevenson's and Toulmin's argument about the nature of ethical disagreement.

There are two replies which the classical naturalist can make about the alleged peculiarity of ethical disagreement. He may contend that the relevant factual matters are so complex that it is impossible ever to be certain that there is complete factual agreement about an issue and that therefore we can never be sure that the ethical disagreement is not factual. For example, a Fiji islander says that a son ought to kill his parents while they are still in the prime of life. Most other people would say that such an act would be about the worst imaginable. Yet the disagreement would be found to turn upon factual beliefs. The Fiji islander believes that one lives forever in another world in the physical condition one was in just before death. Hence it is important not to die a natural death and not to live until one loses one's powers. It becomes a filial duty to see that neither of these things happens to one's parents. If anyone should accept these beliefs, he might agree with the Fiji islander about the obligation of parricide. Here, of course, the factual disagreement is obvious. Stevenson and especially Toulmin do not deny that in many cases ethical disagreement is grounded in factual differences. The point is whether in cases where there are no known factual disagreements we can be certain that an ethical disagreement is not grounded in some hidden or presupposed factual difference. The factual presuppositions of the simplest statement are so extensive and complex that no one could ever fully formulate them or at least could not know that he had formulated them. But it is not reasonable to think that there would be undiscoverable factual disagreements which would be so important that they would give rise to opposed ethical judgments about a particular problem but would not give rise to differences about any of the known facts involved. In any case, the classical naturalist's analysis of the ethical judgment indicates the fact which he thinks it asserts; and two people can agree about that fact and yet disagree ethically about the issue.

The classical naturalist might say that in the case of factual agreement and opposing ethical judgments the apparent ethical disagreement is really linguistic. The source of the difficulty, it might be claimed, lies in the ambiguity of ethical terms. They mean one thing to one and perhaps something else to the other. The situation, it might be said, is like the argument whether a man in circling a tree in which there is a squirrel goes around the squirrel when the squirrel keeps the tree between himself and the man at all times. But if it is this kind of linguistic difficulty, why cannot linguistically sophisticated people locate the sense in which each party is using the term and, with this cleared up, reach an ethical agreement? The fact is that the ethical disagreement cannot be resolved in this manner.

The point of the argument, and I think that it is a good one, is that one is not convinced that x is right or that x ought to be done, regardless of what facts one acknowledges, so long as one does not look upon it with at least some favor. Of course, attitudes toward things are often involved in believing factual statements about them, but they are not linguistically required in the way in which they are with value-judgments. Acceptance of a factual statement about something may be accompanied by opposing attitudes toward it by different people—but not so with value-judgments. It might be said that this is the case because value-judgments, especially ethical ones, are about matters of universal concern; or, perhaps the other way around, people are so constituted that they are universally concerned in the same way about the things value-language is used to talk about. However, there is reason to think that in the very nature of the case the acceptance of a value-judgment involves having an attitude toward that which it is about. It is a linguistic absurdity to say such things as this: 'I ought to do x. That I acknowledge. But I am completely and unalterably opposed to doing it.' Or, 'this is the only right thing for you to do; but, whatever you do, don't do it.' Stevenson and others have taken this fact to be involved in the meaning of the value-judgment itself; however, it may be indicative of the character of the *acceptance* of the value-judgment rather than of the value-judgment. There is something of the same kind of absurdity in saying, "I *accept* the value-judgment 'a is good,' but I have a totally negative attitude toward a" as there is in saying 'I accept the statement S, but I don't believe it.' Having a favorable attitude toward x is, I suggest, the way in which one accepts the judgment 'x is good,' just as believing is the way in which one accepts a factual statement. But the acceptance of no factual statement as such necessarily involves having either a pro or con attitude toward anything. This is what is behind Stevenson's distinction between disagreement in attitude and disagreement in belief. I cannot accept his account of the matter, but he does point up an issue which the classical naturalists have not sufficiently recognized.

Perhaps it was an insight into this same peculiarity of value-language which was behind Moore's naturalistic-fallacy argument. His point may be construed to be that no amount of determination of the facts of a case establishes an ethical judgment or settles an ethical issue about it per se. This seems to be what is involved in the apparent meaningfulness of his recurrent value-question.

### 2.6 Conclusion

We have considered three arguments against classical naturalism: the arguments of reductionism, the naturalistic fallacy, and the nature of ethical disagreement. The first argument was found only to point up apparent differences between the languages of ethics and of science and to challenge the classical naturalist to show that they have no ontological significance. The other two arguments, when properly understood, were seen to reinforce each other in such a way that they are a serious threat to classical naturalism. In fact, I think that they render it untenable. There seems to be something more to the meaning of an ethical judgment than it acknowledges. With his unquestioned assumption that ethical sentences are meaningful and with his theory of meaning (according to which a sentence is meaningful by virtue of the designation of its terms), the only way for Moore to account for this peculiarity was to posit a nonnatural (nonempirical) quality as the designatum of the basic value-term. But such a solution cannot be admitted by a naturalist without giving up his basic epistemological and metaphysical commitments. Furthermore, Stevenson's way of making the point renders such a position just as untenable as that of classical naturalism. For why should agreement about the nonnatural characteristics of a thing require agreement in attitude toward it any more than agreement about its natural properties? Both seem to be equally "factual."

Not only for the sake of saving naturalism, but in order to meet the problem at all, some radically new departure is needed. A point has been reached at which no further progress on the problem seems possible within the framework of the classical naturalist. This calls for re-examination of fundamentals.

CHAPTER III

# EMOTIVE NATURALISM

## 3.1 *Emotive meaning*

Two assumptions are made by both classical naturalists and Moorean nonnaturalists; namely, (1) ethical sentences are meaningful, and (2) every meaningful sentence is such by virtue of the designation of its terms. These have been vigorously challenged. The logical positivists, championing a criterion of meaningfulness which has been implicit in empiricism since the eighteenth century (namely, the empirical verifiability theory) and accepting the criticisms of classical naturalism, boldly declare that ethical sentences, along with a number of other pedigreed varieties, are meaningless. Ayer, in his provocative and influential book, *Language, Truth and Logic,* reasons this way. Every meaningful synthetic sentence is empirically verifiable. Traditionally ethical sentences have been thought to be either empirically verifiable (classical naturalism) or "not controlled by observation, as ordinary empirical propositions are, but only by a mysterious 'intellectual intuition.' "[1] The first alternative is said to be untenable, for it involves the naturalistic fallacy. (Stevenson would add the argument from the nature of ethical disagreement.) The second is rejected because it holds that ethical sentences are both synthetic and meaningful but are not empirically verifiable. So he concludes that ethical concepts are pseudo. "The presence

1. Alfred J. Ayer, *Language, Truth and Logic* (2nd ed.; New York: Dover Publications, 1948), p. 106.

of an ethical symbol in a proposition," he says, "adds nothing to its factual content. Thus if I say to someone, 'you acted wrongly in stealing that money,' I am not stating anything more than if I had simply said, 'you stole that money.' In adding that this action is wrong I am not making any further statement about it. I am simply evincing my moral disapproval of it. It is as if I had said, 'you stole that money,' in a peculiar tone of horror, or written it with the addition of some special exclamation marks. The tone, or the exclamation marks, adds nothing to the literal meaning of the sentence. It merely serves to show that the expression of it is attended by certain feelings in the speaker. . . . Another man may disagree with me about the wrongness of stealing, in the sense that he may not have the same feelings about stealing as I have, and he may quarrel with me on account of my moral sentiments . . . . there is plainly no sense in asking which of us is in the right. For neither of us is asserting a genuine proposition. . . . they have no objective validity whatsoever. . . . they are pure expressions of feeling and as such do not come under the category of truth and falsehood. They are unverifiable for the same reason as a cry of pain or a word of command is unverifiable . . . because they do not express genuine propositions."[2]

This ruthless rejection of the meaningfulness of value-terms (and others) is so shocking that it makes a serious examination of assumption (2) inevitable. It is clear that ethical sentences are "meaningful" in a way in which arbitrary arrangements of the alphabet are not. If ethical terms do not designate, then they must be meaningful by virtue of some other feature. Stevenson sought a generic concept of meaning that would permit us to speak of nondesignating ethical terms as having meaning. This he found in "the psychological reactions of those who use the sign."[3] The meaning of a sign, in this sense, is its power or disposition to affect a hearer which "has been caused by, and

2. *Ibid.*, pp. 107-9.
3. *Ethics and Language*, p. 42.

would not have developed without, an elaborate process of conditioning which has attended the sign's use in communication."[4] So we get two species of meaning—emotive and cognitive; for signs have the specified kind of power or disposition both to express and to arouse feeling and to express and to arouse thought of an object. Ethical sentences are "meaningful," then, in that they have emotive meaning.

This may appear to be nothing more than what Stevenson would call a 'persuasive definition' of 'meaning' for the purpose of relieving the shock of saying that ethical terms are meaningless. However, there seems to be something more behind it. The traditional theory of meaning had been questioned in the teachings of Wittgenstein at Cambridge. He had said to look for the use of expressions, not their meaning. This way of putting it did not identify use and meaning, but it was the origin of the so-called use-theory. It results from a different approach to the problem. Some have thought of the meaning of a term as that which is meant in the role of being meant; others have thought of it as that by virtue of which it is meaningful. The two approaches might terminate at the same point except for the ambiguity of 'meaningful.' Logical positivists think of a sentence as meaningful if it has a meaning in the sense of experienceable truth-conditions. This is in line with the traditional position, according to which the meaning of a declarative sentence is thought of as that which it *means,* which it asserts, in the role of being asserted. This is sometimes expressed as how reality must be different with the sentence true from the way it would be with it false. The logical positivists propose the empirical verifiability principle as a criterion of meaningfulness. Confusion of a criterion of meaningfulness with that by virtue of which a sentence is meaningful and thereby with its meaning gives rise to such views as "the meaning of a sentence is its method of verification" and the operational theory. But for the

4. *Ibid.*, p. 57.

most part logical positivists stick by meaning as experienceable truth-conditions and declare all sentences literally meaningless which are lacking in this respect. However, they talk of the emotive use and even the emotive "meaning" of ethical terms. But here are signs of the use-theory of meaning which arose from another approach because of the ambiguity of 'meaningful.'

'Meaningful' may mean that that of which it is predicated *means* something. But it may also mean that it makes sense, that it is intelligible. In the latter sense, a term or sentence is not meaningful, does not make sense, if it does not fit some pattern, if it does not have a place in the scheme of the language, if it does not have a use, if its occurrence is not rule-governed. Thus the terms and sentences declared meaningless by virtue of their not designating or asserting anything are declared meaningful by virtue of their having a rule-governed use in the language. This rule or habit-governed use for ethical terms is to express and to arouse feelings. Employing the formula that the meaning of an expression is that by virtue of which it is meaningful, the emotivist says that the meaning of an ethical expression consists of the power it has by virtue of rules or habits of usage to express and to arouse feelings and attitudes.

We may say that it is by virtue of either a persuasive definition or an equivocation of 'meaningful' that we speak of *emotive meaning* at all. However, the propriety of the term is a small matter. The important thing is the contention that ethical terms (even though they may have descriptive or designative meaning by virtue of the fact that our attitudes are usually directed to classes or kinds of objects rather than merely to individuals[5]) do not, as *ethical* terms, designate an ethical quality or feature of reality but are used to express and to evoke feelings and attitudes. It matters little whether we say 'ethical and emotive *meaning*' or merely 'ethical and emotive *use*.'

5. *Cf.* Ayer, *Language, Truth and Logic*, p. 21.

### 3.2 The emotive theory of ethics is naturalistic

The emotive theory, then, accounts for the apparent irreducible nature of value-discourse (the apparent meaningfulness of Moore's recurrent question and also the peculiarities of ethical disagreement as stated by Stevenson) from within the general position of ethical naturalism. The emotivist is as firmly committed to the position that the ontology of value-language is included in the ontology of the language of science as the classical naturalist. Where value-language designates at all, it designates purely natural qualities which may be equally well designated by scientific expressions. Even the feelings and attitudes expressed and evoked by value-language are subject to being referred to by scientific terms. Nowhere is there to be found (or even hinted at) a peculiar ontological entity called 'value.' As one emotivist put it: "I acknowledge and obey many moral demands, . . . I make many moral demands myself, . . . I often express my moral demands in the forms 'you ought to do x' and 'y is wrong'; but . . . I hold that from these emotive uses of the words 'ought' and 'wrong' no true descriptive uses of them can be inferred, and nothing follows about what attributes occur in the world except that moral demands and emotions occur."[6] In other words, there is nothing indicated or shown about the world by the language of value which is not also indicated or shown by the language of science. The emotive theory is simply another form of ethical naturalism designed to meet the telling criticisms of classical naturalism.

### 3.3 How value-discourse is practical

There have been few philosophical theories so vigorously championed and so heatedly opposed as the emotive theory. I shall not attempt to catalogue the criticisms which have been made of it. Many of them have been based upon misunderstandings of the theory. Some have been moralistic. But others, I

6. Richard Robinson, "The Emotive Theory of Ethics," *Aristotelian Society,* Supp. Vol. XXII (1948), 95.

think, have made their mark with telling effect. I myself believe the position to be untenable. The remainder of this chapter will be given to what I believe to be valid arguments against it. I shall draw upon the criticisms of others when I find them helpful, but my purpose is to get at the truth of the matter rather than to survey and to appraise the literature of the opposition.

One of the strong points in favor of the emotive theory is its recognition of the practical function of moral discourse. It is an undeniable fact that value-language is not used simply to formulate and to impart factual information. It is not used merely for the purposes of "pure thought." Of course scientific language has a practical employment. The pragmatist will tell us that it is primary. But there is no denying that value-language is the language of feeling, desire, and volition in a way that is not so with the language of science. There is ground for saying that value-language is primarily the language of affection and conation and of thought pertaining thereto, whereas the language of science is primarily the language of perception and of thought pertaining to it. Something of this difference was recognized and marked by the classical distinction between practical and theoretical reason, but it was not sufficiently appreciated by classical naturalists and Moorean nonnaturalists alike. The emotivists are to be credited with calling our attention to this error.

However, they give what is basically a causal account of how value-language is practical. Ayer speaks of ethical statements as "expressions and excitants of feelings which do not necessarily involve any assertions."[7] According to Robinson the emotive theory means that an ethical word has "independent emotive meaning," "the power . . . to arouse emotion independently of what it describes or names."[8] But this power is quite different from the power of words to arouse thoughts of objects. The

---

7. *Language, Truth and Logic*, pp. 109-10.
8. *"The Emotive Theory of Ethics,"* *Aristotelian Society*, Supp. Vol. XXII (1948), 79.

latter is governed by rules and can be changed by changing the rules, by redefinition. But not so for emotive words. " 'Good,' " Robinson says, "has a certain practical force, which we can no more alter by our definitions than most of us can alter the economic system of our country. . . . The nature of this inevitable practical force," he continues, "is that, each time we declare to another man that x is good, *we are doing something that tends to make him* approve x or evaluate it favourably. The influence is often extremely slight, like the force of gravity; but, like the force of gravity, it is always there, and one cannot legislate it out of existence. . . . Whereas the descriptive function of words can be altered by deliberate definition, their emotive function cannot be."[9] Stevenson speaks of the descriptive and the dynamic uses of words, the latter being characterized as the use of words "*to give vent* to our feelings, or *to create* moods, or *to incite* people to actions or attitudes."[10] In the same article he speaks of the "magnetism" of ethical terms. It is clear that he thinks of this as a causal disposition. There are no emotive synonyms, he says, for "each term bears the characteristic stamp of its emotional history."[11] The point here is that the causal disposition of a term which constitutes its emotive meaning is acquired by its use in emotionally charged situations. Again, he says, "Instead of identifying meaning with *all* the psychological causes and effects that attend a word's utterance, we must identify it with those that it has a *tendency* (causal property, dispositional property) to be connected with." Furthermore the disposition, in order to constitute meaning, "must exist for all who speak the language; it must be persistent; and must be realizable more or less independently of determinate circumstances attending the word's utterance."[12]

9. *Ibid.*, pp. 89-90; italics added.
10. "The Emotive Meaning of Ethical Terms," *Mind*, N.S., XLVI, No. 181 (Jan., 1937), 21. Italics added.
11. *Ethics and Language*, p. 82.
12. "The Emotive Meaning of Ethical Terms," *Mind*, N.S., XLVI, No. 181 (Jan., 1937), 22.

Value-terms, then, according to the emotive theory, are tools or instruments, long in the making, for venting one's own feelings and for causally affecting the feelings, attitudes, and actions of others. The utterance of an ethical sentence is, insofar as it is an *ethical* sentence, a purely natural occurrence which gives vent to a feeling of the speaker in the manner of a cry or a groan and causally arouses or produces feelings and attitudes in the hearer. We might say that the utterance is, on the one hand, either simply an effect of the emotional condition of the speaker or an act intentionally done because it has the consequence of venting or releasing pent-up emotional energy; or, on the other hand, it is an intentionally introduced event for the purpose of causally manipulating the feelings and attitudes of the hearer. What appears to be moral reasoning about a matter, except as it involves reasoning about factual matters, is not reasoning at all; for reasoning with one about something is not a matter of trying to produce causally an effect in one but of trying to convince one of something by showing one or getting one to see it. Moral "reasoning," according to the theory, is simply doing something to get a desired effect, throwing ethical words around to produce feelings and attitudes causally in the hearer, like fertilizing, watering, and hoeing flowers to make them grow. There is no question of the *validity* of moral judgments as such, only of their effectiveness. As Ayer says, in the case of a purely ethical dispute, "there is plainly no sense in asking which . . . is in the right."[13] And, as Stevenson says, "if any ethical dispute is *not* rooted in disagreement in belief, then no *reasoned* solution of any sort is possible."[14]

It is universally recognized that in the case of factual beliefs people can be either causally persuaded or rationally convinced. The former is the technique of the advertiser, the propagandist, the indoctrinator. They are concerned with creating conditions which will causally induce people to believe whatever it is they

13. *Language, Truth and Logic,* p. 108.
14. *Ethics and Language,* p. 138.

want them to believe. The question of the truth of the propositions involved and of genuine evidence in support of them is of only incidental importance, if any. They have a task to do: to get people to believe that such-and-such is the case. What they want are efficient means of accomplishing the end-result. They are concerned with cause and effect relations. Rational conviction, on the other hand, is the way of the inquirer and the teacher. They are concerned with finding out what is the case and with *showing* others that it is so, with getting them to "see" that it is so or that it is probably so. The ultimate appeal, whether in logic and mathematics or in an empirical discipline, is to something "seen" or "recognized" to be the case, for which supporting reasons cannot be given. But even here, or should we say especially here, the distinction is clear between acceptance being caused and its being based on "seeing" or knowing. The genuine teacher tries to get one to "see" for oneself, not merely to accept, to believe. If acceptance or sheer belief of a body of statements were the objective, causal techniques, the methods of the propagandist and the advertiser, would no doubt be the most effective means.

Is there a parallel distinction with regard to value-judgments? The emotivist would say not. While he would allow that a moral judgment might be in error or be correct and reasoned about insofar as factual beliefs were involved, he would deny that this was true of a *pure* moral judgment, one which was in no way factual. When all the factual questions about an act and its situation have been answered, there is no further issue to be reasoned about; and when the possibility of factual error is set aside, there is nothing more about a moral judgment which is subject to being appraised correct or incorrect, sound or unsound, for there is nothing more that is cognitive. The pure moral judgment is merely an expression of an effect (a reaction to the object thought about in factual terms) and/or a device or instrument for producing (for causing) a similar reaction on the part of a hearer. Such reactions are thought of as noncognitive natural occurrences in the ordinary causal nexus of events.

The truth of this position, as I see it, turns upon two points: (1) whether emotive states or attitudes which are expressed and evoked by ethical language are merely natural occurrences within the causal nexus and (2) whether pure moral judgments are subject to being reasoned about and to being appraised as sound and unsound or correct and incorrect. These are not distinct problems. They are tied together. The only alternative, I suppose, to emotive states or attitudes being natural occurrences within the sequence of causes and effects is for them to be in some way cognitive and, therefore, subject to being appraised correct or incorrect. And the only way for pure moral judgments (sentences) to be subject to being reasoned about and appraised sound or unsound would be for the emotive states and attitudes "expressed" and "evoked" by them to be cognitive and, therefore, subject to being appraised correct or incorrect. So to argue for (1) is to argue for (2).

### 3.4 How a value-sentence expresses an attitude

The emotivist's account of the relationship between value-utterances and feelings and attitudes is essential to his position. It is one, as we have seen, of *expressing* and *exciting*. The moral utterance "expresses" the speaker's attitude and "excites" a feeling in the hearer or reader. No one, I suppose, would deny this. But the important question is, What does it mean? In what sense does a value-utterance "express" the speaker's attitude and "excite" a feeling in the hearer? The emotivist gives a causal interpretation. He thinks that one's ethical utterance expresses one's attitude in much the same way as one's tone of voice may express irritation or annoyance. Now, a quality of one's voice "expresses" irritation or some other emotional state by being a natural sign of it, a sign of it based on a causal relationship. The quality of voice is itself an effect of the irritation. It shows or "expresses" it in the same way in which a muddy river shows that it has rained recently, the way in which red spots on the body show that one has measles, or the way in which steam rising from a pot shows that it contains hot liquids. Is this the way in which an ethical utterance "expresses" or shows one's attitude? I think not. One intentionally makes the ethical utterance. It is not simply a natural effect of an emotional state. It is not a natural sign. If anything, it is a linguistic sign. Any act or gesture which is intentionally done to communicate something to another is of this type. However, I think the emotivist is right in resisting the view that the ethical utterance means semantically that the speaker has a certain attitude. When I say 'x is right' I do not *state* that I approve of x. The emotivist is also correct in his contention that when I say 'x is right' I in some way "show" or "express" my approval of x. One would not know what to make of it if I should say 'x is right, but I disapprove of it.' It would be the same kind of linguistic absurdity as saying 'Roosevelt died in 1945, but I don't believe it.'

Then, if a moral utterance does not *say* that the speaker has a certain attitude toward what it is about and does not express or show the attitude in the manner of a natural sign, how does it express or show it? I suggest that it does it in much the same way as a factual utterance expresses or shows a belief. When I say 'Roosevelt died in 1945' I do not assert that *I believe* that Roosevelt died in 1945, but I do show or express my belief. To utter the sentence in an ordinary conversational context certainly gives others warrant for believing that I believe it. The utterance makes my belief known to others, but not in the way in which my utterance of the sentence 'I believe that Roosevelt died in 1945' would, nor in the way in which the tone of one's voice might express irritation. It is not even that people ordinarily believe what they say and that therefore others may infer with a high degree of probability that when one says something one believes it; nor is it that one morally should believe what one says, or perhaps the other way around—one should not say what one does not believe. It is that my *saying* 'Roosevelt died in 1945' *presupposes* in some sense that I believe Roosevelt died in 1945. Of course I may say 'Roosevelt died in 1945' when I really believe he died in 1946. But this merely shows that what is presupposed by an utterance may be false. That the belief-sentence is presupposed in some sense is shown by the fact that it would be absurd, as it was pointed out above, for me to say 'Roosevelt died in 1945, but I don't believe it.' Such an utterance is not strictly self-contradictory. It does not both assert and deny the same thing. But it does *presuppose* and deny the same thing. This is a kind of self-contradiction. It is a linguistic absurdity. If the parallel I am pointing up holds, when I say 'x is right,' I do not assert that I approve of x and I do not "display" or "evince" my attitude of approval, but rather I *presuppose* that I approve of it.

There is another sense of the word 'express' in terms of which we can say that a sentence expresses a belief. We can report an event like Roosevelt's death by saying 'Roosevelt died on April 12, 1945.' But I cannot report my believing it in this manner. I would have to use indirect discourse: 'I believe *that Roosevelt died on April 12, 1945.*' This shows that believing has a semantic content or dimension. For me to say 'Roosevelt died on April 12, 1945' may report his death, but it also *expresses* the content of my belief (what it is that I believe) as distinct from "expressing" or showing the autobiographical fact that I believe that he died on that date. This points up a peculiarity of at least some mental occurrences, e.g., believing, thinking, knowing, and the like. They are not merely natural occurrences but have a semantic dimension or content. The question I am now raising is whether one's utterance of the sentence 'x is right' may "express" one's attitude in this sense and thereby show that moral attitudes have a semantic content like beliefs.

The feeling or attitude shown by the utterance of a moral sentence is not simply a pro or con feeling. It must be distinguished from simple likings and dislikings, acceptances and rejections. The most common feelings or attitudes so expressed are those of moral approval and disapproval. The emotivists, in my opinion, have not been very astute in distinguishing them from other kinds of emotive states and attitudes. Stevenson marks the difference this way: "Suppose that a man morally disapproves of a certain kind of conduct. If he observes this conduct in others, he may then feel indignant, mortified, or shocked; and if he finds himself given to it, he may feel guilty or conscience-stricken. But suppose that he dislikes this conduct, as distinct from morally disapproving of it. He may then be simply displeased when he observes it in others, and simply annoyed with himself when he finds that he is given to it. Similarly, if he morally approves of something, he may feel a particularly heightened sense of security when it prospers; whereas if he merely likes it, he may feel only an ordinary sort of pleasure."[15] These distinctions are sound, but Stevenson does not, I think, get to the bottom of what is behind them. He seems to think that the difference is solely genetic, the moral response of approval or disapproval being highly conditioned, with reward and punishment playing an important role.

In the first place, a person does not feel indignant, mortified, or shocked by what others do, nor feel guilty or conscience-stricken for what he himself does, *because* he disapproves of it. Rather to disapprove of x *is* to feel indignant, mortified, or shocked at others doing x and to feel guilty or conscience-stricken upon doing it himself. If disapproval is to be distinguished at all from such specific feelings, it is simply the disposition or capacity to have them. One does say that one disapproves of acts of a certain kind when at the time one has no noticeable feeling of any kind about the matter. In fact we do not have

15. *Ibid.*, p. 90.

specific feelings about kinds of acts any way, only about instances of them. What we mean when we say that we disapprove of acts of a certain kind is that we have a disposition or capacity to feel indignant at another's doing such a thing and to feel guilty at doing it ourselves.

The important question, then, is, How does feeling indignant at another's doing x or guilty for doing it oneself differ from being displeased or annoyed at another or oneself for doing it? Let us consider being indignant and being displeased or annoyed with someone. We are displeased or annoyed when what he does is contrary to some desire or wish of ours. But in feeling indignant about his doing something we think that what he has done is an injustice or a wrong of some kind to someone else. It is not simply that we believe it to be an injustice or a wrong and that this belief evokes a feeling of indignation. This would treat the feeling of indignation as a distinct effect of the belief. Thinking that the act is an injustice or a wrong to someone is an integral part of the feeling of indignation in much the same way as "thinking" that the pen is blue is involved in perceiving the pen to be blue. It is precisely in regard to this content of the feeling that it differs from simple displeasure or annoyance. The difference is not merely that the former is caused by a conditioning process involving rewards and punishments.

In fact, one does not have to be conditioned by rewards and punishments to feel indignant. The very young child may be only displeased or annoyed at his parents when they refuse to let him have his way; but at a certain level of maturity he begins to mark a distinction. At certain kinds of treatment he is displeased; at others he is indignant. If a brother or sister is given candy and he is refused without a good reason, he is not only displeased but indignant. He *feels* that he has been treated unjustly or done a wrong. This is not a feeling which has to be conditioned. All that is required is a certain level of maturity. Perhaps a stronger case can be made for the role of conditioning in the case of feeling guilt or being conscience-stricken for what one does oneself. But even here it may be simply that more maturity is required and that one's attention has to be directed to the wrongs one does to others. Certainly we are naturally more sensitive to the injustices and wrongs we suffer at the hands of others than to those suffered by others. The former cannot escape our attention, but other things can force the latter out of our minds. In any case, feeling guilty about having done something involves thinking that it is wrong in the same way in which feeling indignant does. We may say, in general, that an attitude of disapproval toward x involves feeling that x is wrong and that an attitude of approval involves feeling that x is right.

Now if this is the case, the feelings and attitudes shown and evoked by the utterance of moral sentences are not simply natural occurrences; they are semantic or cognitive. They are feelings *that x is wrong, that x is an injustice, that x is right,* and the like. If this is so, and I think it is, the utterance of an ethical sentence not only shows that one has an attitude of a certain kind but "expresses" or voices the semantic content of the attitude. We may say that the attitude shown by the moral utterance embodies or is constituted by a moral judgment. The judgment is the semantic content of the attitude. The emotive state makes a cognitive claim and, therefore, is not subject to being described and explained in terms of causal laws and antecedent conditions, but subject to being appraised as correct or incorrect, as valid or invalid, as rational or irrational.

### 3.5 *How we appraise moral feelings and attitudes in ordinary discourse*

How can this claim be substantiated? One method, and perhaps the only one, is to look to the way in which moral discourse functions in ordinary usage. How we categorize the phenomena of moral feelings and attitudes is revealed in our ordinary talk about them. And certainly how we categorize them in ordinary experience determines what they are in such a way that we cannot find out by inspecting them that they are miscategorized. Consequently, any theory about their nature must square itself with their categorial features revealed in our ordinary talk about them. So it is pertinent to ask if we, in ordinary life-situations, reason about and appraise our approvals and disapprovals, our feelings of justice and injustice, our feelings of obligation and of guilt, our preferences and decisions, as though they make cognitive claims which can be substantiated or invalidated. If we do, the emotive theory is false; for it not only denies that moral feelings and attitudes are subject to such appraisals but proposes to be an account of how moral discourse functions. At best it would be only a descriptive account of the pragmatic dimension of ethical language; it would be simply false in its contention that this is the whole story and that there is not a semantic or referential phase of the matter.

No one has stated the emotivist position more clearly than Hume in the following passage: "A passion is an original existence, or, if you will, modification of existence, and contains not any representative quality, which renders it a copy of any other existence or modification. When I am angry, I am actually possessed with the passion, and in that emotion have no more a reference to any other object, than when I am thirsty, or sick, or more than five feet high. It is impossible, therefore, that this passion can be opposed by, or be contradictory to truth and reason; since this contradiction consists in the disagreement of ideas, considered as copies, with those objects which they represent. . . . Where a passion is neither founded on false suppositions, nor chooses means insufficient for the end, the understanding can neither justify nor condemn it. It is not contrary to reason to prefer the destruction of the whole world to the scratching of my finger. It is not contrary to reason for me to choose my total ruin, to prevent the least uneasiness of an Indian, or person wholly unknown to me. It is as little contrary to reason to prefer even my own acknowledged lesser good to my greater, and have a more ardent affection for the former than the latter.

A trivial good may, from certain circumstances, produce a desire superior to what arises from the greatest and most valuable enjoyment; nor is there anything more extraordinary in this, than in mechanics to see one pound weight raise up a hundred by the advantage of its situation."[16]

The issues are clear in Hume's mind. If a passion—and for him this would include a feeling or an attitude—is subject to being appraised as correct or incorrect, as valid or invalid, as rational or irrational, then it must be referential or semantic in nature. He is convinced that such "phenomena" are original existences without any "representative quality" and so he concludes that they are not subject to being appraised in this manner. But if it should be found that they are subject to such appraisal, then we would have to conclude that either (a) they are semantic or referential in nature or (b) they need not be semantic or referential in order to be subject to being appraised as rational or irrational.

Let us consider the latter alternative. First of all, we must distinguish between two senses of 'rational' and 'irrational.' Sometimes we speak of the "rationality" of nature or of the possibility of an "irrational" world. Those who talk in this way identify being *rational* with being *intelligible* in the sense of exhibiting discoverable regularities and being *irrational* with being *unintelligible* in the sense of lacking any discoverable laws. An event that "follows" no law is in this sense irrational. However, this is not the sense of 'rational' and 'irrational' with which we are here concerned. Most of us operate upon the assumption that there are no irrational occurrences of this kind, and yet we are quite ready, I think, to appraise certain attitudes or preferences as irrational. Furthermore, 'irrational,' in the sense being explained, does not connote or entail that what is irrational is somehow invalid or wrong. They are purely descriptive terms. However, 'rational' and 'irrational' as appraisal terms do connote

16. David Hume, *A Treatise of Human Nature* (Everyman's Library; New York: E. P. Dutton and Co., 1911), II, 127-28.

or entail that whatever is so appraised is correct or incorrect, right or wrong, in regard to some cognitive claim that it makes. Hume himself equates "being irrational" with "being contradictory to truth and reason," which he says "consists in the disagreement of ideas considered as copies, with those objects which they represent." It is in this sense that we ask if a natural occurrence which is not at all cognitive could be properly appraised as rational or irrational.

From the clarification of what the question means it is evident, I think, what the answer must be. We certainly should not say that it was irrational of the sun to rise this morning nor that it was irrational of the hurricane to blow itself inland and wear itself out when it would have kept going much longer had it gone out to sea. A natural occurrence as such simply is. It has causes and effects. It has various kinds of relations to other events. But it makes no claim of any kind and consequently is not subject to being appraised as rational or irrational, as correct or incorrect. If we find, however, that moral feelings, attitudes, and preferences are subject to being appraised as rational or irrational, we may conclude that they do make some kind of a claim that is either correct or incorrect.

Now what should we say in an ordinary life-situation of the man who prefers the destruction of the whole world to the scratching of his finger? What in fact do we say of the person who prefers running the risk of having polio in the midst of an epidemic to taking three shots of Salk vaccine because the needle would hurt? What should we say of a person who preferred to run over a child in the road to running through a mud-puddle because it would muddy his white-wall tires? What should we say of a person who, no matter how considerate others were, always felt that he was treated unjustly? What should we say of a person who felt only indignation at those who did him kind deeds? What should we say of a person who morally approved of stealing, murder, and the like? Certainly we should appraise such preferences, feelings, and attitudes as irrational. If a person does prefer having polio to taking a shot, of course this is a fact and there is some explanation of it, just as in the case of a pound's lifting one hundred pounds by virtue of its position. But the preference is irrational just the same, for it makes a claim that taking a shot is worse than having polio, which is just not so and should be obvious to anyone. When a person has a visual hallucination, his experience is an occurrence and it has an explanation. But it makes a claim too, and insofar as it is unjustified the experience is irrational. The person who persists in believing contrary to all evidence is said to be irrational; in like manner, the man who persists in preferences contrary to all value-considerations is equally irrational. If one did prefer A to B because it would hurt more, and for no other reason whatever, we should not know what to make of him. It would be like saying, "I know there isn't a table there because I see it there." It just does not make sense.

### 3.6 Conclusion concerning how value-discourse is practical

If there is a correctness or incorrectness about our moral attitudes, and I think the evidence clearly points to this conclusion, then they are not simply subject to being causally induced or influenced but may be reasoned about. A person may come to have a moral attitude of approval toward x by virtue of being convinced, by being *shown,* that x is right. To accept the judgment that it is right is to approve it. The acceptance is the result of "insight" or the weighing of considerations in a way analogous with coming to believe a factual statement on the basis of insight or evidence.

Reflection upon our moral reasoning bears this out. Who, without commitment to certain philosophical theories, can deny that there is a difference between trying causally to induce someone to approve of something and "reasoning" with him to the same end? In the one case, one may want to soften up the "victim" with drinks, entertainment, and flattery. One may want to cite the endorsement or favorable attitude of notable people.

One will try to hide all unfavorable facts. One will try to work on the person psychologically. One's only criterion may be causal effectiveness. Contending that this is the only way we can go about the matter, Stevenson says, "*Any* statements about *any* matter of fact which *any* speaker considers likely to alter attitudes may be adduced as a reason for or against an ethical judgment."[17]

But if the purpose is to convince by reasoning, one wants the person one is reasoning with to have a clear mind and to be in the mood to think the matter through. One wants the whole story brought into the open and irrelevancies left out. One will cite facts in support of a proposed moral judgment and will expect *anyone* else to see and to acknowledge the relevance of the facts cited in support of the judgment. Also, one will expect *anyone* else to acknowledge the bearing of facts cited as being against or as tending to invalidate the judgment. If it is questioned whether a certain fact supports the judgment, a rational person is willing to try to make out the claim. Proceeding with a mind open to new insights, he is ready to give up an argument if he "sees" that it is not valid. All the way through, he is *arguing* the issue as he "sees" it and is not at all concerned with what will be causally persuasive with the person he is talking to. In fact, he may, and indeed does, go through such.a reasoning process with himself, and he may find himself coming out with a conclusion quite different from the one he tended toward in the beginning.

Who, I ask, can genuinely deny that both of these procedures are found in our common experiences and that they are quite distinguishable even though neither may be found without a mixture of the other? It seems undeniable that we do employ techniques of persuasion. It is equally undeniable that we argue for moral judgments; in doing so we appeal to reason as such and expect any rational person to see and to acknowledge our point. Furthermore, whereas we appraise the techniques of persuasion as effective or ineffective, we appraise our arguments as sound

17. *Ethics and Language*, p. 114.

or unsound, as valid or invalid. Any theory of moral judgments which fails to provide for this distinction is woefully inadequate.

## 3.7 Conclusion

If I am correct in my contentions that the emotive states and attitudes expressed and evoked by ethical language are not merely natural occurrences but have a semantic dimension and that the pure moral judgments involved in such states and attitudes are subject to being reasoned about and appraised as correct or incorrect, then the emotive theory must be rejected.

# CHAPTER IV

# LOGICAL NATURALISM

### 4.1 *The position of the good-reasons ethicist*

We have now seen, I think, and there is a fair amount of agreement on this, that neither classical nor emotive naturalism will do. Even so, naturalists are not ready to throw in the sponge and admit that there are values as nonnatural or nonscientific entities in the world. A new form of naturalism, equally as vigorous as its predecessors, has appeared on the scene and is all but carrying the day. I refer to what may best be called 'good-reasons' or 'logical' naturalism.

The good-reasons ethicist is reacting to the emotivist's contention that pure moral judgments are not subject to being reasoned about and appraised as valid or invalid. But his fundamental purpose is not to specify the "meaning" of ethical terms or sentences.[1] He recognizes no particular problem about them. An ethical sentence simply declares that one ought, or ought not, as the case may be, to do something or other, without regard to the personal identity of those involved. If one boggles over 'ought,' which is thought to present no philosophical problem, our theorist simply omits it and says that an ethical judgment declares that something-or-other is the thing to do (or is not the thing to do) under the circumstances, and to encourage others

1. Stuart Hampshire, "Fallacies in Moral Philosophy," *Mind*, N.S., LVIII, No. 232 (Oct., 1949), 466 ff.; and Toulmin, *The Place of Reason in Ethics*, p. 154.

to do (or not to do).[2] There he leaves the matter. His primary purpose is to show that ethical sentences are not simply instruments or weapons to be used in the causal nexus but are subject to rational proof or justification. For the emotivist, as we have seen, all use of value-language is in the same category: it is an attempt to persuade, to manipulate, to induce certain feelings or attitudes. No distinction is marked between its use in propaganda, psychological warfare, advertising, and the like, where admittedly the purpose is to get a desired effect by causally effective means, and its use in counselling, advising, and deliberating. The good-reasons ethicist is on solid ground in seeking to mark a distinction here. Moral arguments are seriously offered as an appeal to reason, and they themselves are subject to rational critique. Some are good and some bad; some valid and some not. And it is not always the causally ineffective which are judged invalid or bad under rational critique; nor is it the causally effective as such which are appraised as good or valid.

Part of the problem of showing that ethical sentences are subject to proof or disproof, to appraisal as valid or invalid, consists of showing their validity-conditions, the facts that would validate or justify them. Of course the philosopher of ethics is not concerned with validating particular judgments as such. That is the task of anyone in the role of making ordinary moral appraisals. "Practical reasoning," according to Baier, "consists in surveying the situation, reviewing the courses of action open to the agent, reviewing the considerations, or reasons, other things being equal, which bear on the issue, weighing and balancing them against one another, and then deciding." "Philosophy," he continues, "can hope to improve our knowledge of what are considerations and what in general are better reasons. But it cannot hope to do all the practical thinking once and for all. . . ."[3] And, as Toulmin says, "The question

2. *Cf.* Toulmin, *The Place of Reason in Ethics*, p. 154.
3. Kurt Baier, "Good Reasons," *Philosophical Studies*, IV, No. 1 (Jan., 1953),
2.

which the analysis of 'x is right' can answer is the question, 'Which kinds of reason are required in order to show that something is right (i.e., the thing to do, to encourage others to do, etc.) ?' "[4]

The important contribution of the good-reasons moral philosopher is the rescue of moral judgments (and other value-sentences as well) from the realm of tools and weapons of propaganda, advertising, and psychological warfare and the restoration of them to their rightful place in the arena of argument and rationality. He agrees with the classical naturalist that there are factual validity-grounds for an ethical judgment. He agrees with the intuitionist in his criticism of the classical naturalist; he agrees that the meaning of the ethical sentence is not to be identified with its factual validity-conditions. Furthermore, he agrees with the emotivist in his criticism of the intuitionist that the meaning of the ethical judgment is not something's exemplification of some nonnatural quality. He is able to accomplish all of this by the recognition of a new kind of argument, an ethical argument, which is neither deductive nor inductive. It is an argument with factual premises which *support* an ethical conclusion, but the "support" is of a different kind from any recognized by the logicians. As Toulmin says, "Although factual reasons (R) may be good reasons for an ethical conclusion (E), to assert the conclusion is not just to assert the reasons, or indeed anything of the same logical type as R."[5] If the inference were deductive, the conclusion would simply reassert something already said in the premises. If the inference were inductive in the ordinary sense, the conclusion would be of the same logical order as the premises. The great blending of the achievements

4. *The Place of Reason in Ethics*, p. 154.
5. *The Place of Reason in Ethics*, p. 55; *cf.* Hampshire, "Fallacies in Moral Philosophy," *Mind*, N.S., LVIII, No. 232 (Oct., 1949), 472 ff.; John Ladd, "Reason and Practice," in *The Return to Reason*, ed. John Wild (Chicago: Henry Regnery Co., 1953), pp. 235 ff.

of the traditional theories is accomplished by recognition of a new form of argument and a distinctively ethical inference.

### 4.2 Why the good-reasons ethicist is a naturalist

Perhaps it is time to give attention to a question which no doubt is already bothering the reader, namely, why call the good-reasons philosopher a naturalist? Does he not contend that ethical sentences are different from scientific ones? Does he not even argue for the uniqueness of ethical arguments? And is it not true that he refuses to face up to the problems for which naturalism would be a possible solution? All of these must be answered in the affirmative. Furthermore, I shall argue later that he has even opened up the possibility of and perhaps even unwittingly presupposes or assumes a new kind of nonnaturalism. Yet I think it is not unfair to say that the general temper of the position is naturalistic. In any case it suggests a new way of making out a case for naturalism. It might be argued, for instance, that the conclusion that A is the thing to do in such and such a situation is a valid "ethical inference" from certain factual statements but that we need not look beyond the factual statements which "ethically entail" the moral conclusion in order to discover the ontological significance of the whole argument. A generalization of this would be the naturalistic thesis that ethical judgments and ethical arguments have no ontological significance other than that of their factual premises. The positions of Toulmin, Hampshire, Baier, and others lend themselves, I think, to this interpretation, even if they themselves would object to raising the ontological question at all. It is the good-reasons position interpreted in this manner that I am calling 'logical' naturalism.[6]

6. I myself at one time proposed a somewhat similar theory. See "The Nature of Ethical Inquiry," *Journal of Philosophy*, XLVIII, No. 19 (Sept. 13, 1951), 569-74; and "Empirical Verifiability Theory of Factual Meaning and Axiological Truth," in *The Language of Value*, ed. Ray Lepley (New York: Columbia University Press, 1957), pp. 94-105. The latter essay was written in 1951; the former, in 1950.

### 4.3 *Two further problems the good-reasons ethicist refuses to consider*

While I concur wholeheartedly in what has been accomplished by the "good-reasons" ethicists, they do not go far enough. There are at least two further problems: (1) there is a need for analysis of the meaning of ethical sentences as such. It is not enough to say that 'x is right' means x is the thing to do, to encourage others to do, and so forth. Nor is it enough to say that it is the thing to do under the circumstances without regard to the personal identity of those involved. Even if 'x is the thing to do, to encourage others to do' does express the meaning of 'x is right,' it is not so simple and clear that its philosophical import (or lack of it) is obvious without philosophical analysis. Toulmin simply does not recognize any problem here. What has been the most troublesome problem throughout the centuries is not solved but simply abandoned. This is the point, or at least part of it, of Hall's charge that the good-reasons ethicists are not really ethicists.[7] And (2) what is involved in a fact's being a good reason or a validity-condition of an ethical judgment? What is the relation between the factual reason and the moral judgment? What is the meaning of 'if . . . then . . .' in the sentence 'If $f_1$ and $f_2$, then A is the thing to do'? Is it like a truth-functional operator or does it refer to some kind of a real connection somewhat as some have interpreted the contrary-to-fact conditional? In short, what, if anything, is required of reality for such a sentence to be true or for an ethical argument to be valid? How would reality be different with the sentence true or the argument valid from what it would be with the sentence false or the argument invalid?

The good-reasons philosopher, if we may take Toulmin as typical, does not simply fail to concern himself with these further problems; he could not be prodded to do so. He rejects them on principle because of his conception of the philosophical enter-

7. E. W. Hall, "Practical Reason(s) and the Deadlock in Ethics," *Mind*, N.S., LXIV, No. 255 (July, 1955), 324.

prise. For him the task of philosophy is to make a language map showing the different kinds of words and sentences according to their uses. Accordingly, he interprets the traditional ethical theories as disguised comparisons to show how ethical concepts function. The point of classical naturalism, he would say, is that ethical concepts are like ordinary descriptive terms; the point of the objectivist (Moore, for example) is that ethical words are like property words but not exactly like them; and the emotivist's point is that value-sentences are like exclamations. They are all well and good, according to Toulmin, so long as they are recognized as comparisons. Value-terms are like all of these. Each comparison points up certain features, and there is no incompatability among them. But their comparative nature is usually disguised under the form of 'a is b' instead of 'a is like b.' Consequently they are said to be downright misleading; and even when understood as comparisons they are quite limited in showing the function of ethical terms. So what is needed, Toulmin says, is "a descriptive account of our ethical concepts . . . some device for bringing out the relation between the manner in which ethical sentences are used and the manners in which others are used—so as to give their place on the language-map."[8] Hampshire too thinks of the philosophical problem in ethics as "What are the distinguishing characteristics of sentences expressing moral praise and blame?"[9] Traditional ethicists of the post-Kantian period have been concerned with analyses "which consist in defining, or finding synonyms for the moral terms of a particular language" which "is no more than local dictionary-making, or the elimination of redundant terms" and "is useful only as a preliminary to the study of typical moral arguments."[10] To conceive the task of the moral philosopher as the definition of moral terms is one of the "fallacies" Hampshire's paper is

8. The Place of Reason in Ethics, pp. 194-95.
9. "Fallacies in Moral Philosophy," Mind, N.S., LVIII, No. 232 (Oct., 1949), 469.
10. Ibid., p. 481.

about. According to him, "When as philosophers we ask how a particular kind of sentence is to be categorized or described, we are asking ourselves by what sort of arguments it is established and how we justify its use if it is disputed; to explain its logic and meaning is generally to describe and illustrate by examples the kind of sentences which are conventionally accepted as sufficient grounds for its assertion or rejection. So we may properly elucidate moral or practical judgments by saying that they are established and supported by arguments consisting of factual judgments of a particular range, while admitting that they are never strictly deducible, or in this sense logically derivable from any set of factual judgments."[11] His conception of method is clearly brought out in this contrast, already cited in Chapter I: "an informative treatise on ethics—on the ethics of a particular society or person—would contain an accumulation of examples selected to illustrate the kind of decisions which are said to be right in various circumstances, and the reasons given and the arguments used in concluding they are right. An uninformative treatise on ethics consists of moral sentences, separated from actual or imaginable contexts of argument about particular problems, and treated as texts for the definition of moral terms. . . ."[12]

Toulmin does, at one point, seem to think of his language-map, his descriptive account of the uses of various types of words and sentences, as simply an aid in doing philosophy rather than as an end in itself: "It will be from such a description, or 'language-map,'" he says, "rather than from a one-sided and disguised comparison, that we shall obtain the understanding that we seek—whether of the generality of ethical judgments, their expressive and rhetorical force, the function and importance of moral principles, the place of the moralist, or the principles of the open 'society'; or, most important, what it is that makes an ethical argument a valid argument, and what things are *good*

11. *Ibid.*, p. 473.
12. *Ibid.*, p. 481.

*reasons* for ethical judgments."[13]  But even here we do not find
the central problems for which we seek understanding, namely,
the elucidation of the moral categories and their ontological
significance and what constitutes or is involved in a "good reason"
or a valid ethical argument.  He does seem to include the latter,
but, as will become evident later, not in the sense with which
I am concerned.  He is trying to throw light on certain questions about moral discourse as it is used in ordinary practical
situations, and he interprets traditional ethicists as having been
concerned with the same problems.  No doubt what he is doing is
important.  For one thing, he shows, I think, that ordinary moral
discourse does not function in the way in which the emotivists
have claimed, although they have no doubt pointed up an important feature of it.  Without claiming that what he and others
of his persuasion are doing is illegitimate, I wish to contend that
the further problems with which the following pages are concerned are also legitimate and important.

### 4.4 *Analysis of 'ought'*

The analysis of ethical terms and sentences is not the barren
process Hampshire would have us believe it is.  It is not simply
a hunt for synonyms or a bit of local dictionary-making.  It is a
matter of locating, delineating, and characterizing an element or
aspect of reality in the enterprise of discovering and formulating
the categorial structure of the world as experienced by us.  And
this I think is most fundamental and important.

The most troublesome of value-concepts is 'ought.'  If its
mysteries can be solved, the other terms will be fairly easy game,
for it seems that there is no particular difficulty in defining them
in terms of 'ought.'  For instance, to say of something that it
is good is to say that it is as it ought to be; to say of something
that it is bad is to say that it is not as it ought to be or that it is
as it ought not to be; to say of an act that it is wrong is to say it
ought not to be done; and to say of an act that it is right is to

13. *Ibid.*, p. 195.

say it ought to be done, or, in a weaker sense, it is not something that ought not to be done.

In his book *What Is Value?*[14] Everett W. Hall suggests the notation 'A[a],' to be read "a ought to exemplify A," for an 'ought'-sentence, which he calls a 'normative,' parallel with the usual 'A(a),' to be read "a exemplifies A," for its corresponding declarative.[15] He takes these as paradigms for normatives and declaratives and argues that the structure of value "is revealed by the structure of the normative, that is, that value is the oughting-to-exemplify or the it-were-good-to-exemplify that obtains between a particular or particulars and a quality or relation (analogously to fact, which is the actual exemplification of a quality or relation by a particular or by particulars)."[16]

Furthermore, the form of the normative, he argues, is just as basic and simple as that of the declarative and indicates just as basic and simple a categorial feature of reality. A normative sentence's "normativity is no more complex than the declarativity of a declarative sentence. . . . value-requiredness is not simple in the way a simple quality is simple. It is rather simple in the way exemplification is simple."[17] Nevertheless he recognizes a kind of complexity in value which is not paralleled in fact, namely, the involvement of fact in value. Ought, he says, is properly expressed by 'ought to exemplify' and is therefore, in a sense, more complex than exemplification.[18] This concerns the way in which a value embraces or involves its corresponding fact. There is an analogy between a normative and a declarative in the apodictic modality. " 'Must be,' " he says, "is not properly analyzed, categorially, as a complex of 'must' and 'exemplifies.' It is just

14. (New York: The Humanities Press, 1952).

15. Most of the following discussion of Hall's position is adapted from my three articles, "The Nature of Ought," *Philosophical Studies*, VII, No. 3 (April, 1956), 36 ff.; " 'Ought' Again," *Philosophical Studies*, VIII, No. 6 (Dec., 1957), 86 ff.; and "Hall's Analysis of 'Ought,' " *Journal of Philosophy*, LV, No. 2 (Jan. 16, 1958), 73 ff.

16. *What Is Value?*, p. 226.

17. *Ibid.*, pp. 172-73.

18. See *ibid.*, p. 173.

in this sense that 'ought to be' is analogous to 'must be.' The requiredness in a normative sentence is different from that asserted in an apodictic, factual sentence, but something like the same peculiar union with exemplification while still preserving simplicity of form is present."[19]   In a footnote he adds, "One difference is obvious. 'a must be A' entails 'a is A.' I am simply saying that all of these sentences are equally elementary in form."[20]   Although there are admittedly some true sentences like 'a is A' and 'a ought to be A,' he contends that there are no true sentences like 'a must be A,' although such sentences are meaningful. His claim is that the actual world contains no objective or factual necessity, although there are possible worlds for which some such sentences would be true.[21]

First of all, I wonder if 'A [a],' or, as Hall would allow, 'A [a,b],' where 'A' names a relation, is an adequate way of representing all simple normatives. We not only say that a given particular ought to exemplify a certain property, but also that there ought to be an individual to exemplify a certain property, e.g., 'There ought to be someone to blow the trumpet.' Perhaps it would be suggested that this sentence could be rendered in the form 'A ought to be exemplified by a,' which differs from 'a ought to exemplify A' only in voice and would not affect the logical form shown by 'A[a].' But 'A ought to be exemplified by something' is not the passive voice of 'There ought to be something to exemplify A,' but rather of 'Something ought to exemplify A.' Now 'There ought to be something to exemplify A' is quite different from 'Something ought to exemplify A.' The latter may be symbolized by '$(\exists x)A[x]$,' combining a familiar symbolism with Hall's notation for normatives; this gives us only a generalized form of A[a], without any particular significance for our purpose. But the former, 'There ought to be something to exemplify A,' is a different matter. Again drawing on

19. Ibid.
20. Ibid., note 1.
21. Ibid., p. 173.

conventional notations and on Hall's suggestion for normatives and improvising to a certain extent, this might be symbolized by '[∃x]A(x)' and read "there ought to be something which would exemplify A." This seems to be a basic kind of normative. It not only is reducible to neither 'A[a]' nor '(∃x)A[x]'; it is not even entailed by either and it does not entail either of them. 'Something ought to exemplify A' does not entail 'There ought to be something which would exemplify A,' for if the something that ought to exemplify A did not exist, it might not be the case that A ought to be exemplified at all. And neither does 'There ought to be something which would exemplify A' entail 'There is something which ought to exemplify A.' It might be *there ought to be a man who would marry Jane* and yet not *there is a man who ought to marry Jane*.

Even though normatives of the form '[∃x]A(x)' or '[∃x] A(x).B(x)' are neither logically nor materially equivalent to x)A[x]' or '(∃x)A(x).B[x],' it might be suggested that they still concern oughting-to-exemplify or oughting-to-be-exemplified in that 'there ought to be an x such that x would exemplify A' can be stated in the passive voice: 'A ought to be exemplified by a nonexistent x.' Now this of course is absurd. A nonexistent x cannot exemplify anything; neither ought it to exemplify any property. Let us try again. It might be suggested that it can be stated this way: 'A ought to be exemplified but there is nothing to exemplify it.' This may be equivalent, but it is not the same thing. 'A ought to be exemplified but there is nothing to exemplify it' entails 'There ought to be an x such that x would exemplify A.' But the *oughting-to-be* is not an *oughting-to-exemplify*.

The oughting-to-be or the oughting-to-exist of a particular seems to be a basic kind of normative which we do manage to assert in ordinary language but which cannot be asserted in Hall's suggested ideal language with 'A[a]' as the standard normative form. His not recognizing this seems to have a significant bearing upon his conclusions concerning the nature of oughtness and, since he identifies the two, the nature of value. There is not the same difficulty about fact. Although what is said in the form of '$[\exists x]A(x)$' cannot be said in the form of '$A[a]$,' I see no difficulty in saying anything that is sayable in the form of '$(\exists x) A(x)$' in the form of '$A(a)$.' An ideal language could conceivably get along with the fact-forms of '$A(a)$' and '$A(a,b)$' but not with the 'ought'-forms of '$A[a]$' and '$A[a,b]$.'[22] This argues against his theory of parallelism between fact and value, against his contention that every value, in a sense, contains a corresponding fact, and especially against the contention that the nature of value is shown by the form '$A[a]$' or '$A[a,b]$.'

In reply[23] to this criticism when it was first put forth in article form, Hall attempted to maintain his position that the basic normative is predicative by introducing a more generic form which would embrace both the existential and the predicative varieties. His new paradigm is " '$(\exists x)M(x,J)$' ought to be true," to be read " 'something [Hall reads it 'somebody' but this would require an additional predication] is married to Jane' ought to be true." And from this, he says, we can obtain the two species (existential, $[\exists x]M(x,J)$; predicative, $(\exists x)M[x,J]$) by appropriate differentiation.

I do not see how this helps his position. His new normative is, of course, predicative, but it is at the meta-level. It concerns a relation between a sentence and the semantic predicate 'true.' It is difficult to see in what sense either the existential or the predicative normative of the object-language could be a species of this normative of the meta-language. The only relationship I see is that the predicative normative of the meta-language may hold by virtue of the legitimacy of either an existential or a predicative normative of the object-language. But this in no sense establishes that the existential normative of the object-lan-

22. It is only fair to point out that Hall was careful to say that a functional logic of normatives has not yet been worked out.

23. "Existential Normatives," *Journal of Philosophy*, LV, No. 2 (Jan. 16, 1958), 75-77.

guage is therefore of the same kind as the normative of the
meta-language. It remains just as much an existential normative as ever. Furthermore, it is essential to Hall's program in
*What Is Value?* for his ideal language to be zero level, for it
is only by this device that he can make his case for the parallelism
between fact and value.

Perhaps his proposal can be better understood if expressed in
the material mode. His position would be something like this:
the fact *something* (again I use 'something' instead of 'somebody'
in order to avoid an extra predication) *is* (or *will be*) *married
to Jane* ought to-be. In this sense what ought to-be is a fact.
Here 'ought' is the analogue of neither the predicative nor the
existential 'is' but of a third, which may be called the 'factual
'is,'' one expressing the "existence" of a fact. There are of
course difficulties involved in saying a fact ought to-be, because
the use of 'fact' would seem to preclude its application to something that is not. Perhaps this is why Hall resorts to a meta-
language to express his point. But in any case, if I may be permitted to speak at the moment in this improper manner, why
is it that Hall speaks of what I call a 'factual normative,' one
which expresses the "ought to-be" of a fact, as generic and as
predicative? He seems to assume that if it is both generic and
predicative, the species must also be predicative. It is not at all
obvious that the factual normative is predicative, but for the
moment let us assume that it is. The relation between a factual
normative and its corresponding existential and predicative
normatives seems to be simply that the factual normative cannot
hold unless its corresponding existential or predicative normative
also holds. In fact, it seems that the factual normative is simply
a way of saying that one of the others holds. It is similar to the
relation between an alternative statement and its alternants. It
is not a new kind of normative in its own right. It does not
show or say anything about reality which cannot be shown or
said by the other two. It is for this reason that Hall's ideal language should not contain the factual normative in either the

formal or the material mode. Even if the factual normative is predicative, there is nothing here to argue that the existential normative is somehow "reduced" to a predicative form.

In what sense is the factual normative predicative? It says that a certain fact *ought to-be,* not that it ought to be such and such. Perhaps what Hall has in mind is the reduction of the factual normative to its corresponding predicative normative along these lines. The only way for a fact to-be is for its elements to be combined in such a way that those which are particulars exemplify those which are properties or relations. This, however, is merely to say that the way for a fact to-be is to be a fact, which is not very enlightening. Nevertheless it might be said in a parallel manner that the only way a fact can ought to-be is for its elements to ought to be factually constituted. Then for a fact to ought to-be is for some particular or set of particulars to ought to exemplify some property or relation. But cannot a fact ought to-be by virtue that there ought to-be elements which would be combined together in such a way as to constitute the fact in question? I think so. Existential and predicative normatives seem to be basic and irreducible kinds. This does not argue well for Hall's theory of value. To say the least, his position is too restricted. There would seem to be a kind of value which his theory does not account for. Moreover, this fact may mean that his theory is in error even about the nature of the kind of value he does recognize.

Even if all normatives could be expressed in the form of 'a ought to exemplify A' or 'a ought to be A,' which we have seen is not so, 'a ought to be A' and 'a must be A' are not simple and elementary like 'a is A.' First, I shall consider 'a must be A,' since Hall admits an analogy between it and his simple normative. It may shed some light on the latter.

Hall admits that apodictic declarative sentences may be meaningful but denies that any are true, because he believes there happens to be no factual necessity in the world as constituted. Nevertheless, he claims that there might have been a priori synthetic truths.[24]

Although he chooses the example 'colored patches must be extended' to illustrate a declarative in the apodictic modality, I think that his general position would require that what is said in this generalized form be expressible in the form of 'if a is A, then a must be B,' 'if b is A, then b must be B,' and so on, and ultimately, in his ideal language, in the form 'a is A,' 'a must be B,' 'b is A,' 'b must be B,' and so forth. We may consider 'a must be A'—a sentence equally as independent and as capable of standing by itself as 'a is A'—to be his ideal form of an apodictic declarative. This interpretation is confirmed by a note[25] in which he explains one way in which "the requiredness in a normative sentence is different from that asserted in an apodictic, factual sentence"; for there he writes, " 'a must be A' entails 'a is A,' but 'a ought to be A' does not entail 'a is A.' " In the same note he says that 'a is A,' 'a must be A,' and 'a ought to be A' are all "equally elementary in form." And it is profusely evident throughout the latter part of the book that he considers 'a ought to be A' as a simple, elementary sentence on a par with 'a is A.'

Even if there were factual necessities, they could not, I submit, be properly expressed by simple, elementary sentences in the form of 'a must be A,' where 'a' names a particular and 'A' names a property. If 'a must be A' as a simple, elementary sentence expresses or shows a necessary connection at all, it expresses it as holding, or shows it to hold, between a and A. Now if we should allow this, I do not see how we could stop short of the position that every true sentence with the form of 'a is A' could be replaced by a true sentence with the form of 'a must be A,' for I can see no truth-condition for 'a must be A' other than a, being what it is, cannot lack A. It might be taken to be something like this: a, being what it is, exemplifies B, and nothing can exemplify B without exemplifying A. But by the same

24. Cf. *What Is Value?*, p. 173.
25. *Ibid.*

reasoning we may claim that for any property F and for any particular x, if x exemplifies F, x, being what it is, it must exemplify F. This would commit us to there being no factual contingencies, but it would do so by trivializing the whole issue. Appeal to intuition is a frequent way of saving a philosophical view, and I would not wish to reject all such appeals. If one should claim to intuit a necessary connection between two properties A and B to the effect that nothing could possibly exemplify A without also exemplifying B, I would at least know what was meant. But if a believer in necessary connections of the kind allegedly shown by an elementary sentence with the form of 'a must be A' should attempt to ground his claim in a basic intuition, I could only say that the matter is unintelligible to me. Basic actual necessities, if there are any, or for that matter if there are not, are the kind of connections which hold between instances of properties so that if a particular exemplifies a certain property, then it must exemplify a certain other one.

Although Hall has 'x must be F' as the ideal form of apodictic declarative sentences, he seems to be thinking in terms of general sentences, for his one example is 'colored patches must be extended.'[26] Even if we should grant, and there is a difficulty involved, that ordinary general sentences like 'All men are mortal' are analyzable ultimately into a set such as 'a is A,' 'a is B,' 'b is A,' 'b is B,' the general sentence 'For all x, if x is a colored patch, then x must be extended,' is not analyzable into 'a is colored,' 'a must be extended,' 'b is colored,' 'b must be extended,' and so on, for the point of the sentence is to assert that it is impossible for anything to be colored and not to be extended; that is, it asserts a necessary connection, not between a particular and the property, *extension*, but between the two properties to the effect that color cannot be exemplified without extension being exemplified by the same particular. The proposed conjunction of atomic sentences does not say this.

26. *Ibid.*

In other words, 'if a is A, then a must be B' is not a truth-functional statement. The truth-value of it is not determined by the truth-values of its components 'a is A' and 'a must be B,' for the truth-value of 'a must be B' is not independent of the truth-value of either the antecedent or the conditional itself. It might be analyzed this way: (1) "'if a is A, then a is B' is necessarily true." In other words, the 'must,' although it is placed in the consequent, might be said not to belong to either component but to the conditional itself. An alternative analysis would be this: (2) "if a is A, then 'a is B' is necessarily true." Here 'a must be B' is treated as a meta-statement about 'a is B' instead of about 'if a is A, then a is B.' Although (1) and (2) are logically equivalent, perhaps (2) shows more clearly the nature and locus of the necessity involved. It shows that the 'must' concerns a relation which holds between the truth-conditions of the antecedent 'a is A' and those of 'a is B.' In other words, the 'must' indicates that the truth of the antecedent in some sense requires the truth of 'a is B' or that the truth of 'a is B' in some sense follows from or may be inferred from the truth of the antecedent.

If this analysis is correct, no sentence like 'a must be A' is simple and elementary like 'a is A.' It cannot stand alone and be verified directly. It is not well formed but elliptical. An antecedent is always understood or assumed. It says that given that certain other sentences which are explicitly mentioned or understood are true, then 'a is A' is necessarily true. Hence, contrary to Hall's view, 'must be' is properly analyzed as a complex of 'must' and 'exemplifies,' or perhaps in some cases as 'must' and 'exist,' analogously with the "ought to-exist" of a particular.

Hall seems to hold that in order to have objective necessity at all we must have elementary, zero-level sentences with the form of 'a must be A.' I do not see this. The position here advocated, as I see it, simply shifts its location. Instead of holding between a particular and a property, objective necessity, if there is such, holds between the factual truth-conditions of the premises and those of the conclusion of what I shall call a 'natural' deductive argument, an argument in which the relationship between the truth-conditions of the premises and those of the conclusion is not grounded in linguistic rules or a tautological consequentiality but in a real connection between facts: for example, 'This is a cube; therefore, it has twelve edges,' interpreted so that 'If this is a cube, then it has twelve edges' is not a tautology. Objective necessity, then, concerns fact-to-fact rather than particular-to-property relationships. Hall no doubt would object on the grounds, which he argued for earlier in the book, that facts cannot be named but only asserted and that therefore in a properly constructed language no property can be predicated of a fact and no relation can be asserted to hold between two or more facts. But this objection misses its mark. I am contending only for relations between facts that can be shown by the 'if . . . then . . .' of a certain kind of conditional statement or by the structure of a "natural" deductive argument in a manner parallel to his position that the syntactical structure of zero-level sentences shows categorial features of reality.

Now, what does this discussion concerning 'must' have to do with 'ought'? Hall himself admits that the two are analogous in a sense. "The requiredness in a normative sentence," he says, "is different from that asserted in an apodictic, factual sentence, but something like the same peculiar union with exemplification while still preserving simplicity of form is present."[27] In the footnote already quoted, he indicates one difference between them to be that 'a must be A' entails 'a is A,' whereas 'a ought to be A' does not. I agree on all these points except that of the simplicity of form. Contrary to his position, I have tried to show that 'must be' is properly analyzed as a complex either of 'must' and 'exemplification' or 'must' and 'exists.' Is the same true of 'ought to-be'? And how can we account for the fact that 'a must be A' entails 'a is A' but 'a ought to be A' does not?

27. *Ibid.*

I do not see how 'a ought to be A' can be a simple, elementary sentence any more than 'a must be A.' It has been generally recognized, and apparently subscribed to by Hall, that any particular's oughting to exemplify some specific property does so by virtue of some other characteristic it possesses. According to Prichard, "For whenever in ordinary life we think of some particular action as a duty . . . we do not think of the action as right blindly, i.e., irrespectively of the special character which we think the act to possess; rather we think of it as being right in virtue of possessing a particular characteristic of the kind indicated by the phrase by which we refer to it. Thus in thinking of our keeping our promise to x as a duty, we are thinking of the action as rendered a duty by its being the keeping of our promise."[28]  Ross puts it this way: "Now it is clear that it is in virtue of my thinking the act to have some other character that I think I ought to do it."[29]  Hare expresses much the same idea by speaking of the 'supervenient character' of value-terms.  "I cannot say 'Smith ought to have given her the money but this might not have been so although everything else might have been the same.' "[30]  This indicates that 'a ought to be A' is not a well-formed, simple, elementary sentence. It could more properly be written 'a, being B, ought to be A,' or 'If a is B, then it ought to be A; and a is B.' Therefore, 'ought' does not show or indicate a kind of relation between a particular and a property parallel with the relation of exemplification shown by 'is' in 'a is A.'

Does the analogy between 'ought' and 'must' extend further, so that we can say that 'a ought to be A' is about 'a is A' in the way in which 'a must be A' is about it? This would be in line with Hall's later suggestion that the form of the basic normative be rendered ' 'a is A' ought to be true.' The fact that 'a

28. H. A. Prichard, *Duty and Interest* (New York: Oxford University Press, 1939), pp. 15-16.
29. W. David Ross, *Foundations of Ethics* (Oxford: Clarendon Press, 1939), p. 168.
30. *The Language of Morals*, pp. 153-54.

must be A' entails 'a is A' but 'a ought to be A' does not entail it argues against the parallelism. Maybe there is something analogous. Let us explore a suggestion made by R. B. Perry, who writes, "The imperative character attaching to . . . [a will which the logic of the situation requires] consists in the necessity with which conclusions follow from premises . . . . [The rational will] is the conviction of the necessity of an act relatively to a principle, when this conviction is felt by an agent who has adopted the principle as his maxim."[31]

The suggestion may be formulated this way: the 'must' of an apodictic declarative sentence indicates or "refers to" a relation that holds between the truth-conditions of the premises and those of the conclusion of a deductive indicative argument, a logical relation in the case of a tautological argument, a real connection between facts in the case of a "natural" argument, whereas the 'ought' of a normative sentence indicates or "refers to" a relation that holds between the premises and conclusion of a "practical" argument.

A practical argument, unlike an indicative one (which contains only declarative sentences), has for its conclusion an imperative. For example:

(1) Be like your father.
Your father was kind to the poor.

Therefore, be kind to the poor.

Notice that the conclusion does not contain the word 'ought.' Neither does the conclusion of the following argument contain 'must':

(2) All mules are barren.
Pat is a mule.

Therefore, Pat is barren.

However, the conclusion of (1) might have been written, (1a) "You *ought* to be kind to the poor." That of (2), (2a) "Pat

31. *General Theory of Value*, pp. 108-9.

*must* be barren." When we do include 'ought' and 'must,' as in (1a) and (2a), we attempt *to say* what arguments such as (1) and (2) both *say* and *show*. We must not, however, assume that 'must' and 'ought' are simply conclusion-indicators such as 'therefore' and 'consequently.' The difference between them is that of the difference between showing and saying. In (2a) we assert the conclusion of (2) and at the same time say, not merely show, that the truth of the premises requires or renders necessary its truth. In like manner, the simple imperative conclusion of (1) becomes in (1a), by the inclusion of 'ought,' not merely an imperative but also a statement about its relation to its premises.

When this analysis was first put forth in article form, Hall replied, "It just isn't consonant with common parlance to treat normative statements as merely disguised conclusions of arguments even if one restricts them to cases where the premises are suppressed." He says that 'don't you think people ought to try to make one another happy?' is simply a complete question and that no one would respond to it in the manner he thinks that my analysis would suggest, namely, "go on; your question isn't complete. Give me your premises."[32] But a careful consideration of this kind of question shows that my analysis is not in conflict with the ordinary use of 'ought' which he points to. The premise I am talking about is built into the question itself. Properly formed, his question is something like this: 'Don't you think that, in general, if one's doing x would make someone else happy, then one ought to do x, unless there are overriding reasons?' Or perhaps 'don't you think that, in general, if x is a person, then one ought to try to make x happy?' The antecedent of the 'if . . . then . . .' is the premise referred to in my analysis. Thus the very example which he cites to refute my analysis supports it.

If this analysis is correct, then the parallel between 'must'

32. "Further Words on 'Ought,'" *Philosophical Studies*, VII, No. 5 (Oct., 1956), 75.

and 'ought' holds up in that 'a must be A' entails 'a is A' and 'a ought to be A' entails 'a, be A' or 'Let a be A.'

This conclusion can be supported by another consideration. 'If a is A, then a ought to be B; and a is A' obviously entails something analogous to 'If a is A, then a must be B; and a is A.' In the latter case, there is an entailment, a conclusion which can be drawn, but it is not 'a must be B.' The whole thing is an analysis of that. The statement 'a is A' does not affirm the antecedent of the conditional in the manner which warrants concluding what appears to be its consequent, for 'a must be B' is not the consequent, for reasons already indicated. The conditional is more appropriately read, "If a is A, then that fact requires assertively that a is B." When we affirm the antecedent, the conclusion which is warranted is 'a is B,' not 'a must be B.' In like manner, when we affirm the antecedent of 'If a is A, then a ought to be B' we cannot conclude that 'a ought to be B,' for the conditional is 'If a is A, then that fact requires prescriptively that a be B.' The conclusion warranted is 'a, be A' or 'Let a be A.' Since 'If a is A, then a ought to be B; and a is A' is an analysis of 'a ought to be B,' we may say that 'a ought to be B' entails 'a, be B,' just as 'a must be B' entails 'a is B.'

I contended above that if there is objective necessity in the world, it is shown by the logical structure of "natural," deductive, indicative arguments (or their corresponding conditionals) rather than by the syntax of certain simple, elementary sentences. To deny that there is objective necessity one would have to deny that any such arguments are "valid." The same, I think, holds for my analysis of 'ought.' Oughtness, or value-requiredness, as a categorial feature of reality could be shown by the structure of "natural" practical arguments, arguments with an imperative conclusion but lacking an imperative premise. It is my contention that the nonnaturalist's position holds that the facts asserted by the premises of a natural practical argument "require prescriptively" that which is prescribed by the imperative conclusion. This is parallel with the way in which the facts asserted by the premises of a natural indicative argument "require assertively" that which is asserted in the indicative conclusion. Accordingly, 'if a is A, then a ought to be B' means that *a's being A* "requires prescriptively" *a's being B*. Note that *a's being A* is not asserted in the antecedent; neither is *a's being B* prescribed in the consequent. If we use the argument form 'a is A; therefore, a ought to be B,'[33] unlike the case of the conditional, *a's being A* is asserted in the premises and I contend that *a's being B* is prescribed in the conclusion. But 'ought' in the conclusion, in addition to prescribing a's being B, says a's being A "requires prescriptively" *a's being B*. It is the same as the way in which in 'a is A; therefore, a must be B,' 'must' asserts *a's being B* and at the same time says that *a's being A* "requires assertively" *a's being B*.

4.5 *What constitutes a good reason for an ethical judgment*

Having attempted to give an analysis of the moral categories, which the good-reasons naturalist failed to do, it is now time to turn our attention to his second neglect, namely, what in general constitutes a validity-condition or "good reason" for an ethical judgment.

Toulmin does, as noted above, discuss the problem of what is a good reason for an ethical judgment. However, he is content, as he himself says, "to see how, in *particular types* of ethical question and argument, good reasoning is distinguished from bad, and valid from invalid—to be specific, by applying to individual judgments the test of principle, and to principles the test of general fecundity." He goes on to say, "I myself do not feel the need for any general answer to the question, 'what makes some ethical reasoning "good" and some ethical arguments "valid"?': answers applicable to particular types of argument are enough."[34]

33. 'Therefore' used with 'ought' in this manner is not a redundancy; nor is it a matter of merely showing what 'ought' says, for it serves the additional function of showing that we do not have a mere conjunction and that the preceding statement is the one 'ought' has reference to.
34. *The Place of Reason in Ethics*, p. 161.

The reason, I suspect, that he does not feel the need for such an answer springs from the way in which he interprets the question. In a summing-up statement he says, "Of course, 'This practice would involve the least conflict of interests attainable under the circumstances' does not *mean* the same as 'This would be the right practice'; nor does 'This way of life would be more harmoniously satisfying' *mean* the same as 'This would be better.' But in each case, the first statement is *a good reason* for the second: the 'ethically neutral' fact is *a good reason* for the 'gerundive' moral judgment. If the adoption of the practice would genuinely reduce conflicts of interest, it is a practice *worthy of adoption,* and if the way of life would genuinely lead to deeper and more consistent happiness, it is one *worthy of pursuit.* And this seems so natural and intelligible, when one bears in mind the function of ethical judgments, that, if anyone asks me *why* they are 'good reasons', I can only reply by asking in return, 'What better kinds of reason could you want?' "[35]

Here he clearly shows the level at which he is operating. If one should say that the state's corporation tax should be lowered because it would attract new industries to the state, another might ask, "Why is that a good reason for changing the tax law?" The answer might be, "because increased industrialization would raise the standard of living of the people." Again it might be asked, "But why is that a good reason for doing it?" And it might be answered, "Raising the standard of living makes life more enjoyable." If the question "Why is that a good reason?" should be asked still again, one might well answer, as Toulmin indicates, "What better reason could you want?" Toulmin is thinking of the question in this kind of practical context. It is a question anyone might ask in the process of practical reasoning. And Toulmin is right. Although one may be able to explain why $f_1$ is a reason for doing a by saying $f_1$ will bring about $f_2$, and maybe $f_2$ is a reason because $f_2$ will bring about $f_3$, etc., at some point one must simply acknowledge, let us say, that $f_n$ is a

35. *Ibid.,* p. 224.

good reason for doing a. If one does not, then others simply cannot reason with him.

But our question concerning what constitutes a validity-condition or a good reason for an ethical judgment is not of this practical nature. It is not one which would ever arise in the practical situation as such. It is a philosophical question. Only the philosopher would ever be bothered about it. Although it may be readily granted that it "seems so natural and intelligible" that if $f_n$, then a is the thing to do, the philosopher still wants to know the meaning of the 'if . . . then . . .' in such a sentence. He wants to know by virtue of what and in what sense the imperative follows from the factual statement. Does the imperative "follow from" the factual statement by virtue of a "logical" or a "real" connection? Toulmin speaks of 'evaluative' or 'ethical' inference. Is it grounded in an "ethical" connection? If so, is the "ethical" connection a kind of linguistic or a kind of real connection? Is it grounded in rules of language or in some extralinguistic feature of reality?

Toulmin, I think, never faces up to these philosophical problems. Perhaps he would not consider them to be genuine because they would not arise in the practical situation. But we are in a philosophical situation, not a practical one; and they do arise at this level.

The above analysis of moral sentences has thrown considerable light on what constitutes a validity-condition or good reason for an ethical judgment. In fact, the analysis of ethical judgments is a necessary condition for any clear headed thought about what constitutes a good reason for an ethical judgment and the nature of "ethical inference." For how can we understand philosophically what will support an ethical judgment or how an ethical judgment "follows from" something or other if we do not have a philosophical understanding of what is involved in an ethical judgment? With this understanding, it is clear, I think, that a validity-condition or a good reason for a value-judgment is simply a fact (or a factual statement) which either by itself or in conjunction with a relevant imperative requires that which is enjoined in the value-judgment. The nature and peculiarity of "ethical inference" have been located. Either it is purely logical, being peculiar only in that it concerns practical arguments, which involve imperatives; or it is grounded in an objective value-requiredness in reality which is expressed or shown by the 'if . . . then . . . ought . . .' of the conditional which states the relationship between the factual premises and the imperative conclusion of a natural practical argument.

Hare, perhaps going further than Toulmin himself would be willing, interprets his position as involving a third alternative to those just proposed.[36] "Mr. Toulmin," he says, "speaks from time to time (e.g. pp. 38, 55 f) of a sort of inference called 'evaluative,' whose virtue is to enable us to pass from factual reasons to an ethical conclusion. It seems to be the chief aim of the book to give rules for making such inferences."[37] These rules, or at least some of them, according to Hare are of the form "if the factual statement 'F' is true, then the ethical judgment 'E' may be inferred." The important thing is the status of such a rule of inference. In ordinary reasoning, the logical rules of inference have quite a different status from the statements of the argument and they do not occur as constituents within the arguments they apply to. Hare, I think, correctly charges that Toulmin, if this is his position, elevates a substantive truth of morals to the level of a rule of inference. This is the same kind of error which would be involved in treating the general laws of science as logical principles. But whether we treat such "moral principles" as rules of ethical inference or as premises of arguments governed by ordinary rules of inference, the important question is from whence they come. Are they ontologically free in the way in which most people interpret logical principles to be? Or does this attempt to assimilate them to logical principles

---

36. In "Review of *An Examination of the Place of Reason in Ethics,*" *Philosophical Quarterly*, I (July, 1951), 372-75, and in *The Language of Morals*, pp. 44-55.

37. "Review," *Philosophical Quarterly*, I (July, 1951), 374.

simply cause us not to ask what is required of reality for one such principle to obtain rather than some incompatible one? Certainly we have to be able to make a case for some such rules rather than others. Is the way in which we do it like the way in which we do it in logic? Or is it more like the way in which we make out a general law in science? Is the "validity" of such a rule in any way dependent upon the structure of reality?

Kurt Baier attempts to have it both ways. "We begin with certain beliefs; let us call them 'consideration-making beliefs' or 'rules of reason.' These are propositions to the effect that if a line of action is of a certain sort then the agent has a reason for or against entering on it. Consideration-making beliefs can function as major premises in our arguments or as inference-licenses in our inferences. The minor premises are the facts which, in accordance with the consideration-making beliefs, we conclude to be reasons."[38] Baier is obviously trying to have his cake and eat it too. He wants both to have his consideration-making belief a substantive moral principle which is true and yet to regard it as an inference license. The former, if fully explored, would involve him, I think, in one of three positions (if we exclude the possibility of what Moore called a 'metaphysical' theory of value-concepts): (a) a classical naturalistic position which finds the meaning of the moral principle to be factual; (b) an objectivistic position according to which there are values in a unique ontological sense; or (c) a logical naturalistic position which holds that the value-principles concerned are themselves the conclusions of valid tautological practical arguments. When facing what to him would be such an unwelcome outcome as either (a) or (b), no doubt he would shift to the inference-license version. But then, when faced with the problem of why one inference license rather than another, he might easily shift back to viewing it as a moral principle which is true. This

38. *The Moral Point of View* (Ithaca, N.Y.: Cornell University Press, 1958), p. 94.

duality of his position might provide for sufficient shiftiness to avoid clear insight into the consequences of either.

Actually, I think, both Toulmin's and Baier's positions (they are really identical) reduce to (c); in the last analysis, although neither has gone this far, for them a good reason for an ethical judgment is a factual statement which in conjunction with an imperative premise logically entails the imperative of the conclusion. This is evident, I think, when we consider the role played in their thinking by the function of moral discourse or the purpose of the practical reasoning game. Toulmin says that the function of ethics is "to correlate our feelings and behavior in such a way as to make the fulfillment of everyone's aims and desires as far as possible compatible."[39] It is, according to him, this function of ethics which determines the inference rules, which determines what facts are to count as reasons for doing something and what facts as reasons for not doing it. "Our very purpose in 'playing the reasoning game,'" Baier says, "is to maximize satisfactions and minimize frustrations. Deliberately to frustrate ourselves and to minimize satisfactions would certainly be to go counter to the very purpose for which we deliberate and weigh the pros and cons."[40] Clearly, then, anyone who genuinely engages in moral reasoning is committed to or is concerned with the goal which it is the function of ethics to attain. We may say, as will be argued in the following chapter, that one who engages in moral reasoning subscribes to the imperative "to correlate our feelings and behavior in such a way as to make fulfillment of everyone's aims and desires as far as possible compatible" or, as Baier would have it, "to maximize satisfactions and minimize frustrations." For a factual statement, then, to be a reason for an ethical judgment is for it, together with this imperative, to entail the imperative of the ethical judgment. Thus Toulmin's and Baier's logical naturalism, according to which good reasons for ethical judgments are determined by

<hr />

39. *The Place of Reason in Ethics*, p. 137.
40. *The Moral Point of View*, p. 301.

rules of ethical inference, is not different from logical naturalism conceived in terms of tautological practical arguments.

It might be suggested that Nowell-Smith,[41] if not Toulmin and Baier, has shown how nontautological practical arguments can be "valid" without their validity's being grounded in an objective value-requiredness as a categorial feature of reality by enlarging the concept of the logical. Although the premises of such an argument do not strictly imply the conclusion, the assertion of them, it might be contended, *contextually* implies it. The difference between the two kinds of implication, as I understand it, is that in the first case, by virtue of *what is said,* the assertion of the premises and the denial of the conclusion constitute a logical absurdity involving a contradiction; in the second case it is a logical oddity, although not a contradiction, by virtue of *the saying of it* (not by virtue of what is said). For example, it is not self-contradictory but it is logically odd for one to say 'Today is the sixteenth of the month, but I don't believe it.' According to Nowell-Smith, for me to say 'Today is the sixteenth' contextually implies 'I, the speaker, believe that today is the sixteenth.'

It might be said in a somewhat similar vein that although a factual statement as such does not imply an imperative, the *citing* of a fact in arguing for an imperative does contextually imply it. Then it would be logically odd for one to cite a fact in support of an imperative and yet reject the imperative. Also, according to Nowell-Smith, there is a point at which it becomes logically odd to ask one why a fact cited in support of doing something is a reason for doing it because in citing the fact there is no other question of this type left to be answered. This is the case when the citing of the fact as a reason directly, rather than mediately, contextually implies the imperative concerned.

But certainly the philosopher should give some account of what is involved in contextual implication just as he is expected

41. P. H. Nowell-Smith, *Ethics* (Harmondsworth, Middlesex: Penguin Books Ltd., 1954); see especially pp. 80-87.

to give an account of the nature of strict implication. It is not enough merely to name it. Maybe the contextual implication holds precisely because in citing a fact as direct support for an imperative one acknowledges an objective value-requiredness as holding between the fact cited and whatever is enjoined by the imperative concerned; or maybe it is as Nowell-Smith himself suggests. His third rule of contextual implication is, "What a speaker says may be assumed to be relevant to the interests of his audience." "This rule," he says, "is of the greatest importance for ethics. For the major problem of theoretical ethics was that of bridging the gap between decisions, 'ought'-sentences, injunctions, and sentences used to give advice on the one hand and the statements of fact that constitute the reasons for these on the other. The third rule of contextual implication may help us to show that there is no gap to be bridged because the reason-giving sentence must turn out to be practical from the start and not a statement of fact from which a practical sentence can somehow be deduced."[42] I suppose the suggestion is that the factual sentence is really practical because it will move the person to whom it is addressed by virtue of his presumed interest. I would myself argue, as I shall do later, that the assumed interest of the hearer provides a suppressed imperative premise which together with the factual premise either entails or provides a kind of "probability" support for the imperative conclusion. If this is so, in this kind of case at least, contextual implication or logical support involves suppressed or assumed premises.

So contextual implication does not seem to offer a third alternative. It seems that we are justified in our contention that the validity of practical arguments is grounded either in their tautological character (or logical support of a "probability" sort), which requires imperative premises, or in an objective value-requiredness.

42. *Ibid.*, pp. 82-83.

4.6 *Reformulation of the issue between naturalism and non-naturalism*

Although the good-reasons moral philosophy may be interpreted as a form of naturalism, and indeed its general temperament and affinities are naturalistic, it opens up the possibility of a new form of nonnaturalism not too far removed from the kind argued for by Hall. Value-language, instead of naming or pointing out nonnatural qualities, may indicate or show nonnatural connections or relations through the syntactical structure of certain arguments or their corresponding conditional statements in a way somewhat analogous to his form of what may be called 'syntactical objectivism.'

The issue between naturalism and nonnaturalism, then, as I have come to conceive it, boils down to this: are there any valid natural practical arguments? The logical naturalist says, "no." He contends that they all have suppressed, if not given, imperative premises so that 'ought' expresses only a *logical* relation between the premises and conclusion of a tautological practical argument and therefore shows nothing unique about reality. The nonnaturalist, as his position is here interpreted, claims that there are at least some valid natural practical arguments so that the 'if . . . then . . . ought . . .' of the conditional which expresses the relation between the premises and conclusion of such an argument indicates or shows an objective value-requiredness in reality. The naturalist can make his case only by producing the alleged suppressed imperative premises where they are not obvious. We shall see how well his case can be made out in the next chapter.

# CHAPTER V

# THE CASE FOR LOGICAL
# NATURALISM

## 5.1 *How logical naturalism is to be appraised*

It must be remembered that the test to which such a philosophical theory must be subjected is its faithfulness to the categorial structure of common-sense moral experience as got at by linguistic and phenomenological analysis and interpretation. It is difficult to know when a theory squares with it; for the theory we are testing, if it is one we are inclined toward, cannot fail to color our interpretation of the common-sense framework, especially in phenomenological analysis. And if we are not inclined toward it, our interpretation in all likelihood will be colored by some rival theory. The best way of proceeding, although it is beset with these difficulties, is a careful consideration of how we use moral language in ordinary situations. Here we may find ways of talking that reflect the common-sense categorial framework with which a philosophical theory must square. Ways of ordinary talk are more objective and a little more unbending to our philosophical propensities than phenomenological inspection. But whatever conclusions we reach from linguistic analysis must also square with phenomenological insight.

One thing philosophers have not always realized is that alternative and rival philosophical theories can be made to appear quite reasonable. All too often, when one finds a plausible position, one immediately assumes that all rival views are false and proceeds to refute them by reading the categorial framework of common-sense experience in terms of one's own theory. Of course on this basis one can refute all rivals. It seems more responsible to test each rival position by sympathetically pushing it against our common-sense categorial structure and then appraise all positions in terms of their weaknesses and plausibility as revealed in the process; in other words, genuinely to try them all and then judge which one does the job best. Such a judgment is still likely to be quite subjective and to reflect some deeper philosophical bias which has not been under review. But perhaps the best one can do is to form one's judgment after going through the process of sympathetically testing each, weighing various considerations, considering all plausible objections which can be raised and considering how well they can be met, and then to hope that the judgment will be shared by others who go through the whole process in the same spirit of inquiry.

Through criticism and reformulation of ethical naturalism we have found that perhaps its most plausible form is that of logical naturalism, which holds, as it was pointed out in the preceding chapter, that the ethical 'ought' and indeed all 'oughts' are really logical. The position can be made out only by showing that there are no valid "natural" practical arguments; for the "validity" of such arguments would depend upon and be grounded in an objective value-requiredness holding between the facts asserted by their premises and the things enjoined in their respective imperative conclusions.

Thus the naturalist must undertake to show that all such apparent arguments either are not valid or actually have suppressed imperative premises by virtue of which they are "tautological" rather than natural. It is evident, I think, from our criticism of the emotivist that some such arguments are valid. Some facts are "good reasons" for doing and some for not doing certain things. For example, the fact that a train is coming is, under most circumstances, a good reason for getting off the track;

the fact that smoking cigarettes causes lung cancer is a good reason for not smoking them. The issues narrow down to whether such arguments are natural or tautological; and, as I have said, this a matter of whether they have suppressed imperative premises.

## 5.2 What is an imperative

First of all we should be clear about what an imperative is. Quite naturally we turn to the imperative sentence for help. 'Come in,' 'close the door,' and 'mix two cups of wheat paste flour in ten pints of water, stirring as the flour is sifted in' are ordinary examples. Such sentences are commonly used to express commands, entreaties, and exhortations and to give instructions on how to do things. In short, they are used to tell people both things to do and the manner of doing them.

These two uses may appear to be quite different and unrelated. It seems that to tell someone to do something is not to convey information or knowledge, whereas to tell someone how to do something is to convey "information," to impart know-how, but it is not to tell him to do something. Yet they are not unrelated. The use of an imperative sentence to give instruction about how to do something, as in a cookbook or in the directions for assembling and operating a machine, may be interpreted in either of two ways: (a) as expressing a conditional imperative, e.g., 'If you want to make a paste for hanging wallpaper, mix two cups of wheat paste flour in ten pints of water . . .'; or (b) as expressing a straightforward imperative addressed to people under certain conditions. It might be said that 'mix two cups of wheat paste flour in ten pints of water' expresses an imperative in exactly the same way as my utterance of 'Come in' does to a man at my door. Although it is written on a label, it is addressed not to any and all readers but only to those who are about to use the contents of the package to make paste for hanging wallpaper. In neither case is the use really different from that to tell someone to do something. This is especially evident when we consider that to tell someone to do something is really to tell him it is something for him to do. If this were not so, how could we account for the fact that whenever one tells another to do something we expect one to be able to validate it with a reason. It is always linguistically appropriate to ask 'why?' If there is no legitimate answer, we think the order is somehow improper. We demand that there be a fact or circumstance by virtue of which the act commanded is something to be done. To tell someone to do something is to convey "information" about what to do under certain circumstances. This is not unlike telling someone how to do something, which, as we have seen, is also to give "information" about what to do in a given situation.

We use declarative sentences to tell people truths or falsehoods, *to assert* facts; we use imperative sentences to tell them things to do, *to prescribe* facts. This way of putting the matter suggests that there are two parts of both, namely, what is asserted or prescribed and the asserting or prescribing of it. In regard to declaratives, it is not uncommon to say that the meaning of the sentence is what is asserted. And in terms of one school of thought, the meaning of a sentence is a proposition. C. I. Lewis[1] (and H. S. Sheffer in his lectures at Harvard before him) says that a declarative sentence asserts a proposition. For instance, the meaning of the sentence 'Mary is baking pies now' is analyzed into the proposition, *Mary's baking pies now* or *that Mary is baking pies now,* and the assertion of it. *Mary's baking pies now* is treated as a property which can be exemplified only by the world as a whole. (The outcome of this would be a kind of Spinozistic position to the effect that there is actually only one logical subject, namely, reality itself. What appear to be logical subjects in ordinary talk, such things as Mary and desks, are only pseudo-subjects which might well be called 'modes' as Spinoza did.) The assertive factor in the sentence is

1. *An Analysis of Knowledge and Valuation* (La Salle, Ill.: The Open Court Publishing Company, 1946), pp. 48 ff.

taken to be a pragmatic operator indicating the stand of the speaker, his endorsement (to use Sheffer's term) of the possibility expressed by the proposition.

R. M. Hare[2] has applied a similar analysis to both indicative and imperative sentences. He would analyze the indicative sentence (1a) 'You closed (or will close) the door at time T' in this manner: (1b) 'Your closing the door at time T . . . yes'; and the imperative sentence (2a) 'You close the door at time T' as (2b) 'Your closing the door at Time T . . . please.' It will be noticed that (1b) and (2b) are the same in the first part, what he calls the 'phrastic.' They differ only in what he calls the 'neustic'; where one has 'yes' the other has 'please.'

This analysis of a sentence into a phrastic and a neustic is misleading precisely because it leads us to think that the whole sentence refers or means in the way in which the phrastic does and that then there is only a pragmatic role for the so-called neustic. But when we look at either an indicative or an imperative sentence, especially the latter, from the perspective of a person who accepts what he is told, we see that this will not do. The one who accepts what he is told by an indicative sentence accepts the components as actually related in the way which its corresponding phrastic presents as a possibility. And the one who accepts what he is told by means of an imperative sentence accepts that which is presented by its corresponding phrastic *as something to be done* or *something to be brought about.* This is what is told, what is meant.

An imperative, an analogue of a proposition, is something thought or expressed as *something to be done* or *something to be brought about.* The peculiarities of the grammar of imperative sentences, which are restricted in tense and person especially, are functions of their use in ordinary language, which is that of telling people things to do. But there may be occasion to talk about *things to have been done* or things as prescriptively required

2. *The Language of Morals*, pp. 17 ff.

in all tenses and persons. If we find need for usages which go beyond those of ordinary discourse, we may have to conceive of imperatives in ways for which we do not have linguistic guides. We are here up against what Waismann calls the open texture of ordinary language.

We may say that a person is operating under an imperative whenever he accepts something as something to be done or something to be brought about. One is presented with an imperative whenever one is presented with something as something to be done or brought about, whether or not one accepts it as something to be done. An imperator, in the sense of a person commanding, entreating, exhorting, is not necessary. These are simply some of the ways in which one can be presented with something to be done. One often says 'It is imperative that I do so and so,' 'This is something for me to do,' and the like. Such expressions indicate that even according to ordinary discourse an imperator is not required for an imperative to exist.

### 5.3 *The search for suppressed imperative premises*

In attempting to determine whether the naturalist's case can be made out, we must look for imperatives which function as premises (along with factual truths) in our practical reasoning. Some such premises themselves may be obtained by inference from still others. But it seems so evident that it is not worth arguing that in such a setup some imperatives must be accepted, subscribed to, or had in some way other than by inference from still others. Of course if naturalism is to be made out, they cannot be inferred from purely factual premises alone. The problems then are these: do we subscribe to a set of noninferred imperatives in terms of which all our practical reasoning proceeds? If so, what kind of status do they have?

We do not have to look far for some such noninferred imperatives. As Hobbes clearly saw,[3] the language of desire and of aversion is imperative just as the language of perception is

3. Thomas Hobbes, *Leviathan* (London, 1951), Pt. I, Chap. 6, p. 29.

declarative. A desire is not simply an occurrence, an event, like a book's falling off a table. The difference is not merely that a desire is somehow mediated by a cognition of its object. It is wrongheaded to think of it merely as a response to a stimulus —even though there is cognitive mediation—as though the inclination toward or in favor of the object were simply an effect of certain causal conditions. To do so is to miscategorize it. It is somewhat similar to a perception, a belief, or an approval. These are different from natural events, as we saw in Chapter III, in that they have a semantic aspect, as it is evident from the language required to report them. An ordinary event like the book's falling off the table is reported by the sentence 'The book fell off the table.' But perceptions, beliefs, and desires have to be reported differently. 'He saw *the book fall off the table*,' 'I heard *him coming*,' 'I believe *he went to Washington*.' Sentences like these are complicated in a peculiar way. What comes after the mental verb either is or can be translated into a declarative sentence, which expresses *what* was perceived or thought— the semantic content of the mental act. Desires and aversions are not quite like perceptions and thoughts. Their content cannot be expressed by declarative sentences. Consider some examples: 'He wants you to run for the office,' 'I desire to bring this meeting to a close,' 'I prefer to have steak for dinner,' and 'It was his desire to continue where he was.' What is wanted, desired, or preferred is for something to-be (or the negative of these). It takes imperative sentences to express them. When a person sees a book fall off a table, he expresses himself by saying 'The book fell off the table.' When one wants someone else to run for an office, one expresses oneself by saying 'Run for the office.'

To have a desire, then, is to entertain and indeed, in some sense, to subscribe to an imperative, just as to have a perception or belief is to entertain and to accept, in some sense, a proposition. So every desire, as distinct from an idle wish, presents something as *something to be done, to be brought about,* or simply *to-be.*

Many have taken likes and dislikes rather than desires as the primary or basic value-experience. The two kinds of experience are closely related. When one desires that a be F one might say 'I want a to be F' or 'I should like a to be F.' What is desired or wanted is something which would be liked if it were. Whenever one says 'I like a,' one might say 'a is what I want'; or instead of saying 'I like a the way it is,' one might say 'a is the way I want it.' To like something is to find it to be what one wants or to be as one wants it to be. And if to desire something involves the acceptance of an imperative, to like something involves finding it to be in accord with an imperative which one subscribes to. 'I like a' is the subjective counterpart of 'a is good' ('a is what ought to-be' or 'a is as it ought to be'), whereas 'I desire a' is the subjective version of 'a ought to-be.' Just as 'ought' is a more basic value-term than 'good' (since the latter involves both 'existence' and 'ought'), desires are a more basic kind of value-experience than likes. For this reason I shall concentrate on desires.

We desire many things because we believe them to be factually connected with other things we desire. But there must be some desires which are underived if there are any at all. These are simply had. We find ourselves with them; they occur without deliberation. I shall call them 'primary' desires. They present us with noninferred imperatives in terms of which practical reasoning can get started.

However, on the basis of the imperatives provided by what I shall call 'zero-level' primary desires, no more than a start can be made. Given in a primary desire the imperative that something be or be brought about and certain factual truths, some other imperative may follow logically and be accepted in the form of a new but derived or reasoned desire. The negative of this derived imperative, however, may follow from the imperative of some other primary desire and the relevant factual truths.

If so, how can the deliberation proceed? How can we determine what ought to-be or ought to be done? What imperative follows? It would seem that none follows; for if the premises yield contradictory imperatives, they cancel each other and we are left with nothing prescribed. There is no reason for doing one thing rather than another. We have no conclusion about what is to be done or not to be done. And practical reasoning is at its limit.

Perhaps in such situations deliberation proceeds in a manner which distinguishes it from practical reasoning (from *inferring* imperative conclusions from premises). When we reflect upon what happens in our minds in some situations, it does seem that we simply survey the facts and that in the process of the discursive review of them the former conflicting interests simply evaporate and some new primary desire occurs, which provides us with an unopposed imperative to act upon. Certainly personal deliberation is not always, and perhaps never is, a simple matter of taking a set of well-formed imperatives presented by a set of pre-deliberative desires (which remain constant throughout the deliberative process) and of deducing the imperative conclusions which follow from them. Often, primary desires emerge, undergo modification, and disappear during the deliberative process. The naturalist can say with a great deal of plausibility that the original conflicting desires and the ones that replaced them were simply *caused* by cognition of the facts; the former, perhaps by an incomplete or erroneous cognition of the situation, and the latter, by a more complete and correct view of the matter.

Although deliberation is not always (and perhaps never) all practical reasoning, it is equally certain that we do sometimes engage in practical reasoning, especially when we reason with someone, when we try to help someone reach a decision or try to reach a group decision, and when we appraise conduct rather than deliberate it. Practical reasoning is more obviously present in such situations than in personal deliberation; for we are not as likely to confuse it with the noninferential kind of decision-procedure.

The same problem of conflicting imperative conclusions occurs in cases of more or less pure practical reasoning. If such a matter is to be resolved by reasoning (and it obviously is done in some cases), according to the naturalist's account there must be subscription to some higher-level imperatives in terms of which a reasoned decision can be made.

A young man may have a positive interest in being a doctor, for example. It may be his settled purpose which functions as a governing propensity over a considerable area of activity. In terms of it he may deliberate many of his actions involving conflicting imperatives of a lower level. But it is not basic, for it itself is subject to critique. He might by deliberation decide that he ought not to be a doctor. One might operate under an imperative to be fully loyal to one's country and yet by deliberation in terms of other principles decide to change one's citizenship. But are there any imperatives not subject to deliberation and rejection in this manner which can provide deliberation and practical reasoning with a steady and stable framework?

Some have thought commitment to such imperatives to be inherent in man as a rational being. It does seem that man, by virtue of what he is, operates under rational imperatives, if not always in the ordering of his thought and conduct, at least in that he recognizes the validity of rational critique of both his thought and action. He is uncomfortable with charges of being irrational and is pleased with being appraised rational. Consequently, 'irrational' and its family are condemnatory words, whereas 'rational' and its cognates are commendatory. Insofar as one recognizes the pertinence of rational criticism of oneself, one acknowledges the principles in terms of which the criticism is made. But this whole program of rational criticism, according to the naturalist, presupposes the acknowledgment of certain principles in terms of which it is defined. Therefore, the principles themselves cannot be subject to such criticism. It was such a principle that Kant was concerned with in his search for a categorical imperative. "The final and universal imperative," C. I. Lewis says, "is one which is categorical. It requires no reason; being itself the expression of that which is the root of all reason; that in the absence of which there could be no reason of any sort or for any thing."[4]

What is the basic rational imperative, if there is one entitled to this description? Lewis has offered several formulations which he seems to think amount to the same thing: "Be consistent, in valuation and in thought and action"; "Be concerned about yourself in future and on the whole."[5] These are not obviously the same. Apparently what he means by 'being consistent' is for one to valuate, to think, and to act in such a manner that one will not later have occasion to be sorry. The consistency involved is a practical one: whatever one does at any time—in valuing, thinking, and acting—one should do it in such a manner that it will be consistent with one's future valuing, thinking, and acting. One who does something and then later regrets it evaluates the act differently at the two times. Lewis thinks that this imperative for practical consistency amounts to the same thing as 'Be concerned about yourself in future and on the whole.' Elsewhere he says, "The basic imperative is . . . simply that of governing oneself by the advice of cognition, in contravention, if need be, to impulsion and inclination of feeling."[6] This I suppose is thought to be equivalent to the other formulations only by virtue of the fact that following the advice of cognition is believed to be the only way of achieving the practical consistency of the other imperatives.

The import of Lewis' position is that man is by nature concerned to be rational. "The ground of the validity of these imperatives," he says, "must somehow lie in our human nature. Human nature *calls for* principles of right decision. The necessity of that acknowledgment, if it should be challenged, must lie

4. *An Analysis of Knowledge and Valuation*, p. 481.
5. *Ibid.*
6. "The Rational Imperatives," in *Vision and Action*, ed. Sidney Ratner (New Brunswick, N.J.: Rutgers University Press, 1953), p. 158.

finally in the fact that to decide is unavoidable."[7] It is not clear from this passage whether Lewis means that human nature, or some factor in it, is a validating or justifying ground for the basic rational imperative (or imperatives) or whether the *explanation* of our acknowledgment of it (or them) is to be found in the way in which we are constituted. However, elsewhere he has said, as we have already observed, that there can be no reason for the imperative without which there would be no reason for anything. Although his wording is ambiguous, it seems that his intent is that of naturalism.

The important problem is what constitutes rationality. Lewis has attempted to give only a pragmatic account of it. It is true that he has assumed that a person cannot be pragmatically consistent without following the advice of cognition. But what if a person should be able to persist in stupidity and obtuseness in a pragmatically consistent manner? Would we say he was acting rationally? Of course, Lewis would say this is not possible; but I suspect he could support such a claim only by a similar pragmatic account of stupidity and obtuseness. It seems to me that it is at least possible (in the sense that it is meaningful to say it) for a person to make stupid decisions without ever being sorry (in the sense of coming to value differently the things involved). He might insist that he made the right decision but merely had bad luck or that the world was against him or in some other way he might persist in his original thinking and valuation.

Lewis' pragmatic consistency is simply a test of whether a reason for thinking or doing something is a good one. If we consider something to be a good reason for thinking or doing something and later find out that the thought was false or that the thing ought not to have been done, then that something was not a good enough reason for thinking or doing the thing in question. The fundamental imperative involved would seem to be to have good reasons for whatever one thinks or does (to

7. *The Ground and Nature of the Right* (New York: Columbia University Press, 1955), pp. 86-87.

be justified under rational critique). This is simply the imperative to be rational.

But what constitute "good reasons" in the realm of action? A reason is simply a truth which either by itself or in conjunction with an imperative (as the naturalist would insist) "entails" prescriptively the act in question. A good reason for doing something is one that is not cancelled or overridden by some counter reason. In short, it is a reason which in the situation concerned justifies the act in question. The naturalist's position, as it is here interpreted, would contend, for example, that the fact that an act promises one pleasure, apart from other considerations, would be a good reason for one to do it (and that it would give one pain, taken by itself, would be a good reason for one not to do it), because by virtue of one's biological or psychological nature, one operates under an imperative to seek pleasure and to avoid pain. We would have a practical argument which could be formulated this way:

> Seek pleasure.
> Act a promises to give me pleasure.
> ───────────────
> Therefore, I ought to do a.

or:

> Avoid pain.
> Act b will cause me pain.
> ───────────────
> I ought not to do b.

It should be noted that apart from the imperative 'Seek pleasure,' according to the naturalist, the fact that a promises me pleasure would not be a reason for my doing it; and apart from the imperative to avoid pain the fact that b will cause me pain would not be a reason for my not doing it.

A desire or an interest, I have argued, involves at least a tentative acceptance of an imperative. Therefore any act which would satisfy a given interest, relative to that interest and apart from other considerations, ought to be done. This, I take it, is the valid point of naturalists who have attempted to define value-concepts in terms of interest, especially Perry's definition of value as any object of any interest. He contends that everyone should recognize an object to be good insofar as some interest, regardless of whose, is taken in it. However, an interest operates as an imperative only to the person whose it is. Suppose it could be satisfied only by an act of another person. Although the other person might recognize in a purely factual way that the act ought to be done relative to the given imperative, he might not at all accept the imperative to do the thing required. If he did not, he would not fully accept the statement that the act ought to be done; for the 'ought'-statement would entail the imperative, and to accept fully or to believe the 'ought'-statement would involve accepting the entailed imperative. It is the same kind of thing as for one to believe that a factual conclusion follows from certain premises but not to accept the conclusion. For the value-judgment to function in one's deliberation or appraisal, one must accept the imperative, for only an accepted imperative can provide one with something that one can count as a reason for doing something. This is the significance of the contention of Stevenson and others that to accept something as good involves having an inclination to bring it about or to promote it, that one cannot say, "yes, I agree; it is good, but I don't give a hoot about it." This would be a linguistic absurdity.

Hobbes built this relativism into his value-theory. "But whatsoever is the object of any man's Appetite or Desire; that is it, which he for his part calleth *Good*: and the object of his hate, an aversion, Evill; and his contempt, *Vile* and *Inconsiderable*. For these words of Good, Evill, and Contemptible, are ever used with relation to the person that useth them: There being nothing simply and absolutely so; nor any Common Rule of Good and Evill, to be taken from the nature of the objects themselves; but from the person of the man (where there is no common-wealth)."[8]

We now have before us not one but two problems. We were first concerned with how there can be a reason for doing some one thing rather than another when contradictory actions are prescribed by zero-level primary desires and the relevant factual truths. We now have the further problem of how an interest or desire of someone can provide another with a reason for doing something. So far our appeal to man as a rational animal has yielded only the imperative that one have a good reason for whatever one does. But this does not help at all in providing any reasons whatever for doing any particular thing. If the naturalist's account is to be made out, man must have some primary or underived imperatives from some source to provide him with ways of solving problems of both intra- and interpersonal conflicting interests.

The problem is, what constitutes *rationality* in such situations? The only way to find out is to examine our rational critique of action. We find the best examples in the judgments of informed, impartial spectators. Our task is to uncover and to formulate the rational principles in terms of which they make their appraisals.

Certainly we think it is not rational for one to refuse to suffer a temporary pain, like having a bad tooth extracted, for the sake of good health or for one to sacrifice a successful career for the sake of indulging in temporary pleasures. There is something more involved here than what Sidgwick spoke of as the imperative "of impartial concern for all parts of our conscious life"[9] or Lewis' formulation, "conduct yourself, with reference to those future eventualities which cognition advises that your activity may affect, as you would if these predictable effects of it were to be realized, at this moment of decision, with the poig-

8. *Leviathan*, Pt. I, Chap. 6, p. 24.

9. Henry Sidgwick, *The Methods of Ethics* (7th edn.; London: Macmillan and Company, 1922), p. 121 note.

nancy of the here and now, instead of the less poignant feeling which representation of the future and possible may automatically arouse."[10] Such a principle helps only in weighing considerations of the present with those of the future. It simply tells us to weigh them as though they were all present. But this is of no help unless we already know how to weigh considerations of the present and how to stack them up against one another to determine what ought to be done in light of the total situation.

Perhaps when we confront the total situation without distinguishing between present and future factors a new primary desire replaces the conflicting ones. Or perhaps some one of the conflicting ones is singled out and accepted as the one to act on by the simple occurrence of a feeling of approval toward acting on it. If so, there is no practical reasoning as I am conceiving it. But there are situations in which we reason out such matters —especially when we appraise what was done in such a situation, if not when we deliberate it. But I think we do it even in deliberation. And there are rational principles involved. No one, I suppose, would question that we do in fact operate under and often appeal to such imperatives as the following, at least in appraising conduct as rational or irrational: do not sacrifice a greater good for a lesser one; do not sacrifice a great good in order to avoid a small evil; do not suffer a greater evil in order to avoid a lesser one. These need some refinement, I am sure, but the idea should be clear. Also, no one would quarrel with a principle like this one: if you claim that the fact that a proposed action of another would hurt you is, apart from other considerations, a good reason for the act's not being done, and if you expect him and others to recognize it as such, then acknowledge that the fact that some proposed act of yours would hurt another is, apart from other considerations, a good reason for your act's not being done. This is the kind of thing Kant was getting at in his categorical imperative. It amounts to this: act yourself according to

10. *The Ground and Nature of the Right*, p. 89.

and only according to those imperatives which you approve of others acting by in similar situations.

We could not reject any of these by reasoning in terms of other principles, although we might on occasion act contrary to them. Contrary to all the arguments of the relativists, they do not seem to vary from person to person or from culture to culture. We all recognize that behavior contrary to any of these principles is irrational and that to say that an act is contrary to any one of them is to condemn it. This, I take it, is to admit that they are basic rational imperatives and that not to employ them in deliberating and appraising conduct would be to be nonrational.

However, the situation is not as happy as it might at first appear. These basic and universal rational imperatives presuppose that we are able to determine what the greater and lesser goods and evils are and what imperatives we approve of others acting by. Unless we already have determined the greater and lesser goods and evils and what it is right for others to do, these principles are of no practical help. Too, I rather suspect that their universality depends upon their peculiar character. To determine what are the greater and the lesser goods and evils is to determine which things are the more and the less imperative; and to determine that doing a particular thing is more imperative than doing another is to determine that it rather than the other is the thing to do, if they are incompatible. Also, in determining what is right for another in a given situation involves determining what would be right for anyone in that situation. In the very nature of the case, if it would not be right for me to do a in a similar situation, it would not be right for the other fellow to do it. So these basic rational imperatives are universal, no matter how we go about determining greater and lesser goods and evils and determining what is right and wrong for other people to do. They ride piggy-back, so to speak, upon any principle or set of principles by which we determine these other matters. Kantians have been trying to formulate these basic rational imperatives. Others, like the self-realizationists and the utilitarians, have been trying to formulate the principles in terms of which we actually determine the greater and the lesser goods and evils and what it is right for others to do.  The relativists also have been talking about principles at this level.

It might seem that no such intermediate principles are needed, that the imperatives presented by desires and the basic rational imperatives are sufficient.  One might try to make out such a position by arguing that whether one good or evil is greater or less than another is a matter to be determined solely by cognition and reason, even though nothing is good (as it ought to be) or evil (as it ought not to be) except in relation to some imperative premise.  But there are difficulties with such a position.  One obvious way of accounting for comparative and superlative values, according to the naturalistic view as it is here interpreted, is for something to be more or less as it ought to be, or more or less like what ought to be.  This is something to be determined by cognition, once we know how something ought to be or what ought to-be.  But this kind of comparative value is not what is needed.  It is determined in relation to an "ought" that is not quantitative—a logical relation between premises and conclusion of a practical argument.  What is wanted is a way of determining the comparative value of two things even though each is exactly and absolutely as it ought to be in the above sense (that is, relative to the respective premises of each).  This would seem to require weighing the imperative premises, weighing their imperativeness.  This, I take it, is what Perry was getting at in his account of comparative value.  However, he confused quantity of interest with degree of imperativeness and consequently confused imperativeness with psychological factors.  This position is not open to the consistent logical naturalist; it forsakes the reduction of value-concepts to logical concepts.  If the quantity of value varies with some nonlogical feature of the imperative premise, like its imperativeness, then value-concepts do not express merely a logical relation between the premises and the conclusion of a practical argument.

It would seem that the only way in which one could say, on this account, that a is a greater good than b, when their goodness is appraised relative to different imperative premises, would be for the imperative premise of b to be subordinate to the other in such a way that (although the doing or being of each follows from its respective premises) when the imperative and factual premises of both are combined the doing or being of a rather than b follows prescriptively from the combined set. Thus, 'a is a greater good than b' means a is more nearly what ought to-be, relative to this new set of premises, than b. But all this presupposes that we know what premises are to be combined and what follows from them and that what follows from them is to be done (or to-be) rather than that what follows from either subset taken by itself is to be done. The determination of these matters requires the intermediate principles spoken of above. Without them, on the naturalistic account, we cannot know any of these things.

With regard to the imperatives presented by the desires of one person, we usually assume a prudential interest or self-concern which provides the needed imperative for combining all the imperatives presented by his own desires, for determining what imperative follows from the combined set (plus the facts of the situation), and for determining its superior rank to those that follow from some subset. Philosophers have never felt any peculiar need to ground or in any way validate this imperative or its superior status. It is simply there. It is existential. It is the source of reasons for other things, but it itself apparently has no justifying reason.

Why combine the imperative premises presented by the interests of different people? How do we determine what follows from the combined set and the facts of the situation? And why count the imperative conclusion of the combined set as superior to that of the subsets?

Some have tried to make the prudential imperative do the job. It might be put something like this: each person desires that others consider his own interests, and the only way for this to be realized is for each to consider the interests of others. But this still would not help in determining what really follows prescriptively from the combined set of imperative (and factual) premises. How do we determine that one imperative is to have precedence over another? This is not something that can be determined by either the facts or the logic of the case.

The simplest account of the matter would be to say that what we do is simply to survey the facts and the various conflicting interests and find that we would have a feeling of disapproval toward certain interests being acted on and a feeling of approval toward some. According to this account, the feelings of approval and disapproval would present imperatives of a higher level, imperatives concerning other imperatives, and thereby function as superior in rank. They would be general in nature and apply to a particular imperative only as an instance of a kind. Some naturalists might be content to say that we simply appeal to such feelings of approval and disapproval in each individual case of deliberation and appraisal and that they may be quite erratic, varying from time to time with the same person, or from person to person, or from culture to culture. Others may think that there is more uniformity and consistency in our approvals and disapprovals, especially when we eliminate extraneous considerations, as in the case of a disinterested spectator.

Hume thought that by virtue of sympathy with all of one's kind (which provides an explanation, not a justification) one approves and disapproves of acts in terms of their effect on the general happiness of mankind. Bentham, in speaking of the principle of utility, says that it is not susceptible of any direct proof, "for that which is used to prove everything else, cannot itself be proved: ... To give such a proof is as impossible as it is needless. Not that there is or ever has been that human creature breathing, however stupid or perverse, who has not on many, perhaps on most occasions of his life, deferred to it. By the natural constitution of the human frame, on most occasions of their lives men in general embrace this principle, without thinking of it: if not for the ordering of their own actions, yet for the trying of their own actions, as well as those of other men."[11]

Contrary to Bentham, Mill offers what seems to be a proof of the principle of utility. He says, "No reason can be given why the general happiness is desirable except that each person, so far as he believes it to be attainable, desires his own happiness. This, however, being a fact, we have not only all the proof which the case admits of, but all which it is possible to require, that happiness is a good: that each person's happiness is a good to that person, and the general happiness, therefore, a good to the aggregate of all persons."[12] Many problems have been raised about this argument. However, the only one I am concerned with is how he gets from the proposition that each person's happiness is a good to that person to the proposition that the general happiness is desirable to the aggregate of all persons. We find a clue in Chapter III of *Utilitarianism,* where he says, "for whether there be any other ground of moral obligation than the general happiness or not, men do desire happiness; and however imperfect may be their own practice, they desire and commend all conduct in others towards themselves by which they think their happiness is promoted." What he is saying is that with each person desiring his own happiness, the only modes of conduct in society which can win the approval of all or most people are those which conform with the greatest happiness of all. In other words, the basic moral principle is that presented by *commonly shared approvals in society.*

Others have held that we may simply make up our minds about how we want to live and that that will constitute our basic principle. R. M. Hare says, "if pressed to justify a decision completely, we have to give a complete specification of the

11. *An Introduction to the Principles of Morals and Legislation,* p. 4.

12. John Stuart Mill, *Utilitarianism,* in *The English Philosophers from Bacon to Mill,* ed. Edwin A. Burtt, Modern Library (New York: Random House, 1939), Chap. IV.

way of life of which it is a part. . . . If the inquirer still goes on asking 'But why *should* I live like that?,' then there is no further answer to give him. . . . We can only ask him to make up his own mind which way he ought to live; for in the end everything rests upon such a decision of principle. He has to decide whether to accept that way-of life or not; if he accepts it, then we can proceed to justify the decisions that are based upon it; if he does not accept it, then let him accept some other, and try to live by it."[13] This, I take it, is much the same as Donald Williams' theory that ethics "is a system of resolves rooted logically in certain fundamental resolves which are postulates, and which may be *pure* postulates in the sense that, although there may be *causes* of them, there literally is no *reason* for them. They are what happens with the blank indemonstrability and the blank irrefutability of a natural event."[14]

### 5.4 *Summary and conclusion*

Practical reasoning, then, according to the naturalistic picture, proceeds within a framework bounded on one end by imperatives presented by zero-level primary desires and on the other by the imperative to be rational, to have a good reason for whatever we do. Falling in between are the piggy-back rational imperatives; the "existential a priori" imperatives (whether presented by feelings of approval and disapproval of the individual or commonly shared approvals and disapprovals in a society; or had by virtue of an inherent sentiment of humanity and self-concern or by the natural constitution of the human frame or by pure personal or societal resolution, or what have you); and various levels of imperatives presented by more or less settled purposes, which may function in an a priori manner in many areas but are, under some conditions, subject to rational review and a reasoned decision.

13. *The Language of Morals*, p. 69.
14. "Ethics as Pure Postulate," *The Philosophical Review*, XLII, No. 4 (July, 1933), 404.

The naturalist, it would seem, can find an abundance of imperatives to serve as premises of practical arguments. He can make a somewhat plausible case for his contention that there are no valid natural practical arguments in our ordinary deliberations and practical reasoning and that, therefore, there is no reason to believe that there is an objective value-requiredness in reality as experienced by us.

# CHAPTER VI

# THE CASE AGAINST LOGICAL NATURALISM

6.1 *Does the logical naturalist really find the alleged suppressed imperative premises*

Although the logical naturalist can, as we saw in the preceding chapter, make a somewhat convincing case for his position, we must not yet grant him a full victory. There are further problems to be considered.

First of all, does he really *find* the *suppressed* imperative premises as he makes out? Of course there are often such premises involved in our practical reasoning, but are they always there? Are we so well stocked with imperative premises that every new fact which alters our conclusion about what we ought to do, what ought to-be, what ought to have been done, or what ought to-have-been does so by virtue of some imperative we already subscribe to? The naturalist would have to say, I suppose, that we find out what imperatives we are committed to by finding out what facts count as reasons for something's being done or just plain being. But how does he know, then, that we are really committed to those imperatives in such a way that they are there as suppressed premises? Does he not simply posit them because his theory requires them? Does he have any other basis for saying they are there? If his only ground for claiming their existence is that his theory requires that they be there in order for the facts concerned to count as reasons, he cannot appeal to the fact that he can always find the suppressed imperative in making his case for his theory. It would simply cite the theory in support of itself. The data appealed to would be shaped and constructed in terms of the theory being tested. This is the most vicious hazard involved in doing philosophy. It seems to be almost unavoidable. We are all more or less guilty of it even while we are pointing it out in others. This no doubt is one reason why progress in philosophy is so tortuous and uncertain.

Let us consider an alternative to the stockpile theory of suppressed imperative premises. Suppose we adopt or subscribe to the needed imperative right on the spot, so to speak. Instead of going around with a stockpile of imperative premises which we do not even know we have until we catch ourselves using them in practical reasoning, which in itself is not an absurd possibility, maybe we simply adopt them as they are needed. This seems to be the position of Hare.[1] The peculiarity of his position is that moral reasoning must terminate in, not *a* decision, but a *double-barrelled* decision—not that merely sometimes in deciding a particular case we modify some previous principle of conduct, but that every time we make a decision it is twofold. We make a decision about the matter at hand and in doing so make a decision about the principle employed in deciding the particular matter. Suppose, for instance, to use Hare's example, that I am in doubt about whether to tell some particular falsehood. Any moral principle which would help me to decide the matter, along with some factual premises, would have to enjoin me not to tell (or to tell) the falsehood. But "since I am in doubt, *ex hypothesi,* whether or not to make this false statement, I must be in doubt about assenting to the command, 'Do not make this statement.' But if I am in doubt about this command, I must *eo ipso* be in doubt, either about the factual premise 'This statement is false' (and this alternative is ruled out *ex hypothesi*),

1. The discussion of Hare's position that follows is largely adapted from my article, "Mr. Hare on the Role of Principles in Deciding," *Mind,* LXV, No. 257 (Jan., 1956), 78-80.

or else, as must be the case, about the imperative premise 'Never say what is false.' "[2] If there is a decision to be made about the particular matter, there is also a decision to be made about the general principle.

It seems to me that Hare must admit that there are some single-barrelled decisions—either some without the benefit of a guiding principle or suppressed imperative or some with a guiding principle which involves no decision about the principle itself. Let us suppose that he rejects the first alternative, which I think he does. On this position, no decision can be made without an imperative premise. Therefore, in order to make a decision about an act A, according to Hare one would have to decide on a principle $P_1$; but in order to decide on $P_1$, one would have to decide on $P_2$; in order to decide on $P_2$, one would have to decide on $P_3$; and so on *ad infinitum,* with the embarrassing consequence that no decisions could ever be made. It might seem that a "self-evident" (a self-determining) principle somewhere down the line could break the infinite regress, but Hare has closed this avenue of escape by what he believes to be a conclusive refutation of all forms of "Cartesianism" in ethics.[3]

Clearly, some slip has been made. Part of the problem arises from the kinds of principles selected for consideration. In the above example, although he considers his conclusion to be 'Do not make this statement' and speaks of 'This statement is false' as a factual premise, it is clear that he takes as his paradigm, as I pointed out in Chapter II, the application of the principle 'Never tell a falsehood' to the problem of *whether to tell this falsehood.* As he contends, it is much easier to decide not to tell a particular falsehood than to decide never to tell a falsehood; for the decision of principle in this case must wait upon the decision about telling this and many other particular falsehoods and is subject to being overthrown in its full universality by the decision about any particular one. Yet he also maintains that

2. *The Language of Morals,* p. 41.
3. *Ibid.,* p. 33.

to decide to do or not to do a particular thing is to adopt a principle for all of its kind.[4] There seems to be an inconsistency here, but perhaps it is due to an implicit recognition of two kinds of principles, which he does not distinguish.

Hare is quite right in contending that when one decides not to tell a particular falsehood one does not decide never to tell a falsehood. But in deciding not to tell the particular falsehood, insofar as it is a reasoned decision, one would do it for such and such a reason, perhaps because it is a case of deception under such and such conditions; and, according to logical naturalism, an appeal would be made to the principle 'Never do an act that is a case of deception under such-and-such conditions.' This itself, according to logical naturalism, is a principle which would be adopted for some other such and such a reason or reasons, and thereby an appeal would be made to a still higher principle, in terms of which a later modification might be made. The two kinds of principles related to a decision about a particular act, then, are (1) a generalized principle pertaining to all acts of the kind under consideration and (2) a generalized principle pertaining to the reason for doing the particular act.

With this distinction between the two kinds of principles, Hare's paradigm should have been one of the following:

(1) Never tell a falsehood. Therefore, do not make this statement, because it is a falsehood.

(2) Never tell a falsehood under such-and-such conditions. Therefore, do not tell this falsehood because it would be to tell a falsehood under such-and-such conditions.

rather than:

(3) Never tell a falsehood. Therefore, do not tell this falsehood.

In (1) the problem would be *whether to make this statement,* not *whether to make this false statement.* In (2) the problem would be *whether to tell this falsehood.* In (3) Hare should

4. *Ibid.,* p. 70.

have had either the problem of (1) or the principle of (2). In either case, although operating with the assumption that a guiding principle is always required for a decision, his theory of the double-barrelled nature of decision would not have suggested itself; for with the above distinction between two kinds of principles and the resulting modification of Hare's paradigm, a distinction can be made between *deciding* that a particular act shall come under a certain principle and *recognizing* that it does. Suppose that a judge is in doubt about what law applies to a particular case. From what does his doubt arise? Lack of knowledge of the case or the vagueness of the law? If the former, his doubt can be removed by further study of the case, resulting in its proper characterization and, consequently, *recognition* of what law applies; if the latter, his doubt is removed by a *decision,* resulting in a refinement of the law.

If there were situations in which we decided a particular case A in terms of a principle $P_1$, which we recognized to apply to A, or if we should find ourselves with a doubt that required a decision about applying $P_1$ to A and found a principle $P_2$ which we recognized to apply to the case of $P_1$'s application to A, then a decision could be made. But assuming that a guiding principle is required for a decision, without recognizing that some principles applied to some cases so that some single-barrelled decisions could be made, we would be in the predicament of the infinite regress outlined above.

The outcome of this discussion is that with the assumption that a guiding principle or suppressed imperative premise is necessary in all cases of practical reasoning, the stockpile theory of suppressed imperatives is inescapable. I feel that there may be some significant insight involved in Hare's contention that we do in fact make at least some double-barrelled decisions, that we do adopt principles on the spot. But, as I have shown, holding to such a view involves giving up the logical naturalist's contention that there is always a suppressed imperative premise; for the decision of principle contained in the double-barrelled decision would have to be made without the benefit of a guiding principle.

Consider case (2) cited above, where the problem was *whether to tell a certain falsehood:* it was characterized by a factual premise as *a falsehood under such-and-such conditions.* Now, what about the alleged imperative premise never to tell a falsehood under just these such-and-such conditions? How does it get into the picture? Do we adopt it by inferring it from some still more general principle? Or is it involved in (or perhaps simply is) what we decide? Perhaps our argument is merely this:

> Telling this falsehood would be to tell a falsehood under such-and-such conditions. Therefore, do not tell this falsehood.

This is a natural practical argument. In accepting it as valid, as in the case of any natural practical argument, one accepts what I have earlier called its corresponding conditional, namely, 'If telling this falsehood would be to tell a falsehood under such-and-such conditions, then it ought not to be told.' Insofar as the reasons contained in the antecedent are complete (that is, insofar as there are no suppressed factual premises of the natural practical argument), the conditional has the force of a general principle. We are likely to say that we adopt or decide on the generalized conditional and then use it in deciding the particular case. In this way we get an imperative premise for the practical argument, and the naturalist seems to have made his case so far at least. However, the decision of principle was nothing more than acceptance of the natural practical argument as valid. The 'if . . . then . . . ought . . .' of the conditional simply expresses the fact that the truth of the factual premises normatively demands that prescribed by the imperative conclusion of the argument. It is no more a premise of the argument than the conditional 'If all men are mortal, and Socrates is a man, then Socrates must be mortal' is a premise of the argument 'All men are mortal; Socrates is a man; therefore, Socrates is mortal.' Perhaps it was this apparent dualism (the acceptance of an imperative conclusion on the basis of factual premises or reasons and the acceptance of the corresponding conditional in its generalized form) that Hare was getting at with his theory of a double-barrelled decision. But, as we have seen, the dualism is only apparent. There is only one decision or acceptance, but it may be expressed in two different ways.

If the naturalist is careful to avoid the error of taking the corresponding conditional of an argument to be a premise of it, will he be able to produce the alleged imperative premises of all our practical arguments? Consider especially the cases in which we make exceptions to general rules which we do have stockpiled. We may very well have a rule which we have always taken to be universal; yet in a particular situation, because of certain circumstances, we may refuse to accept the thing enjoined by the rule as the thing which ought to be done. For example, a person might fully subscribe to the imperative 'Never tell a lie' and yet find himself in a situation in which he would (to his great surprise) conclude that he ought to tell a certain lie. The decision would of course involve a modification of the original principle. We modify our rules this way all the time. The point I wish to raise is this: do we make these modifications of rules in terms of principles already accepted? Or do we simply *recognize* that what the accepted rule enjoins in certain circumstances simply is not what ought to be done in those situations? Can we find rules to cover the modifications if we are careful not to count the corresponding conditionals of our apparent natural practical arguments as premises of them? The same question applies of course to the formation of a new rule as well as to the modification of an old one. And we do make new rules all the time. Whenever we decide to do something for a reason (and I suppose that *deciding,* in at least one sense of the term, involves having a reason), the corresponding conditional has the force of a rule. I am inclined to think that it is more plausible to hold that there are valid natural practical arguments and that we derive our general principles from them. It seems that we do simply recognize that since such and such is the case, we ought to do so and so. We do this over and over again. The child does it very early, even where he has not been taught principles. The hunt for the suppressed imperative premises seems to be prompted only by a theory. And the only grounds I can see for holding that there are always such is that logical naturalism requires them.

## 6.2 Moore's recurring question in a new form

Furthermore, the spirit of Moore's recurring question returns to haunt logical naturalism. It will be recalled that Moore argued against the traditional version of ethical naturalism (which defined value-concepts in terms of scientific ones) by contending that for any scientific concept 'C' which might be offered as a definiens of 'good,' it would be meaningful in ordinary discourse to ask, 'But is Cx good?' This proved to be a serious obstacle to traditional naturalists in their attempts to square their definitions with common-sense value-categories as revealed in ordinary language. A similar criticism, or the same one in a different form, applies to our new formulation of naturalism. Of any underived but simply presented or postulated imperative, it seems to make sense to ask, 'Ought one to do what it enjoins?' or, 'Why ought one to do what it prescribes?' Of course this does not refute the naturalist in any clear-cut fashion. In fact it may not refute him at all. He can make a somewhat plausible defense against it.

The first thing he can do is to say that of course we can render the underived imperatives of the deliberative framework in 'ought'-form by virtue of their self-entailment. 'If P, then P' is a fundamental law of logic. It holds equally for statements and imperatives. But this is a trivial matter and gets us nowhere, unless perhaps to explain why basic imperatives may be stated in the 'ought'-mode with some legitimacy. However, the feeling is that in ordinary discourse the 'ought'-question about any such imperative can be *significantly* asked—that it poses a genuine and an important question. Also, an underived imperative's self-entailment provides no account of the apparent meaningfulness of the question 'Why ought one to do what the imperative enjoins?'; for if 'ought' is applicable only in the self-entailment sense, a practical reason of the ordinary kind (a factual truth) cannot be given. Of course, the naturalist might say (and with some plausibility) that there must be limits to such questions. At some point or other the question 'Why ought one to do so and so?' can only be answered by saying, "one just ought to; that is all there is to it." The naturalist might contend that such limits are constituted by existential imperatives which can be put in 'ought'-form only by virtue of their self-entailment. He might contend that the fact that such questions appear to be meaningful and significant in ordinary discourse is due to the looseness and untidiness of a natural language and that for philosophical clarity we should construct an ideal language in which such questions either could not be asked or would appear for what they are.

The naturalist might reason in this manner: reasons are given for doing what is prescribed by an imperative in order to get people to accept what is prescribed (either tentatively or for action) as something to be done. But the existential imperatives of the deliberative framework are already accepted. This is simply a fact. We do not try to get people to accept them. Since deliberation presupposes their acceptance, there is no point in giving reasons to back them up. When we realize this, it might be contended, we see that the lack of practical reasons of the ordinary kind is precisely what is required for them to constitute the deliberative framework.

## 6.3 *The authority of the basic rational imperatives*

But somehow the above defense does not seem satisfactory. It does not give to the basic rational imperatives of the framework the authority we expect of them. If practical reasoning and deliberation proceed within a framework bounded on one end by rational imperatives which are simply accepted or subscribed to by virtue of our nature, because of our social context, or by pure resolution or postulation and on the other by imperatives presented by primary desires which are simply caused, whence the *authority* of reason over impulse? It would seem that unless the basic rational imperatives can be significantly expressed in 'ought'-form (which is not possible according to the naturalist's account under consideration) and that unless the basic or primary acceptances of imperatives (including the rational or moral attitude itself) are not simply natural occurrences (states of mind which may be explained or accounted for solely in terms of natural causes or conditions) but are themselves subject to being appraised as correct or incorrect, as valid or invalid—in short, unless our basic rational attitudes are themselves *cognitions* of an objective value-requiredness, unless they make cognitive value-claims which may be sound—then there cannot be any *authority* to moral or rational judgments at all.

We have already seen in the chapter on emotivism that *ordinary* moral approvals and disapprovals make such claims. This fact, however, can be accommodated within the framework of logical naturalism. The 'ought'-judgment contained within the approval may be logical. It may express the relation between the premises and the imperative conclusion of a tautological practical argument. If so, the approval is correct or incorrect according to whether the argument concerned is valid or not. But logical naturalism cannot account for cognitive claims, if there are such, of either basic rational attitudes or primary desires. If such claims must be admitted, logical naturalism must be rejected.

Some naturalists have taken seriously the problem of the apparent authority of the rational imperatives of the deliberative framework and have tried to account for it. According to Henry Aiken, moral judgments have authority, are binding upon us, because they express common demands of a unified social order: "just as what we call 'the' meaning of a word in ordinary language is an interpersonal rule which thereby functions prescriptively for those who use the word," he says, "so also the moral authority of an ethical judgment is primarily due to the fact that it is a general rule of conduct which is binding upon the individual only because it is binding upon all."[5] This, I take it, is part of what Kant was getting at. Whatever rules are binding on others are binding on me. However, it fails to account for the reason why they are binding upon all. It is this problem with which I am concerned.

Perhaps it is as with the rules of a game. To have a game there must be rules, and they are binding on all who play it. However, just what the rules are is a matter quite arbitrarily determined. Everyone who attempts to play the game subjects himself to the rules and makes his play subject to criticism in terms of them. The rules have authority because they are the *accepted* rules of the game. The persons who play acknowledge the rules as binding on all. Whatever authority they have is derived from this fact. No other is needed. However, if the naturalist rests his case on this, it seems that he has given up his position, for it involves admitting what is apparently a valid natural practical argument, which is this: these imperatives (rules) have been accepted or consented to by all (of the race, of a society, etc.). Therefore, everyone (of the race, of the society, etc.) ought to act in accordance with them. The *fact* of acceptance by all validates them.

But perhaps the rules of a particular game gain their authority from being acknowledged by all the players by virtue of the fact that there are rules about playing games in general. Perhaps one such rule is that any rule of any game which is acknowledged by all the players shall be binding on all. What is the source of the authority of such rules? Perhaps all that can be said is that it is just the way to play games. If one does not do it that way, one is not playing a game. It is part of what we

5. "The Authority of Moral Judgments," *Philosophy and Phenomenological Research,* XII, No. 4 (June, 1952), 522.

mean by 'game.' When one refuses to go along with it, one ceases game play and begins to do something else. And one is thrown out of the game. He is not said to be a poor player of that particular game, but a poor sportsman, a poor gamesman. In rejecting a rule of the particular game as binding on himself he violates the rules of gamesmanship.

Although the rules of a particular game may be arbitrarily chosen within certain limits, the rules of gamesmanship do not seem to be quite so arbitrary. Do they get their authority from common acceptance? Could they be altered by universal consent of gamesmen? Somehow such rules seem to be quite different from those of a particular game. It seems that the former are more *recognized* than constituted by common consent. Even a failure to consent on the part of many would not undermine one's recognition of them.

The basic rational imperatives, including the moral ones, seem to be more like the rules of gamesmanship than those of particular games. There is this difference, of course: one can refrain from playing games but one cannot refrain from acting; even to commit suicide is to act. And action is rule-governed behavior. There are imperatives which we are under not merely as gamesmen (or not merely as something else about which we have a choice) but as human beings. As beings who make decisions, who deliberate our conduct, we seem to be under the rational imperatives in the same way as one who plays games is under the rules of gamesmanship. But there is this difference. We not only deliberate our conduct, we are under an imperative to do so. We condemn impulsive behavior as unbecoming a mature person, even if it is what the person would have done had he deliberated the matter. What of these imperatives? Are they merely existential? Or do they have some authority? Are they subject to validation?

Some have tried to account for the authority of basic rational imperatives by baptizing them 'metaphysical tendencies.' This, I take it, is the position of John Wild. Although he has no sympathy with modern naturalism, his reading of classical Aristotelianism seems to have been colored by it. "Active tendency," he says, "is a *third* metaphysical principle coordinate with essence and existence, which necessarily results from them, and enters into the constitution of any finite being. . . ."[6] He goes on to say, "Value is the fulfillment of existential tendency. . . . That towards which an entity is essentially tending, which will realize its nature, is good for it. . . . By value, we mean what is fit for a thing, what is due to its nature, the further existence that will complete its basic tendencies, and its incidental tendencies as well, so far as these do not conflict with the former."[7] All that this seems to do is to involve the acceptance of or commitment to certain imperatives in our essence; that is, we could not be otherwise and still be human beings. So what will fulfill them is said to be good for us. It fits the essential tendency. If this is what he means, I do not see where his position is any better off for being "metaphysical" than the naturalist's. In fact, his position seems to be simply Perry's interest-theory cast in metaphysical garb. For Perry an interest, a motor-affective tendency, sets something up as a goal, an end, and this is for it to have value. For Wild a metaphysical tendency sets something up as a goal; this is for it to be good. Perhaps he has the cart before the horse. Maybe he should not define 'value' in terms of 'tendency' but 'tendency' in terms of 'value.' Maybe it is not that the tendency sets up something as an end, as a value, but rather that something as an end, as an "ought to-be," elicits activity toward itself. Maybe the tendency is the pull of the "ought" upon existence. Indeed, was this not the classical teleological view? Was this not what Aristotle meant by 'final cause'? And was this not why he seemed to identify the formal and final causes? On this position there would be no problem about the authority of the basic imperatives; for they

6. "Tendency: The Ontological Ground of Ethics," *Journal of Philosophy*, XLIX, No. 14 (July 3, 1952), 471.
7. *Ibid.*, p. 473.

would be subject to validation. But Wild's position, as I have interpreted it, carries all the problems of naturalism with it over into the "metaphysical" realm.

Wild's position in this regard, although not in many others, is not too much unlike those of Kant and Lewis. They all find commitment to the basic imperatives involved in the kind of being we are. Kant appeals to a universal legislation of reason which we all share. Lewis says, "The ground of validity of imperatives must somehow lie in our human nature. Human nature calls for principles of right decision. The necessity of that acknowledgment . . . must lie finally in the fact that to decide is unavoidable. . . . That we must decide, and for a reason, is a distinctive feature of our human mentality."[8]

I think the intent of all three is that we do operate under these imperatives. Furthermore, this fact is no contingency but a kind of metaphysical necessity. If this is what they mean, they offer only a metaphysical explanation of why we accept them rather than a validation of them. And a metaphysical explanation provides no more authority for the imperatives than a scientific one.

Their position could be read to mean that the fact that commitment to these imperatives is involved in our nature validates them. If so, then we have a valid natural practical argument of the form: commitment to such-and-such imperatives is involved in our nature; therefore, we ought to act accordingly. Or is there still some suppressed imperative premise? If so, what could we make of it?

So it seems that the basic imperatives can have only a de facto status within a consistent naturalism. Yet this does not seem to do justice to the problem of their authority. Why do the higher-level imperatives have precedence over the others? Is it simply a fact that we give them precedence or that they operate in this way? Or do they in some way have a genuine authority? Can their superior rank be justified or validated? Do

8. *The Ground and Nature of the Right*, pp. 85-86.

they make valid claims to their superior status? Unless they do, it would seem that if one chose to satisfy one's "lower" desires at the expense of one's "higher" propensities, there would be no good reason for not doing so. Of course if one kept one's higher propensities and in terms of them condemned oneself for one's choice, we might say that there was, relative to them, a "reason" for not doing it. If the basic imperatives have only a de facto status, then whatever is derived from them can be recommended only on the ground that not to accept it would involve some kind of inconsistency; and unless we have a de facto imperative to be consistent, this would leave us cold. There would seem to be no authority and no valid or well-grounded imperative in the whole system.

Suppose an unauthorized person took over an army in the sense that he gave orders and others accepted them and carried them out. Suppose this involved a complete reorganization of the army, including a change in rank and assignment for everyone. Would there be any valid commands in the reorganized army? Or would the whole system have only a de facto status? If one chose to disobey an order, of course one might be punished, but would one be defying authority or merely force? Some such distinction is marked by a nation which refuses to recognize a government of a country established by revolution and imposed only by force and yet does business with it as a de facto government. Is there a genuine distinction here? And does it apply to the deliberative framework itself?

What is behind the kind of misgivings I am trying to express is the conviction that a purely existential imperative which itself has no validity cannot be the ground or source of the validity of any other imperative. The situation seems to be somewhat analogous to the fact that one statement's following from another does nothing to establish its truth unless the other statement is itself true.

Although I have been talking mostly about rational attitudes, the same general problem occurs in regard to primary desires.

They do not seem to be simply natural occurrences, merely effects of certain causal conditions. If they were, it would be difficult to see how they could impose any obligation upon anyone. If they were, why could not I ignore the desires of another in deliberating my own action in the same way I ignore other natural occurrences, like the grass under my feet and the stone in my path? Somehow we think a desire, regardless of whose it is, makes or presents a claim which must be recognized by a rational person. Its claim may be overridden or invalidated in some way, but it may not be simply ignored. How can this be, unless the desire in some way presents what may be a valid imperative? And how can this be unless the imperative has validity-conditions? And if it is a primary desire, which is what we are talking about, must not these validity-conditions be purely factual? And what, I ask, can the desire itself be, if not in some way a cognition or an awareness that the factual validity-conditions normatively demand or prescriptively require the thing presented?

6.4 *The character of primary desires and of basic rational attitudes*

There is a further problem which must be faced, namely, the character of the primary desires and the basic rational attitudes which present the imperatives constituting the deliberative framework. We have already seen that attitudes and desires are not merely natural events within the causal nexus. They have a semantic dimension like beliefs and perceptions. Where the latter embody factual propositions, attitudes have for their semantic content value-judgments and simple desires have imperatives.

An attitude, as distinct from a simple desire, has to do with the position one takes concerning something. It involves an appraisal of it as good, or bad, or just so-so, as better or worse or equally as good or as bad as something else. If it is something envisaged but nonexistent, it involves appraising it as something that would be good or bad, better or worse, and the like. An attitude need not involve an inclination to do anything at all, such as an attitude toward a past event. But a desire does. In fact a simple desire may be purely the acceptance of an imperative to do something or to bring something about.

I shall consider desires first. To desire that x be F is not to prescribe that x be F but rather to accept the imperative 'x be F.' It is to accept x's being F as something to-be or to be brought about, just as to believe x is F is to accept the proposition 'x is F.' In most desires, the acceptance is only tentative; it is subject to deliberative review in terms of a wider perspective. We have to distinguish it from the final acceptance involved in decision or will. The former does not involve readiness to act (if action is appropriate) as in the case of the latter, but only an inclination to do so.

Through sensory perception we are presented with our elementary or basic factual truths; through primary desires we are presented with basic imperatives, things to-be or to be done. Philosophers have raised the question whether to-be is to be perceived. It is a similar question I am raising here: whether for some envisaged object to be something to-be or to be done is for it to be desired or whether its being something to-be or to be done is prior to and independent of its being desired. The problem has been debated in the form of whether 'x ought to-be' (or, more often perhaps, 'x is good') means *x is desired* or *x is desirable*. The former view is axiological idealism. There have been three views of the meaning of 'x is desirable': (1) x is worthy of desire, or x is a proper or fitting object of desire; (2) x is such that it can be desired; and (3) x is factually such that any "normal" person under "normal" conditions would desire it. The first is a nonnaturalistic position; the other two are just as naturalistic as the view that 'x ought to-be' means that x is desired.

The nonnaturalistic position needs some clarification. What is it to be worthy of being desired or to be a proper or fitting object of desire? Most intuitionists have taken the position that it is a matter of a simple quality of objects and that therefore it does not lend itself to anlaysis. However, it may be fruitful to think of it in comparison with a belief. Certainly the proper or fitting object of a belief is a true proposition or a fact. What is not a fact is not ultimately worthy of belief, although believing it may be proper or justified under certain conditions: for example, when it is highly supported by a considerable body of evidence. By way of analogy, perhaps the proper or fitting object of desire is that which is prescriptively required in an objective manner. In other words, perhaps an imperative which is worthy of acceptance at the level of primary desires is one which has factual validity-conditions; perhaps a primary desire itself stands justified by virtue of the fact that the imperative accepted may appear as the conclusion of a valid natural practical argument. Certainly if the thing desired is something to-be or to be done or to be brought about independently of its being accepted as such, there must be certain facts which normatively demand or prescriptively require it. And for *primary* desires there could not be other interests to provide imperative premises which would render the validity of the imperative conclusion purely logical. Any validity it would have would have to be grounded in a value-requiredness as an objective, real connection.

The question to be considered is whether the acceptance of the imperative for something to-be or to be done which constitutes a primary desire is simply an effect of certain causal conditions. If so (even if part of the causal conditions were a cognition of a factual state of affairs), it would seem that we could not significantly talk about the desire (the acceptance of the imperative) as justified or not or as having a proper or fitting object or not. Natural occurrences, events which are the effects of natural causation, simply take place. They may be explained or accounted for, but they are not correct or incorrect, justified or unjustified.

Consider the case of believing. We do, of course, appraise beliefs as correct or incorrect, as justified or unjustified, as well grounded or not, and the like. But when a person's beliefs are causally determined, as in the case of some of those whom we call insane, although what is believed is said to be false (or even true in some instances), we cease to appraise the beliefs as incorrect, as unjustified, or as not well grounded. For a belief to be properly subject to such appraisals the acceptance of the proposition involved must be based on *reasons* for believing it or at least it must be subject to being dislodged by counter reasons. One cannot be incorrect or unjustified in believing a false proposition unless one was *trying* to get at the truth under the guidance of grounds or reasons. If the acceptance of the proposition which constitutes the belief were purely an effect of natural causation it would involve no effort, no trying, no undertaking, no claim which could be correct or incorrect; there would be nothing in terms of which one could be said to be justified or unjustified.

In like manner, if a desire (the acceptance of an imperative) is simply the effect of natural causation and is completely in the causal nexus, it too, I am urging, is not subject to appraisal as correct or incorrect, as justified or unjustified, as valid or invalid. And vice versa. If it is subject to such appraisals, then it is not simply an effect of natural causation but rather an attempt to get at (and makes the claim that there is) an objective value-re-quiredness. In short, if a desire is subject to such appraisals, it is a cognition of something as prescriptively required.

The naturalist's position on this matter is clear. Desires are simply natural occurrences causally produced. They are to be taken as mere events to be described and explained in a scientific way. They may be somewhat controlled as natural events in general. Certain conditions will induce them; certain others will eradicate them—like blue mold on tobacco plants or rot on apples.

However, can this account of the matter square with the presence of the semantic dimension? The event or condition we are talking about is the acceptance *of an imperative*. It can be reported in full only by some such locution as 'He desires *that so and so be*,' 'He desires *to do so and so*,' or 'He prefers *that so and so be or be done.'* Such events or dispositions can be incompatible with one another in a way in which ordinary natural occurrences cannot. They can be logically inconsistent. Natural happenings can be opposed causally in that what one tends to produce the other tends to destroy, but they cannot be logically inconsistent.

The naturalist might say that the inconsistency of two desires consists of plans (or accounts) of things to be done, all of which cannot be realized or carried out for purely logical reasons, and that this has no bearing upon whether the acceptance of such plans is causally determined. However, what is relevant is that when known, such inconsistency counts as a reason for altering the desires. A person who does not alter them for this reason is said to be irrational. A person who desires both good health and what he knows to be the cause of bad health (that is, one who with full knowledge of what is involved continues to accept both as something to-be in light of all the facts) is illogical. It is similar to continuing to believe two propositions known to be incompatible with regard to truth-value. The irrationality does not consist of accepting incompatible imperatives or propositions but of failure to count their incompatibility when known as a good-enough reason for altering the desires or beliefs. If we are rational, when we desire A and clearly see that B is a necessary condition of A, we either desire B or cease to desire A, just as when we believe P and see that P entails Q, we then either believe Q or cease to believe P.

It seems that the very presence of the semantic dimension in both beliefs and desires puts them in a realm where reasons rather than natural causes are the "determining" factors. But perhaps it is conceivable, in a sense, for a person's beliefs to be completely of the causal nexus—for them to be produced and altered only causally. But I am not sure of this. If so, they would be like the "beliefs" of dreams. I am willing to grant that the latter are largely, if not entirely, of the causal realm. But we do not consider them to be genuine beliefs. One's "thinking" that such and such is the case in a dream or in any purely causally determined belief is not a genuine effort to get at the truth of the matter. It is not a case of considering (or of being ready to consider) grounds and evidence for thinking such and such to be or not to be the case. Although we might say that what was "thought" or "believed" was true or false, we would not say that the one who had such beliefs was unjustified or irrational in holding on to his beliefs in the face of contradictions but rather that he was nonrational.

What I am suggesting is that desires, including primary ones, belong in the same general category as beliefs, perceptions, and thoughts in general. We have seen that they are all alike in that they have a semantic dimension and are subject to being appraised consistent or inconsistent; furthermore, a person is subject to being appraised as rational or irrational in respect to all of them. None of these things is true of purely natural occurrences.

Our perceptions, beliefs, and thoughts in general are not only subject to logical appraisal in terms of their relationships to one another, they are also subject to appraisal as correct or incorrect in terms of what they claim singly. This is a matter of their semantic correctness. In the case of a thought, it is a matter of whether what is thought to be the case actually is so. In fact it is only by virtue of what they individually claim semantically that they can be logically incompatible. Are desires as such, especially primary ones, like thoughts or beliefs in this respect? This is a crucial matter. If they are (and preferences and attitudes as well, which will be considered later), I do not see how the form of ethical naturalism under consideration could be maintained. How could this feature of them be interpreted without admitting at least some valid natural practical arguments? And to admit this is to admit an objective value-requiredness in reality. It should be kept clearly in mind that we are concerned with primary desires (and attitudes), not derived ones. Of course, there could be a kind of correctness about derived ones without there being any valid natural practical arguments or objective values in the world. One might be "correct" in desiring a because one desired b and a was a necessary condition of b without being a sufficient condition to preclude anything else that was desired as much as or more than b. But this kind of "correctness" or rationality is not what is now being considered.

There is a distinction between desires on the one hand and likes and dislikes on the other. A desire is, as indicated earlier, the acceptance of an imperative for something to-be or to be brought about. To like something is more complex. It involves recognition that the thing in question is more or less as it is prescribed by some imperative which is accepted or subscribed to. Desires are more basic or primitive then but closely related to likes and dislikes. What one desires to-be or to be done is what one would like if it were or if it were done. Also, what one likes is what one would desire if it were not. This fact may prove to be of some significance in connection with the corrigibility of both desires and likes and dislikes.

Perry, in *General Theory of Value,* contends that the only way in which a desire or an interest in general may be correct or incorrect is in terms of the correctness or incorrectness of the factual judgment which mediates it (what he calls the 'interest-judgment'). For instance, one may be highly interested in a certain painting because one believes it to be a Titian, when in fact it is not. For Perry the incorrect judgment does not really render the interest incorrect; it merely makes it less secure. If the error is discovered, the interest will evaporate. If the error remains unknown, the interest is entirely unaffected.

What I am concerned with is whether a desire may be said to be correct or incorrect in a way quite independent of the correctness or incorrectness of the factual beliefs which mediate it. Perry's position is that of a thoroughgoing naturalism. The interest is simply something which occurs in the situation, and it is to be understood solely in terms of causal conditions. But if the desire (or interest in general) is subject to being appraised as correct or incorrect in its own right and apart from its compatability or incompatability with other desires, then it seems it itself must be regarded as a cognition and not merely as mediated by cognition. How could this be? Perry thought it would require some unique value-quality (what Moore called a nonnatural quality of things), and he could not find any. He may have been right in regard to the latter contention.

We now have another possibility open to us. Perhaps the desire is neither an apprehension of a value-quality of the object cognized (or judged) in Perry's mediating interest-judgment nor simply an occurrence occasioned by it, but rather a cognition to the effect that the object of the interest-judgment is normatively (or prescriptively) required by some fact or state of affairs which one is more or less clearly aware of or believes to be so. In other words, perhaps the acceptance of the imperative for the thing to-be or to be done, which constitutes the desire, is not simply an occurrence but rather a *recognition* that relative to the facts concerned the thing in question is something to-be or to be done. If this is so, the desire may in fact be incorrect by virtue of several different things. It may be incorrect in that the thing desired is not what it is thought to be. It may be in error by virtue of the factual situation which is thought to require it prescriptively being otherwise than it is taken to be. Most importantly, the desire may be wrong even though the factual situation is as it is taken to be and the thing desired is as it is judged to be, by virtue of the fact that the factual situation does not prescriptively require the thing concerned. The task at hand is to determine whether we do recognize these kinds (especially the last) of correctness and incorrectness of primary desires. If we do, there seems to be no escape from admitting that there are valid natural practical arguments and consequently that there is an objective value-requiredness in reality.

It seems obvious enough that a desire may be in error with regard to what Perry calls a mediating interest-judgment. One might desire some fruit from a bowl on the table, only to discover that it is made of wax. The desire for the particular object would immediately vanish. Like a belief, it could not persist in the face of the discovered error. In like manner, a man might desire a tie of a certain color because he thought the suit he had just purchased was tan when in fact it was grey. Discovery of the error might alter the desire for the color of tie concerned, for it was the acceptance of something as something to be had when it was not. The acceptance was not warranted because the thing concerned was not prescriptively required.

This much, I suppose, will be readily allowed. But if it is true that there may be a question about the correctness or incorrectness of a primary desire when all the relevant factual judgments are granted to be correct, the matter will require some showing. The most obvious place to turn for examples of this kind is the whole area of perversion. Broadly speaking, there are two major types of mental sickness: one in which a person is given to perceptual illusions or systematic distortion of factual beliefs, although he may evaluate things and act in a quite proper manner for the kinds of situations he believes himself to be in; one in which a person's perceptions and factual beliefs are normal but his desires, aversions, and attitudes are perverted. Obvious examples of the latter are the sadist, the masochist, and the homosexual. It may be assumed that at least sometimes all the relevant factual beliefs of such a person may be correct. It is the desire (or liking) as such which is perverted. Now what do we mean by 'perversion' here? Is it merely that it is contrary to the usual pattern? If so, why count it a perversion? May not the unique, the unusual, or the extraordinary be the most proper or fitting thing? Can we justify our concern for the normal in these matters if the normal is simply the usual or ordinary? Can we make sense out of our talk and thought about the normal and the abnormal in this area without construing the normal to be the proper and fitting way? Is not an abnormal desire or liking, such as that of the homosexual or the sadist, a matter of (or at least involves) accepting something as something to-be or to be done when in fact it is not? Why is it condemned, if this is not so? Those "sophisticated" persons who find nothing in such desires and likes but the unusual do not condemn them as such. Could it be that those who do disapprove sense or in some way detect an impropriety or unfittingness about them?

In any case, the logic of 'normal' and 'abnormal' when used in this area seems to be very similar to that of their use in other mental areas, particularly the areas of perception and belief. Here a person is mentally abnormal if there are certain conditions which systematically distort or render incorrect the cognitions involved. The similarity of the use of 'normal' and 'abnormal' in the two areas supports the claim that in the case of perversion of desire and of pleasure it too is a matter of systematic distortion of cognition by causal conditions.

We cannot talk about distorted or perverted primary desires and likes in the sense in which we do without treating them as subject to appraisal as justified or not. A primary desire cannot be said to be justified or not in the sense in which we appraise an action, for what we desire or like in a primary way is not a matter of choice. This is the point of the Humean doctrine that we can do what we please but cannot please what we please. The only sense, it seems, in which a primary desire or pleasure can be said to be justified or not is in the sense in which it can be said of a perception or thought, namely, in terms of the correctness or incorrectness of its semantic claim. It would seem that a primary desire could be correct or incorrect in and of itself and thereby be justified or unjustified only by virtue of the thing desired being or not being desirable and that a thing can be desirable in this sense only in the way in which truth is believable, namely, by that which is desired (that which is accepted or subscribed to as something to-be or to be done) actually being something normatively demanded or prescriptively required by some actual state of affairs.

Not only the fact of perversion, and our talk about it, but also the kind of therapy this kind of sickness lends itself to argues for the cognitive nature of desires and pleasures. Perversion of desire and of liking and disliking, as I remarked earlier, is a matter of causal conditions systematically distorting them. If psychoanalysts are to be trusted, knowledge that one's perverted desires, aversions, and pleasures are the effects of such-and-such causal conditions sometimes works a cure. It breaks the causal connection. The perverted effects tend to evaporate. Even some aversions which express themselves in the form of allergies may be cured in this way. For a patient to become fully aware of the causes of polio, pneumonia, and other illnesses has no such result. Do we find anything similar to this strange therapy in any other field of experience? I suggest the area of belief. A person may be causally induced to believe certain things. If he becomes fully aware of the causal conditions of these beliefs and fully aware that the beliefs are solely the effects of them, the beliefs tend to evaporate unless he finds reasons for them as distinct from causes.

It seems to me that we cannot make sense of psychoanalytic therapy of perversion of desire, aversion, pleasure, and indeed the emotions as well unless we think of them as having a semantic correctness or incorrectness like believing. It does not make sense unless we think of them as attempts to get something right so that when it is seen that there is no basis for thinking the attempt gets it right, or indeed that the "attempt" is not a genuine attempt at all but only an occurrence, it is discontinued.

If perverted desires, aversions, and the like have a semantic incorrectness about them, certainly the unperverted have a similar trait. We do, I think, sometimes recognize an incorrectness of an unperverted primary desire. One may, for instance, desire something very much only to find that the fulfillment of it is not at all satisfying. This can be so even when there are no false factual judgments involved. Knowing quite well all the relevant facts, one may desire x and yet upon obtaining it feel no satisfaction and indeed even definitely dislike it. In such a situation, one would likely say, 'I thought I wanted x, but I have found out I didn't. I was mistaken.' This of course is not to say that one did not in one sense of the word desire x. It is to say that the desire was illusory or incorrect. It was the acceptance of something as something to be had when it was not. The lack of felt satisfaction or the definite dislike of it upon getting it would be construed as a valid recognition of it as not something to be had or as something not to be had, whereas felt satisfaction or liking it upon getting it would be construed as corroboration of the desire, as "confirmation" of its correctness.

As it was remarked at an earlier point, much of what is called 'deliberation' is not a matter of inferring imperative conclusions or value-judgments from imperative (or value) and factual premises or a matter of weighing the claims of conflicting desires against one another, but simply a matter of reviewing the facts of the situation, which sometimes gives rise to new desires and terminates old ones. This has an important role in determining what it is we desire or prefer in a given situation. We often think a person's desire is not "rational" simply because there are facts he is ignorant of or has failed to consider. Often he can be talked out of a desire or preference simply by getting him to consider certain facts. Also, a person can be talked into having a certain desire. In some cases, at least, it seems we must admit that to be aware of certain facts gives rise to some desire or preference; and to be aware of some facts terminates certain desires and preferences. We cannot, I think, consider this a purely causal process nor make very plausible the claim that there are always overriding interests which provide imperative premises. It seems more plausible that in some such cases one "sees" or at least thinks that the facts considered prescriptively require the thing desired.

The way in which one develops new interests in general seems to support the same conclusion. A person may for whatever reason desire to have an interest in literature. Perhaps it is because his wife has such interests and he wishes to develop areas of common interest. How can he acquire such interests? The only way is to read, to study, and to discuss literature. When one becomes acquainted with it one may become interested in it. It seems that the acquaintance gives rise to the interest, but I do not think it is simply caused or derived logically from other interests.

It may be helpful to point out in this connection that we do at least sometimes expect a person to give a reason for desiring something even though his desire is a primary one. Such a reason is always some fact which is regarded as validating the desire. Part of what we call 'deliberation' is a matter of weighing the validity-claims of desires to see which ones stand validated in light of the whole situation. We cannot do justice to deliberation if we interpret it simply as a tug of war between conflicting interests in which the stronger ones win out. This simply will not do. We hunt down the reasons for each, and some desires are appraised as dominant over others in regard to rank, authority, or validity and not merely in terms of strength. In fact the strength that a desire can maintain throughout a deliberative process seems to be relative to the appraisal of its validity.

It is now time to turn our attention to the rational attitudes. There are, as we found earlier, three levels of rational imperatives: the imperative to be rational, to have a good reason for what one accepts or does; the so-called piggy-back imperatives, such as 'Do not sacrifice a greater good for a lesser one'; and the general principles involved in determining the greater and lesser goods. Are the attitudes which consist of the acceptance of these imperatives merely causally determined, simple groundless resolutions, or perhaps in some way inherent in human nature? Or are they also cognitions?

The basic rational attitude, the acceptance of the imperative to have a good reason for whatever one does, might be a cognition to the effect that being a human being prescriptively requires having such a good reason. This would be much like a primary desire except for the fact it is at a higher level: it pertains to or is about believing, desiring, and acting. The imperative involved is, I think, not merely universally subscribed to but subscribed to *as valid,* with the possible exception of some who have been contaminated by certain philosophical views (and they only when in their philosophical closets). It is a fact of common experience that we expect everyone to recognize the appropriateness of rational criticism. I do not see how such criticism could be appropriate unless the imperative to have good reasons for one's beliefs, desires, attitudes, and actions was valid for human beings. (This involves the issue of the *authority* of the rational imperatives discussed earlier.) We consider it improper or not befitting a man to believe, to desire, to feel, or to act in the manner we call irrational. Of course, if a person is lacking certain human capacities, we do not consider him to be properly subject to rational criticism. Does this not indicate that we *recognize* that those features which if present make us subject to rational criticism and if absent render such criticism inappropriate prescriptively require that we have good reasons for our beliefs, desires, attitudes and actions? It seems to me that we do think that there is such a prescriptive requiredness involved. This thought is obviously either correct or incorrect. What better confirmation can there be for its correctness than that such an elemental matter is so universally thought or felt in the face of constant experience! What better grounds can be had, for example, for believing this paper is white than that it is universally acknowledged to be white by those having direct experience of it?

As I said earlier, the so-called piggy-back rational imperatives are (in a sense) tautologies. 'Do not sacrifice a greater good for a lesser one,' for example, is valid precisely because 'x is a greater good than y' entails 'x ought not to be sacrificed for y.' The rational attitudes that consist of the acceptance of such imperatives may be appraised as correct, for they involve cognitions of analytic principles.

This brings us to those basic intermediate imperatives in terms of which the logical naturalist claims we judge what are the greater and the lesser goods and what it is that ought to-be or to be done in those situations where all the things prescriptively required by something or other cannot be. As it was pointed out earlier, these imperatives are found or given in our basic or underived approvals—approvals of things of a certain kind per se and not because they are a subset of some other kind of thing which happens to be approved. Of course it may be that there is only one such imperative, i.e., the principle of utility, as Hume and Bentham thought. But there is the possibility that the principles of our approvals and disapprovals are not reducible to some one grand principle in this manner. There may be several or even many. But if they conflicted in what they prescribed, how would one determine what on the whole one ought to do in the situation? It would seem that the conflict would be unresolvable. The question I am concerned with at this point, however, is not how many basic imperatives we subscribe to and employ in deliberating and appraising action but rather what the status is of such an imperative. Is it simply accepted as an effect of causal conditions, by pure resolution, or is it inherent in human nature? Or is the attitude which embraces it a cognition to the effect that what the imperative enjoins is prescriptively required by something or other?

We have already seen that none of the naturalistic positions can account for the apparent authority of approvals and disapprovals over ordinary desires and preferences. They, in effect, have to explain it away. Yet it seems an undeniable fact that our rational approvals and disapprovals speak with authority. They have a position of superior rank which cannot be reduced to a matter of greater strength or force. Indeed they may be very weak compared to the interests which they overrule. I think the authority of such attitudes is something that our philosophy of ethics must account for, and any position which has to explain it away is to that extent unsatisfactory. This in itself seems to me to be a sufficient ground for rejecting naturalism. What positive reasons are there at this point for accepting a nonnaturalistic position? Any consideration which would support the view that such a basic attitude involves a cognition to the effect that what is approved of is the thing prescriptively required by the situation as a whole would be such a positive reason. This is the problem to be explored.

It has been suggested already that attitudes, along with interests of all types, can be logically incompatible with one another by virtue of their semantic dimension in a way in which natural occurrences cannot. A person who at one time approved an action because it was thought to make for human happiness and on another occasion approved of an action because it was thought to make for human misery would be considered logically inconsistent. If one were to approve of something he thought made for the greatest human happiness of all possible alternatives and another were to disapprove of it while agreeing that of all alternatives it made for the greatest human happiness, we should say, as C. L. Stevenson has pointed out, that they had a disagreement in attitude. The point I am concerned to make is that purely natural occurrences are not logically inconsistent or in disagreement in this manner. Being for and being against something involve thinking that the thing in question is or is not something to-be or to be done. It is by virtue of this factor that even basic approvals and disapprovals may be logically inconsistent and in "disagreement."

The important question, however, as in the case of primary desires, is whether basic or primary approvals and disapprovals can be inconsistent or in disagreement in this manner unless each taken by itself has some kind of validity or invalidity. This is a matter of the semantic correctness of each. As I have analyzed them, they have a semantic dimension in much the same way as desires; they make a semantic claim. If no such claim were made, how could they be logically inconsistent or in disagreement? And if such a claim is made, is it not either valid or invalid, correct or incorrect in some sense?

Stevenson, as we observed earlier (Chapter III), holds that we may reason about a disagreement in attitude so long as it is grounded in disagreement in belief. The reasoning may correct one's beliefs and thereby *causally* alter one's attitude.[9] But he contends that there is no correctness or incorrectness about the attitude as such. It is simply a natural phenomenon.

But is it not true that in ordinary experience we recognize a correctness or an incorrectness about basic attitudes as such, as attested by the fact that it is quite proper in ordinary language to appraise such attitudes as appropriate or inappropriate, as justified or unjustified? Without calling into question any of one's factual beliefs, we think that he ought to have such and such an attitude. We think a father ought to disapprove of his son's acts of cruelty rather than to encourage him in them. If the father says he morally approves of cruelty, we do not know what to make of it. Our first reaction would likely be that he is not serious. If we were convinced of his sincerity and seriousness, we would likely think he does not know what it is "to approve morally" of something. What would be our reaction if we were convinced that he was serious and knew quite well what it was to approve morally of something? Would we simply conclude that strange and unexpected things happen and that no doubt there is an explanation for it? Or would we not say that his attitude of moral approval is obviously illusory or erroneous, that he is irrational or mentally deranged in a peculiar way, that he has a perverted moral sense? We would certainly feel that the attitude was inappropriate and unjustified, because cruelty is not a proper or fitting object of moral approval. I do not think it can be maintained with any plausibility that our feeling of inappropriateness in such a situation is itself merely a natural occurrence; it is no more so than our feeling that false statements are inappropriate for belief.

9. See *Ethics and Language*, p. 5.

When we feel that one ought to have such and such an attitude toward something, the 'ought' is not the kind which applies to an action, for a man does not deliberate and choose his basic attitudes. He finds himself with them just as he finds himself with his perceptions and beliefs. It is the kind of 'ought' which applies to beliefs. There are things people ought to believe, but they do not; there are things people ought not to believe but they do. One difference between the 'ought' of belief and the 'ought' of action is that to punish one who does what one ought not to do makes sense in a way in which it does not to punish one for believing what one ought not to believe. Believing what one ought to believe is a matter of insight, of correct thinking, but doing what one ought to do is not wholly a matter of correct thinking. Punishment cannot help one to think correctly, but it may help one to act correctly. This is why we feel there is such a difference between "political criminals" and other kinds. It simply does not make sense to punish a person for believing what he does, nor for doing what he feels he ought to do. Such a person may need instruction, enlightenment, or even restraint to protect others in some cases, but punishment seems highly inappropriate.

I suppose few would quarrel with the contention that 'ought' as applied to a belief (in the sense that one ought to believe so and so) indicates that such a belief would be justified in what it claims (that it would be semantically correct). It seems to me that 'ought' as applied to an attitude such as a basic moral approval means much the same thing. I do not see how any other interpretation can make sense of it.

Also, we recognize that a person may be perverted in his basic approvals and disapprovals as well as in his desires and pleasures. Such a person, as distinct from the sadist or masochist, as distinct from the ignorant or the foolish, and as distinct from the morally weak (who may know what is right but does not have the character to withstand the promptings of his desires) is called *wicked*. He may be a man of conviction and of strong character. He may be thoroughly committed to what he believes to be morally right. Perhaps Hitler was of this type. Perversion at this level is all-pervasive, manifested in all of one's appraisals and decisions. What do we say of such people? Are they not mad? Are they not as much mentally deranged as the one who is so perverted that he systematically gets all the facts wrong? Is not his perversion precisely that he gets all the *values* wrong? His attitudes are wrong in the sense in which the beliefs of a person with another type of mental derangement may be wrong. In both cases they are wrong in that they are semantically incorrect; in both cases they are not subject to being corrected by reasoning, for the perversion lies in the victim's insight.

There may be an *incorrectness* in basic moral attitudes which is not properly a perversion, for it may be corrected by instruction and insight. I have in mind, for example, a person who morally approves and disapproves with a primary regard to the welfare of his own group or race, such as many white people in the South today. When others are considered at all, they are regarded as having only a secondary status. Many can by instruction and reflection come to "see" the incorrectness of approvals and disapprovals made in this manner. To "see" the incorrectness undermines them, and a change takes place in one's approvals and disapprovals. I think we recognize an important difference between a change which comes about in this manner and one which is simply causally effected. And it is a change which can take place in regard to one's basic approvals and disapprovals.

It is evident, I think, that we expect our moral approvals and disapprovals to square with those of others. We are continuously concerned to get the advice of others, to put our moral judgments to the test of rubbing against those of others. To find ourselves in disagreement with others about such matters gives us a reason for suspecting our own. We seek out the appraisal of the impartial spectator. Why should his judgment be valued more than that of a partisan if there were no correctness or incorrectness to our moral attitudes? Do we not recognize that vested interest may give rise to error in our feelings and attitudes, especially in regard to our basic or primary ones? The above considerations indicate that both primary desires and basic approvals and disapprovals are not simply the effect of certain casual conditions but are subject to being appraised as correct or incorrect. Natural occurrences or states of affairs (those completely and exhaustively treatable by the descriptive-explanatory method of modern science) are not subject to being appraised in this manner. It is now time to consider the nature of this peculiarity in more detail.

### 6.5 The nature and modes of the semantic dimension of experience

The discussion has suggested that primary desires and basic rational attitudes, as well as all others, are somewhat like perceptions and also somewhat like beliefs. Perceptions and beliefs themselves are alike in that they involve "thinking"[10] that such and such is the case and may involve knowing it. This is their cognitive aspect, which may be correct or incorrect. Although I have already intimated some things about it, I shall now attempt to clarify it somewhat more so that we may all the better see if something like it is involved in desires and attitudes and, if so, how it is involved.

First of all, a disclaimer: I am not talking about thinking in the sense in which it is a matter of reasoning or inferring but in the sense in which it is somewhat like believing or knowing. We may say 'I think that P,' 'I believe that P,' or 'I know that P' without reporting any reasoning or inferring. Thinking concerns some kind of a relation one has to what is thought, believed, or known.

Sometimes 'I think that P' may be synonymous with 'I believe that P.' But there is a sense in which the two should

10. Much of the following discussion of 'thinking' is adapted from my article, "On Knowing That," *The Philosophical Quarterly*, VIII, No. 33 (Oct., 1958), 300-6.

not be identified. 'Believe' is primarily a tendency verb. As Ryle points out,[11] we qualify 'belief' with such adjectives as 'obstinate,' 'wavering,' 'unswerving,' 'stupid,' 'fanatical,' 'wholehearted,' 'childlike'—qualifications appropriate for states, habits, inclinations and the like. To believe that P, by the very meaning of the expression, involves being in a state of preparedness or expectancy. Believing as such is not itself a mental act, although it does no doubt involve one. 'To think,' however, in the sense I have in mind, is an episodic term. It refers to a mental act, a doing of some kind. It occurs in many modes: in perceiving, in remembering, in deducing—in any and every mode of knowing. In perceiving that the rose is yellow, I think that the rose is yellow; in remembering that it was yellow, I think that it was yellow; or I think that it is yellow when someone tells me that it is. It is not that I may think it is yellow *because* I see it as yellow nor that I think it was yellow *because* I remember it to have been. Thinking that it is yellow is involved in and essential to perceiving that it is yellow and in remembering that it was yellow. It is the semantic aspect of these modes of experiencing. Thinking, in this sense, is no doubt involved in believing, but there is more to believing. Perhaps one cannot think that P in the sense intended without the something more that makes up believing that it is so, except perhaps in illusory perception in which one is aware of its illusory character. But the two should not be identified.

Also, thinking that P is involved in knowing that P, but it is not to be identified with it either. Using Ryle's distinctions between task and achievement verbs on the one hand and episodic, capacity, and dispositional terms on the other, I suggest that 'know(s) that' may be used either as a capacity or as an episodic achievement verb. This needs some explaining. Task verbs, such as 'play,' 'look,' 'argue,' refer to some activity or undertaking and may be used in reporting it. Achievement

11. Gilbert Ryle, *The Concept of Mind* (New York: Barnes and Noble, 1949), p. 134.

verbs, like 'win,' 'find,' 'convince,' do not refer to some activity distinct from that referred to by their corresponding task verbs. They are used to report the success of the undertakings concerned. To play a game is to *do* something; to win a game is not another activity over and above that of playing it; it is simply to play the game successfully. But this is not like playing it slowly, awkwardly, or quickly.

The distinction between episodic, capacity, and dispositional terms should be clear from the terminology. An episodic word is one that refers to an episode, an occurrence, an event, such as 'skate,' 'fall,' 'sleep.' A capacity term indicates not an activity but an ability to do something, like 'strong,' 'intelligent,' 'musical.' A dispositional expression refers to a tendency, for example, 'loyal,' 'stubborn,' 'docile.'

In saying that 'know,' in the sense here under discussion, may be used as a capacity achievement verb, I mean that it may be used to refer to a capacity for some kind of an achievement, a capacity for successfully carrying out some undertaking; or, as Ryle says, it signifies "that the person described can bring things off, or get things right."[12] We might say of a person, "He knows that Atlanta is west of Cleveland," even when he is asleep or occupied in thought with something else.

'Know,' as I said, can also be used as an episodic achievement verb. Ryle argues against this. He contends that none of the episodes or occurrences from which the capacity use is derived bears the name of 'know.' It is like 'grocer,' he says. A grocer is never described as 'grocing' but as selling sugar and so forth. The knower, according to Ryle, sees, hears, infers, deduces, and the like at certain times, but not simply knows.

Perhaps what bothers Ryle is that a knowing "episode" is not merely an occurrence or act, but, strictly speaking, a complex of at least two elements, say, ab, with only one, say, a, an occurrence or act. The other factor, b, does not seem to be such

12. *Ibid.,* p. 133.

that it precludes the combination's (ab) being an episode. The a, I suggest, is *thinking that P,* and b is the success of it. Although winning a game is not a different episode from that of playing it, we do speak of winning as an episode. We say, 'John won yesterday.' The issue is whether *successfully thinking that P* or merely the thinking involved is to be considered an episode. It would seem that a successful undertaking is still an undertaking and thus still an episode.

Successfully thinking that P is not merely thinking that P with 'P' in fact true. It does of course involve this, for 'I know that P' entails 'P,' and it would be an absurdity to say, 'I know that P but I don't think that P.' But the mere fact that a person thinks something that is the case does not prove that he knows that which he thinks. This might be taken as an argument against the view that to know that P is to think that P successfully. But it is also the case, I think, that merely to think something that is the case is not to think it successfully. If a man should engage in a business undertaking which lacked promise and happen to make a fortune out of it, despite no business skill of his own, we should hesitate to say that he had successfully carried out the undertaking. We should certainly not recommend him as a successful enterpriser on the basis of the adventure. We should say that he had been lucky rather than successful. For one to shoot an arrow which hits the bull's eye is not necessarily to shoot at the bull's eye successfully. The point is that an action cannot be validly appraised as a success unless the manner in which it was done was responsible for the outcome. If a person repeatedly comes up with true statements about a subject, we conclude that he knows what he says. His making true statements, or thinking them, does not constitute his knowing them; it is only evidence that he knows. Others may think that one knows when he himself knows that he does not, just as others may think that one shot at the bull's eye successfully when he knows that he did not. The archer who shot an arrow which hit the bull's eye might know when no one else did whether he had "hit the bull's eye" in the achievement sense by virtue of his awareness of how he had shot. If he had aimed at the outer ring or if he had not aimed at all, he would know that he had not successfully shot at the bull's eye. In like manner, the man who made a true statement might know whether he knew what he had said by virtue of being cognizant of how he had thought it. If it were a guess, a hunch, an attempt to bluff, or, in general, a groundless assertion, he did not know, even if it were true. To be a case of knowing that P, the thought that P would have to be based on good grounds for or evidence of the truth of 'P.'

So far I have only distinguished thinking that P from other things. Can we do any more than isolate and identify it? Can we break it down? Or must we leave the word which indicates it undefined and simply locate in experience what is meant by it by pointing out what it is not and what it is involved in? Perhaps this is where we have to leave it. However, saying the same thing with different words may shed some additional light on the matter. To think that P, in the episodic sense with which I am concerned, is, I believe, to refer assertively to P. I do not mean merely to assert it overtly in the sense of making a statement. One could do that while knowing that 'P' was false. Neither do I mean merely thinking of P as a possibility. I am not talking about thinking *of* something, but *thinking that* something is the case, referring to a fact by asserting it, when this is done primarily to oneself, as it were, and done seriously with the intent to be right and usually with acceptance of or subscription to what one thinks (with the possible exception of perceptions known to be illusory). It is an undertaking, an attempt to think, to assert, what is the case. This is the episode, the occurrence, the undertaking, which is done in such a way that it succeeds in a case of knowing that P.

By way of summary, then, we may say that thinking is an activity involved in perceiving, remembering, believing, and all other modes of knowing. In perceiving, there is sensory stimulation or sensation as a ground of the thinking. However, there may be thinking in which the grounds are entirely conceptually represented. That which is thought may be fully accepted or subscribed to in the sense that one is in a certain state of preparedness or expectancy appropriate to its truth. If so, there is belief. This applies when there is sensory stimulation as well as when the grounds are completely represented conceptually. When the thinking is successful by virtue of its guiding grounds, there is knowledge.

The purpose of this sketchy analysis of perceiving, believing, thinking, and knowing is to see whether desires and attitudes are in any way parallel with them. We have all along spoken of a desire as the acceptance of an imperative. This is much like the acceptance of an assertion (what is thought) in the case of believing. Is there anything in desiring analogous to the thinking involved in believing? It seems to me that there probably is. Just as in believing, we cannot accept what is thought without in some way thinking it; in desiring, we cannot accept something as something to-be or as prescriptively required without in a sense thinking it is such. We may be successful or not in so thinking.

In thinking that something is something to-be or to be had, the something may be cognized perceptually or completely by conceptual representation. Also, the state of affairs that prescriptively requires it may be either perceptually or completely conceptually cognized. Certain apparently primary desires like desire for food (hunger) may always involve a kind of "perceptual" cognition of the state of affairs which prescriptively requires food. Here the perception is of a peculiar nature. We call it perception, for the grounds of the thinking involved are sensations. But the pang of hunger is not simply a factual perception. It is a value-perception. It is the apprehension by sensation that a state of affairs involves a deficiency, a lack—that it is not as it ought to be. What is desired is something apprehended as prescriptively required by the state of affairs involving a deficiency. Here the primary value-cognition is that of the state of affairs as not being what it ought to be—the "perception" which provides knowledge of the grounds which normatively demand or prescriptively require something else.

This analysis of desire is not too unlike that of Dewey's. He says, "When we inquire into the actual emergence of desire and its object and the value-property ascribed to the latter . . . , it is as plain as anything can be that desires arise only when 'there is something the matter,' when there is some 'trouble' in an existing situation. When analyzed, this 'something the matter' is found to spring from the fact that there is something lacking, wanting, in the existing situation as it stands, an absence which produces conflict in the elements that do exist. When things are going completely smoothly, desires do not arise, and there is no occasion to project ends-in-view, for 'going smoothly' signifies that there is no need for effort and struggle. . . . There is no occasion to investigate what it would be better to have happen in the future, and hence no projection of an end-object."[13]

What I am urging is that there is cognition of a perceptual nature (involving sensation) in the case of what we may call biological desires (hunger, sex, and other desires connected with biological functions). There is perception of a situation or state as not being as it ought to be. I am not sure we can distinguish between being aware of a situation's not being as it ought to be and being aware that it prescriptively requires something. They may be one and the same. In any case, there is a kind of "perceptual" awareness of a state of affairs as prescriptively requiring something. I do not know how to do justice to this without admitting what may be formulated as a valid natural practical argument. Therefore, it seems that biological desires are perceptual cognitions of an objective value-requiredness in reality.

Although in biological desires we may not be able to distinguish between perceiving a bodily condition not to be as it ought to be and perceiving that it prescriptively requires some-

13. *Theory of Valuation*, p. 33.

thing or other, it seems clear that we do sometimes perceive a condition not to be as it ought to be or to be as it ought not to be without being aware that the situation prescriptively requires something. This seems to mark the difference between biological desires on one hand and physical pains and general feelings of physical misery on the other. Nothing is presented in these as something to be had or to do. We are simply aware of a bodily condition as not being as it ought to be. In like manner, pleasures and general feelings of well being may be thought of as perceiving states and processes to be as they ought to be or more as they ought to be than is sometimes the case.

There are those, to be sure, who contend that physical pleasures and pains are merely occurrences which are themselves liked and disliked respectively. However, it seems that pain unmixed with pleasure could not be a proper object of liking nor pleasure unmixed with pain a proper object of disliking. Indeed it seems that the liking is built into pleasure and disliking into pain in such a way that we cannot significantly talk about either liking or disliking pleasure or pain. When one has a pain, is it not that one dislikes the condition perceived by the pain as being as it ought not to be? And when one has a feeling of physical pleasure, is it not that one likes the condition cognized by the pleasure as being as it ought to be? At least this way of talking seems to square better with some of our ways of thinking about pleasures and pains, especially in regard to perversion.

The person who feels pleasure upon being hurt or injured is thought to be perverted. How is this appropriate unless pleasure has a fitting object? Pleasure, it seems, is unjustified when it is one's way of being aware of a condition which is as it ought not to be. And is it not appropriate to think of pleasures artificially induced by drugs and intoxicants as being illusory? Are they not perceptions of conditions being as they ought to be when they in fact are not? Are not pain-killing drugs merely ways of keeping people from being perceptually aware that their bodily conditions are as they ought not to be? At least this way of thinking about pleasures and pains seems to fit the experiences and to square with some of our talk about them.

If I am correct about this matter, the perception of a bodily condition to be as it ought to be, not to be as it ought to be, or to be as it ought not to be through pleasures and pains involves some condition rather than another being prescriptively required. I do not see how we can think of it other than as being prescriptively required by some set of factual conditions.

I have been talking about desires, pleasures, and pains which may be called 'perceptual' because they involve awareness through sensation. In the desires concerned, the awareness is of one's own internal bodily conditions as prescriptively requiring something else. Of course the thing desired might be perceptually cognized by the external senses. We have desires, and primary ones at that, in which the state of affairs which prescriptively requires something is perceptually cognized by the external senses. For example, the painter looks at his partly finished canvas and "perceives" that it, as it is, prescriptively requires such and such; the composer plays his incomplete composition and as he listens to it "perceives" how it should go from there; the interior decorator looks around the room and perceives that a red chair is needed in the corner. But one may have desires (and experiences of satisfaction and dissatisfaction) when both the requiring condition and the condition required are only conceptually represented. In such cases, the factual conditions are thought and believed, and the prescriptive requiredness is "felt" to obtain. This feeling involves thinking the requiredness obtains and acceptance of what is thought to be prescriptively required as something to-be or to be done relative to the requiring conditions. As in the case of factual matters, the only ways to check such a matter are (1) simply to review the facts to see whether one continues "to feel" that they prescriptively require such and such; (2) to see how such "feelings" square with certain others—such as how one "likes" the situation after what is thought to be required is obtained; and (3), in some cases, to check one's own desires, preferences, likes, and dislikes against those of others. The last is possible only when all are equally acquainted with the requiring conditions and things required. Even here, if a person differs with others, he may think that he alone is getting at the "truth" of the matter. But he is more likely to distrust his own desires and preferences where they are greatly out of line with others whom he respects. There seems to be nothing essentially different here from the testing procedures of ordinary beliefs about matters of fact.

Attitudes of moral approval and disapproval are unlike simple desires and preferences. They are not simply the acceptance of something as prescriptively required *by some aspect or other of the situation.* They are rather the acceptance of something as the morally right or obligatory thing to do in a situation, which is to accept it as prescriptively required by the total human situation in such a way that it overrules all incompatible prescriptive requirements (or, in the case of disapproval, the acceptance of something as a morally wrong thing to do, as something that morally ought not to be done in light of the total relevant human situation). It is important to notice, however, that a moral approval does not arise from merely factual knowledge of the existing situation. There must be knowledge of value-requiredness about the situation as presented by desires, aversions, pleasures, pains, and the like before there are any feelings of approval or disapproval.

It is this aspect of the situation which makes plausible the view that morality is a matter of economy of values. In our review of a situation which leads to a moral approval or disapproval of a course of action, we consider the pleasures and pains involved and likely to follow and the interests relevant or likely to be affected. This is a way of getting at the various values involved; for the pleasures and pains and interests are value-cognitions. We appraise these as valid or invalid. A perverted pleasure of a sadist, for example, is not given the same consideration as other pleasures. It is discredited. An unreasonable or irrational desire is also discredited. But after the valid pleasures and pains and interests are determined, they are weighed against one another to determine what it is that ought to be done in terms of the total situation. In this process we find ourselves approving of sacrificing some for the sake of others. In the end we may find that there are many actions we would disapprove of and one or maybe several we would approve of in light of the total situation.

I suggest that approving and disapproving in this manner involves thinking that certain things are in a sense "more" prescriptively required than others and therefore have priority over them. We confirm our thinking in this connection as in all others, namely, by seeing whether we still have grounds for so thinking, and continue to acknowledge it when the situation is viewed from all possible angles and by seeing whether others have the same experience.

If this account of the matter is correct, we do not have to have a general principle like that of utility or some other already subscribed to. We can approve or disapprove of particular actions. We simply recognize in the particular situation that certain values involved are greater than others and therefore have priority over them. No doubt this recognition may not be merely that one particular value is greater than another. Sometimes at least, we recognize that any value of a certain kind is greater than any of another kind. This would involve recognition of a general principle. We do, no doubt, develop general principles and then appraise particular cases by application of them. But we can develop general principles only on the basis of insights and recognitions in particular instances.

By way of summary, then, there are considerable grounds for holding that primary desires and basic rational attitudes are cognitions. Chief among these reasons are: (1) they have a semantic dimension somewhat like that of perceptions and beliefs; (2) they may be logically incompatible with one another in a way in which natural occurrences cannot; and (3) they may be appraised as semantically correct or incorrect. The cognitions involved in primary desires seem to be of something as prescriptively required by certain factual conditions of which one may be more or less perceptually aware or may simply believe to be the case. It should be noted, however, that perhaps we are often only dimly aware of the requiring conditions and may not at all distinguish them from other aspects of the complex situation. The basic rational attitude (subscription to the imperative to have a good reason for our beliefs, attitudes, desires, and actions) seems to be a cognition that something about human nature prescriptively requires that we have good reasons for what we do. The rational attitudes such as disapproval of sacrificing greater goods for lesser ones have been seen to involve cognition of analytic principles. And our basic or fundamental moral approvals have been seen to involve cognition that certain things prescriptively required have priority, a greater "ought" about them than certain others.

## 6.6 Summary and conclusion

The design of this study has been to push all plausible forms of ethical naturalism to their limits to see how good a case can be made for them. We have considered it in three forms: classical, emotive, and logical naturalism. Emotivism grew out of valid criticisms of classical naturalism, and logical naturalism, out of valid criticisms of emotivism. We have now seen at least four serious weaknesses in the case for logical naturalism, namely, (1) there is reason to believe that the logical naturalist cannot genuinely produce the suppressed imperative premises for practical arguments in the manner claimed; (2) a new version of Moore's recurring 'ought'-question haunts the position; (3) (which is closely related to 2), it is unable to account for the authority of basic approvals and disapprovals and of primary desires; and (4) there are strong reasons for believing that the primary desires and basic rational attitudes which present the imperatives constituting the deliberative framework are cognitive in nature and consequently that the imperatives presented by them are not merely existential but are valid (or invalid) in a way that involves purely factual validity-conditions which prescriptively require or normatively demand that enjoined in the imperatives. All of this, I think, not only makes logical naturalism untenable, but indeed naturalism as such; for it adds up to what I believe to be a fairly strong case for nonnaturalism.

Moore thought of nonnaturalism as the opposite of classical naturalism, which attempted to show that value-terms designated natural qualities. So his nonnaturalism was conceived in terms of value as a nonnatural quality. The nonnaturalism outlined here is conceived as the opposite of logical naturalism (the view that 'ought' refers to or indicates the kind of logical requiredness which holds between the premises and the conclusion of a tauto-logical practical argument). It holds that what is indicated or referred to by the ethical 'ought' is an objective value- (or norma-tive) requiredness which holds between one fact or state of affairs and some other actual or possible fact or state of affairs, as shown by the structure of what I have called a valid "natural" practical argument (or its corresponding conditional of the form 'If x is F, then x ought to be G').

Three general criticisms have been made of nonnaturalism: (1) we cannot locate in experience what is allegedly meant by value-language; (2) it leaves value-knowledge unintelligible; and (3) like classical naturalism, it does not account for the way in which value-language is practical—the way in which it is tied in with the springs of action.

I suggest that (1) is a product of the critic's view that the meaning of language must be located in either sensory experience or introspective states taken as sheer data causally produced. According to the view I have proposed, it is to be located in the semantic content of affective-conative experiences. If the epis-temological view I have argued for is correct, the criticism is undermined; it in no way applies to the nonnaturalistic value-theory I have proposed.

In regard to (2), it should be clear that knowledge of value-requiredness, as it is conceived in this work, is not something occult or mysterious. It is acquired, I have argued, through our feelings, desires, likes and dislikes, felt satisfactions and dissatisfactions, and pleasures and pains. Value-thought and its verification are not too unlike that of its factual or scientific analogue. Whereas modern science concerns sensory (and to some extent introspective) perception and thought pertaining to it, value-disciplines concern affective and conative experience and thought pertaining to it. The nonnaturalism of this work is grounded in the interpretation of this experience as cognitive— as making cognitive claims about reality which are at least sometimes substantiated. It is claimed that through value-experience we know a categorial feature of reality, namely, value-requiredness, which is not taken account of or indicated in the framework of modern scientific thought.

Also, (3) is not a criticism of the nonnaturalism of this work. The theory here proposed accounts for the practical character of value-language through (a) its analysis of other value-judgments in terms of 'ought'-judgments; (b) its contention that 'ought'-judgments entail imperatives; and (c) its account of what it is to accept an imperative.

When I began this study I was confident that some version of ethical naturalism was correct, but I must confess that in the process of the study I found myself being forced by the unfolding argument into a nonnaturalistic position. I must leave it to the reader to judge whether the argument justifies the shift I have made.

# CHAPTER VII

# METAPHYSICAL IMPLICATIONS

## 7.1 Introduction

Having concluded that a better case can be made for a non-naturalistic than for a naturalistic philosophy of ethics, the next step is to consider the implications of this for the modern naturalistic world-view. This is an extensive and difficult task. It is an area in which it is easy to get lost but very difficult to come up with a convincing argument. Many think that it is so hopeless and treacherous a province that it is better to steer clear of it altogether. But the path I have followed has led me to the edge of this wilderness, and it would only display cowardice to stop now. Perhaps the best I can do is to make some suggestions.

## 7.2 Value, change, and causality

Now that we have found reasons for believing that there are objective values in reality independent of our experience of them, if I may be permitted to speak of philosophical matters in this misleading way, the question I wish to raise at this point is whether such objective values have any bearing or influence on change. This probes at the very heart of modern naturalism, which differs from the classical world-view of the Greeks and of the Middle Ages precisely in that it holds that there are no objective values involved in the processes of nature. This is why modern science is value-free. Science is descriptive-explanatory in character. If values have nothing to do with natural change, if they have nothing to do with why things are as they are and not otherwise, then, of course, value-judgments have no place in a descriptive-explanatory account of anything. If values are thought to have no place or role in the processes of nature, it is quite natural to question their existence (to question whether the category of value has any genuine objective employment). But now that we have grounds for believing that there is a valid objective employment of the category (that value-requiredness is marked out or delineated in our experience of reality), it is quite proper to inquire whether it is involved in natural change and, if so, how. In other words, what are the implications of 'value' as an ontological category for the categories of 'change' and 'causality'? It would seem reasonable that to admit a new category like 'value' into a basic framework of thought like modern naturalism would require some retailoring of its other categories. It is a historical fact that the deletion of it in the early modern period wrought a change in others. The classical world-view conceived of natural change as teleological, as value-oriented and controlled. It was thought of as realization of what ought to-be. Consequently, for it value-judgments were essential in a scientific account of natural phenomena. The categories of 'change' and 'causality,' the meaning of 'why' and what constitutes an explanation, were different. Can the category of 'value' be readmitted to the fold without similar or somewhat related adjustments in reverse? This is the problem before us.

Modern science operates on the assumptions that there are a few basic modes of change and that all complex processes can be accounted for or explained in terms of them and their laws. In its simplest and most naïve form it assumed that the basic mode of change was that of locomotion. Mechanics was thought to be the basic science. Its success in formulating the primary laws of motion in the seventeenth century was heralded as the discovery of the secret code of the universe, the key which would unlock all secrets. The task ahead was simply that of breaking down complex processes into their simple mechanical components, for the whole was thought to be nothing more than the sum of its parts. This particular view of the matter is no longer entertained by anyone, but something of the same general nature prevails. It is still held that there are basic modes of change isolated and studied in physics and chemistry and that all other processes are to be explained in terms of them and their laws.

Although the reductionistic character of the scientific account of complex processes has a bearing (as we shall see later) upon the role of values (especially "higher" values) in natural change, it is not what rules out values per se in the scientific account; for values might have a part in the primary modes of change themselves. If so, the analysis of complex processes into the simple modes of change would not eliminate them. But modern science also eliminates values here. Contrary to the classical view, it conceives the primary modes of change in a nonteleological way.

We may illustrate this shift in the conception of the primary modes of change with the example of the suction pump. It was known to practical men for centuries that water could be lifted from a well by creating a vacuum in a pipe standing with one end in the water by lifting a valve-piston in it. The classical Aristotelian science explained this by saying that nature "abhors" a vacuum. This was a psychological way of saying something more fundamental. The Aristotelian scientist was not actually a pan-psychist. He did not posit a feeling of abhorrence in nature. He did think that there was objectively in reality that which would be experienced by a feeling of abhorrence, namely, that the vacuum ought not to-be (the negative correlate of there ought to be a plenitude of being). Furthermore, this objective "ought" was thought to be dynamic in the sense that it was in some way capable of influencing change, of being an agent in its own realization. In other words, the value-requiredness expressed by 'there ought to be a plenitude of being' was thought in this case to bring about a measure of plenitude of being, namely, the filling (or at least partly filling) of the vacuum with water. The water's rising in the pipe was to be accounted for in terms of the "pull" or requiredness expressed by 'ought.' But why would water rise in the vacuum only about thirty-four feet at sea-level and even less upon a mountain? Why did nature "abhor" a vacuum just so much, and abhor it less upon a mountain than at sea level? The Aristotelian had an answer for this also. Each kind of substance, it was thought, has its own natural place—its own proper or fitting place, or place where it ought to be. With the kinds of substance distinguished as earth, water, air, and fire, it was thought that the natural or proper place for earthy things was at the bottom, then water, air, and fire in that order. When something is other than where it ought to be, it is moved toward where it ought to be by the "pull" or value-requiredness involved, unless there is a counteracting force. Therefore solid or earthy objects fall when suspended without support in air. Fire and hot air move upward. Each kind of thing moves as though it were "seeking" its proper place. When water is rising in the vacuum pipe, there are two opposing "oughts" influencing its movement. There is the pull of the value-requirement for a plenitude of being and the pull of the requirement for the water to be at its natural place. These two opposing "oughts" are found to "compromise" at about thirty-four feet at sea-level. Higher up on a mountain, the water is farther from its natural place and the pull of the "ought" is greater. So the compromise is at a height less than thirty-four feet. Heavier liquids cannot be lifted as high as water because, it would be said, they are farther from their natural place and therefore the two "oughts" "compromise" at a lower height.

Two of Galileo's disciples, Torricelli and Viviani, were the first to give a modern scientific explanation of the phenomenon of the suction pump. They said that air has weight and that there is a column of air sitting on the water exerting an even pressure at all points. But when the piston is lifted in the suction pump, the column of air in it is lifted and the pressure is taken off the water at that point. The weight of the air at other points pushes the water up in the pipe until the pressure is equalized. The height of the water in the pipe is in effect a measure of the weight of the column of air over the water. Up on the mountain the water will not rise as high in the pump as at sea level because the column of air that sits on the water is shorter and lighter.

What is the real difference between these two explanations? It is often said that the difference lies in that the one lends itself to experimental testing, whereas the other does not. Torricelli and Viviani, for instance, conducted an experiment which was taken to be a confirmation of their explanation. They reasoned that if the height of the water column in the pipe was proportionate to the weight of the column of air sitting on the water, then a heavier liquid like mercury, which was known to be fourteen times as heavy per volume-unit as water, would be lifted only one-fourteenth as high as water in a vacuum pipe. They resorted to experiment. They took a glass pipe sealed at one end and filled it with mercury. When it was inverted with its open end submerged in a container of mercury, the column in the pipe fell to about thirty inches, leaving a vacuum in the upper end of the tube. This was what had been predicted. But did it confirm Torricelli and Viviani and refute the Aristotelian account? Certainly not in any straightforward sense. The Aristotelian scientist could accept the results of the experiment and give them an interpretation in terms of his categories. The height of each column would be for him the compromise point between the opposing "oughts" influencing it. The fact that the water column was fourteen times as high as the mercury would indicate the relative force of the value-requiredness with regard to natural place for the two substances, since it would be assumed that the force of the requirement for the plenitude of being would be constant. In fact, the results could be taken to confirm the Aristotelian position just as readily as the modern scientific account, for according to it, one would expect mercury, since it is more "earthy" than water, to have a greater pull toward its natural place. This is just what the results show.

It might be said that the difference lies in the quantitative approach of modern science. Torricelli and Viviani were able, for example, to predict the exact height of the mercury column. But the Aristotelian scientist could do this too by means of empirically observed correlations. Torricelli and Viviani made their prediction on the basis of an observed correlation of the weight of a volume of water and an equal volume of mercury. The difference between them would lie in their interpretations of weight. To the modern scientist the weight of a thing is a function of the pull of gravity upon it. No pull of gravity, no weight. To the Aristotelian it is a function of the pull of the "ought" with regard to place. In other words, the fundamental difference between the two approaches is how one is to think of or to categorize the force acting upon things by virtue of which they are said to have weight. Actually there is nothing more mysterious in talking about value-requiredness with regard to place as a force which moves objects about than in talking about gravity as a force which pulls objects together. Both approaches lend themselves equally well to quantitative and empirical methods.

I am not, of course, saying that an Aristotelian science such as this was ever developed. But I see no reason why it could not be. Some details no doubt would have to be changed. Maybe the idea of a fixed natural place would have to be given up for a relative natural place and maybe the idea that physical objects ought to be together would have to be introduced, and so forth. All of this could be worked out while maintaining the fundamental thesis that physical things have places where they ought to be and that such "oughts" influence changes in their positions.

As we have already indicated, there are for the Aristotelian other forces than the requiredness involved in regard to a thing's natural position. We mentioned the "ought" pertaining to the plenitude of being. There are others. Also for the modern scientist there are forces other than that of gravity. We need not go further into these for our purposes. The important thing is that change is interpreted teleologically by the Aristotelian scientist. Changes occur for the realization of what ought to-be. Value-requiredness is the force of nature. Causality is to be conceived in terms of it. Consequently, explanations of why things are as they are and not otherwise must involve value-judgments about what ought to-be. For the modern scientist, change is conceived nonteleologically or "mechanically." To say 'mechanically' here, however, is not very enlightening. The problem is the nature of mechanical change as it is conceived in modern science. We can put it negatively by saying that it is change which occurs by virtue of the interaction of forces which are "blind" or value-free—change independent of any value-requiredness, change which is not the realization of what ought to-be. The most important thing about it for our purposes, to put it more positively, is that change is thought of as a transformation in the organization of matter, in which its new state is thought to be determined by or to be a "necessary" consequence of its antecedent states. Even if immaterial forms of behavior or functions of material systems such as "relations of meaning, dreams, joys, plans, aspirations" are admitted to emerge and to be indefeasible parts of nature, as the sophisticated naturalist would allow, the belief in "the existential and causal primacy of organized matter in the executive order of nature" is maintained. The point is that only a change in the organization of matter can be the cause of anything; furthermore, it is maintained that changes in the organization of matter can be broken down to relatively simple forms of change, all of which are conceived of as involving a "mechanical" (or perhaps it would be better to say a physico-chemical) "necessity" rather than value-requiredness. As a result science is made value-free. It is not its business to make any value-judgments; for, according to this view, values, even if it is granted that there are any, have nothing to do with anything's being as it is.

Some have thought that the "mechanical" theory of change and its correlative mode of explanation are demonstrably inadequate for some complex systems, biological organisms in particular. It has been said that they operate causally in a way which is not analyzable into or accountable for in terms of the causal operations of their components; that, to the contrary, the causal operations of the components are determined by the causal operation of the system. Suppose, for example, a system S characteristically operates in the manner F. Suppose further that necessary conditions for $F(s)$ (s to operate in manner F), within certain boundary conditions, are subsidiary operations G and H carried on by components a and b respectively. Also, let us suppose that $G(a)$ and $H(b)$ are causally independent so that an alteration of the one does not directly alter the other but does alter $F(s)$ so that $G'(a)H(b)$ results in $F'(s)$. When this happens there is, let us say, a modification in $H(b)$ so that we have $G'(a)H'(b)$, which results in a shift from $F'(s)$ back to $F(s)$. It has seemed to many that the causal relation between the change from $G(a)$ to $G'(a)$ and the change from $F(s)$ to $F'(s)$, and others like it, lend themselves more readily to a nonteleological interpretation than the causal relation between the change from $F(s)$ to $F'(s)$ and the change from $H(b)$ to $H'(b)$ and thus the change from $F'(s)$ back to $F(s)$. It does seem natural to think of the latter change functionally, to think that $H(b)$ changed to $H'(b)$ because it was prescriptively required for maintaining $F(s)$, when $F(s)$ itself ought to-be. But it has been demonstrated, I think, that many competent scientists can satisfy themselves about such processes by thinking of them in terms of what we are calling "mechanical" causality. I do not think that a case can be made for the view that the person who employs the "mechanical" concept will encounter some "empirical" fact which will be recognized as recalcitrant to his category. It is not that kind of problem. Categorial questions never are.

Nagel[1] has argued that teleological explanations are not necessary in biology or elsewhere, because they can be translated into
equivalent nonteleological ones "without loss in asserted content."
"A teleological explanation," he says, "states the *consequences*
for a given biological system of one of the latter's constituent
parts or processes; the equivalent nonteleological explanation
states some of the *conditions* (though not necessarily in physico-
chemical terms) under which the system persists in its characteristic organization and activities. The difference between teleological and nonteleological explanations is thus comparable to
the difference between saying that B is an effect of A, and saying
that A is a cause or condition of B."

While I agree with Nagel that in some sense there is an
equivalence between teleological and nonteleological accounts
of natural processes, I think there are important differences he
ignores. The equivalence is not like that between saying 'A is
the cause of B' and 'B is an effect of A.' It consists only of the
facts that for every occurrence both a teleological and a nonteleological explanation can be given and that the facts of the
case as empirically discovered will bear out the one as well as
the other. The truth of the matter is that the facts bear out
neither in any straightforward sense, because they are not scientific hypotheses but categorial issues.

Contrary to what Nagel suggests, a teleological causal relation
need not hold in the reverse order of its equivalent "mechanical"
causal relation. He suggests that if A is seen as the mechanical
cause of B, then B may be considered the teleological cause of A;
for the teleologist would say that A was as it was for the sake of
B, or because it was a condition for B. But as I am interpreting
the teleologist's position, when the naturalist would say A (within certain boundary conditions, to be sure) is the "mechanical"
cause of B, the teleologist might say that A is the teleological
cause of B, rather than that B is the teleological cause of A.

1. "Teleological Explanation and Teleological Systems," in Sidney Ratner,
ed., *Vision and Action*, pp. 192-222.

The difference would lie in how A causes B, the "mechanism" of causality. On this basis only the actual could be a teleological cause. This frees teleology of the apparent absurdity of that which is not yet actual being the cause of that which is.

Teleologists have been led to think of that which is not actual as the cause of that which is, by thinking of something which ought to-be, B, for example, as causing the condition of itself, A, for instance. But, if my analysis is correct, for A to ought to-be is for it to be prescriptively required by some actual thing or state of affairs. So when A is a condition of B and B is prescriptively required by S, then A is prescriptively required also. Even if prescriptive requiredness is causal, it is not proper in the situation described to say that B is the teleological cause of A, but that S is the teleological cause of both B and A. The explanation that A is brought about for the sake of B is simply to explain why S prescriptively requires A.

Also, it would seem that if causality is interpreted teleologically, the causality of a complex state of affairs cannot be analyzed into the causality of the components of the state of affairs to the same extent that it can be if it is interpreted mechanically. Proceeding with a "mechanical" view of causality, apparently we can go a long way in showing that the causality of a complex state of affairs is the resultant of the causality of components. The success of modern science is testimony to the fruitfulness of this approach. But it does not seem that what is prescriptively required by a complex situation can be broken down as a summation of the prescriptive requirements of various aspects or components of the situation. The situation as a whole may have its own unique prescriptive requirement in addition to that of its components. No doubt there are many instances in which a complex operates in a unique causal way in a "mechanical sense," especially in the area of chemical changes. All that I am contending is that this would seem to be more universal in the case of the teleological framework.

Perhaps the root and most important difference between the teleological and the mechanical points of view (or so it would seem until it is shown otherwise), lies in what is said when it is said that A is the cause of B or, for that matter, what is said when it is said that B is an effect of A. The difference is in the category or causality, in the "mechanism" of change, so to speak. The one thinks in terms of value-requiredness and the other in terms of "mechanical" necessity.

The positivist may protest that neither the teleological nor the "mechanical" models of causality are integral to science itself, that both are equally metaphysical and nonsensical; for we cannot find any ground in "experience" for an objective employment of either, and consequently both are contentless and for that reason indistinguishable. Nonetheless the "mechanical" model has been a central part of the metaphysics of modern science. The positivist who talks only of correlations or mathematical functional relationships—and these as simply brute facts —without employing any category of causality is not simply stripping science down to its naked self. He is actually dressing it up in new metaphysical clothes. He in effect rejects causality in any form. Changes, for him, occur neither by mechanical necessity nor by value-requiredness. Change is in effect a simple, unanalyzable category. This, I contend, is simply an alternative metaphysics for science, not a stripping of it of all metaphysics.

However, there is an experiential base for both concepts of causality in terms of which they have a content and are distinguishable. We are not mere spectators of reality. We are "in" a dynamic universe. We feel "forces" operating on us. We feel a heavy object on our shoulders *pushing* us to the ground; we feel the force of a blow; we feel ourselves pushing and the push of the falling tree we are trying to hold up; we feel ourselves pulling and the pull of others on a rope in a game of tug of war and we see it stretch and break. We feel *forces* that cause changes and from such "feelings" we get our mechanical concept of causality in the literal sense. For various reasons we liberalize it until we have the physico-chemical (what I have indicated by ' "mechanical" ') concept. On the assumption that through felt forces we have a categorial insight into the nature of change, in ordering and categorizing the stuff of experience we extend the employment of the category to instances and areas where forces are not directly felt. The test of such an extension is to be in terms of the fruitfulness of categorizing in this manner for making sense of our world rather than an experiential base in every instance. In other words, although the category has meaning in terms of an experiential base, it does not function in much of its employment primarily as an ostensive concept (one the employment of which is always justified or not according to whether its experiential ground can be pointed out) but rather as an interpretative concept (one that is justified or not in terms of its interpretative power—the extent to which it can help us in making sense of our world).

Also, it is an undeniable fact that we experience "forces" of a different type. We feel the force of value-requiredness in desire, aversion, sense of duty, the voice of conscience, approval and disapproval, and the like. We feel constrained, compelled, or moved to do or not to do this, that, and the other. However, we must be careful not to make a mistake here. If I am right in what I have argued for in this book, the value-requiredness, although there independently of being experienced, is a prescriptive or normative requiredness that does not necessitate; in other words, it is not causally operative in and of itself. It becomes causally operative only through desires, aversions, or feelings and attitudes. It must be experienced or known in order to initiate or influence change. A person is not moved to do what he ought to do except insofar as he is aware that he ought to do it or at least is not aware of being so moved.

If one finds a categorial insight into the "mechanism" of change in his being moved by an experience of value-requiredness which lends itself to being universalized, it would seem to involve one of several things: (1) the error of assuming that the actual "pull" or constraint felt in experiencing the "ought" is there in a causally effective manner quite independently of being felt, so that it is reasonable to assume that value-requiredness is causally operative in nature where there is no cognitive experience of it. This would be to take one's value-experience as a root metaphor for interpreting change in general in a manner parallel with the naturalist's treatment of experienced pushes and pulls and the like, except that the former would seem to involve an error that the latter does not. (2) An assumption or postulation that there are feelings or psychic phenomena throughout nature by means of which value-requiredness is causally effective. This seems to be at least part of what is involved in all forms of animism all the way from the most primitive kind to beliefs in one God or pan-psychism. (3) An assumption to the effect that the independent causal ineffectiveness of experienced value-requiredness is not essential to it as such but is true of it only in certain instances, only when it holds between certain kinds of things or states of affairs. It might be held, for instance, that for $F(x)$ prescriptively to require $G(x)$ under certain conditions does bring about or at least tend to bring about $G(x)$. However, under other conditions and with different values for 'F' and 'G,' the prescriptive requiredness might be entirely ineffective without cognitive mediation. The teleologist of this type might indeed say that affective-conative experience itself has been brought about precisely because it is required for value-requiredness at certain levels or of certain types to be causally effective, but that at the purely physico-chemical or even biological level value-requiredness is quite effectual without cognitive mediation.

The issue between the naturalistic and the teleological theories of change is, as I have repeatedly said, categorial; consequently, it is not subject to being settled by a direct appeal to empirical facts, for the facts themselves are shaped by the categorial framework employed. They differ in that they take as a categorial insight different experiences of change. Of course the issue between the teleologist and the naturalist is not one solely within analytic philosophy. Actually, our philosophy₁ is ambivalent on this matter. It is both. From the traditional Greek and Christian frameworks of thought, we are teleologists; from the modern scientific mind, we are naturalists. Consequently the matter cannot be settled on an analytic basis. It can only be dealt with dialectically in terms of other categories we are committed to and in terms of how well a whole framework of thought will work in categorizing the stuff of experience. At some point in such cases one has simply to make a categorial commitment and proceed accordingly. This is at least part of what is involved in believing that there is a God, for instance. It is to accept in some form the teleological framework, to accept value as an objective category, and to accept the view that value-requiredness is in some way the inner "mechanism" of change.

### 7.3 Free will and the naturalistic theory of change

One test a categorial commitment has to meet, as already indicated, is its consistency with other categories and their experiential base. On this point the naturalistic theory of change, taken as universally adequate, has to square itself with the apparent category of free will. Naturalism holds that human behavior (along with all other events) is, in principle at least, subject to scientific explanation and thus to its underlying naturalistic (or what I have called in a somewhat liberalized sense 'mechanical') theory of change. If this is so, every human act is determined by antecedent conditions in the physical world in accordance with the laws of "mechanical" causality. Under the past conditions or states of organized matter and the causal laws of nature, it is argued, neither human behavior nor anything else could have been otherwise than it has been. Nothing which has occurred has been avoidable.

This view of the matter seems to be contrary to our sense of freedom in choosing among alternatives and to our sense of responsibility for our decisions and actions. Some naturalists have simply denied freedom and responsibility; others have tried to reconcile them with scientific determinism.

Apart from the Kantian solution, which is not naturalistic, perhaps the most notable attempt at reconciling the two is the Hume-Mill theory. According to it, a person is "free" in performing an act if and only if the act is the result of his own desires. Being free in action is not a matter of not being determined by antecedent conditions in accordance with causal laws but a matter of being determined causally by certain special conditions. Some, however, have thought of freedom not so much in terms of the action itself. While granting that a given act was the result of one's desire to do the thing in question, they might hold that one was free *in desiring* to do it. Hume and Mill would deny this. What one desires or wills to do, they contend, is determined in a straightforward naturalistic way. The questions of freedom and responsibility do not even arise here. One may be free to do what one desires in the sense that there is no counteracting cause to prevent it, but it does not make sense, according to the theory, to talk about being free *to desire* something or other. We simply find ourselves desiring something, and if we have conflicting desires the interaction between them results in some one desire which issues into action in the absence of some counteracting cause. The desires we find ourselves with are taken to be the effects of certain prior conditions.

It is at this point that the cognitive theory of value-experience presented earlier has a bearing upon the problem. I have argued that a desire is the acceptance of something as something to-be or to be done, the acceptance of something as prescriptively required by something or other; that a preference is the acceptance of something as being more like what is required than something else; that a rational decision for something to-be or to be done is the acceptance of something as prescriptively required, not merely by some fact or limited state of affairs which might be cancelled by some other aspect of the total situation, but in light of all known relevant facts; that an approval of an action is the acceptance of it as being as it ought to be; and so forth. In other words, desires, preferences, decisions, approvals, and the like make cognitive claims which are either correct or incorrect and may be appraised in these terms. Thus the problem of freedom of desire and will is one with the problem of freedom of thought in general.

We have had a great deal of argument about freedom of the will, but very little about freedom of thought in a metaphysical sense. As I indicated in the first chapter, one of the central and most obstinate problems for metaphysical naturalism is the whole area of the mental. If thought itself as a mental activity is the effect of antecedent conditions in accordance with naturalistic laws, it would seem that it could not be meaningfully appraised as correct or incorrect. Natural events which are thought of as causally determined are thought of as simply being. They have no correctness or incorrectness about them. If thinking is causally determined in this manner, must it not also simply be? This is the kind of problem with which behaviorists in psychology and the sociologists of knowledge have been plagued. If they are correct in their thinking, then their thinking is simply a natural occurrence with causal conditions but without correctness or incorrectness. In other words, such positions are self-refuting. In order for knowledge to be possible, thinking must not be simply the effect of natural causation. It must be an attempt to get something right, an attempt which has the possibility of being right or wrong, an attempt shaped and guided in a nonnaturalistic way. It is shaped and guided by what is and by what ought to-be, by facts and values; but their relationship to the thinking is not causal in a naturalistic sense. No doubt much of the "thinking" of all of us is causally determined; for we do not always genuinely think. And no doubt there are some whose thoughts are all or nearly all causally determined. These we consider to be mentally abnormal and to be responsible neither in thought nor action. But whenever there is either genuine knowledge or genuine error, and there are both, there is freedom of thought—

there is thinking which is not causally determined by antecedent conditions in the manner of a purely natural event.

It is my suggestion that freedom of desire and will is of the same nature as that of thought; for I have argued that they are indeed modes of thought. They are thoughts about values as distinct from the usual kind about facts. They have a correctness or incorrectness about them, as I have tried to show in the preceding chapter. They are attempts to get right what is prescriptively required. As attempts they have the possibility of being right or wrong and are guided and shaped by considerations which are related to them semantically and logically rather than naturalistically. This is not to deny that they have a causal dimension. Indeed at times they may be almost entirely causally produced. And they are always no doubt grounded in the natural causal nexus of events. But they are not of the causal nexus. They have a peculiar dimension of their own, the cognitive—the semantic and the logical. Because they are in the causal realm but not of it, they are causally effective in producing physical action and in altering man's physical environment.

It may be objected that a person can choose to do what he knows he ought not to do and that this involves a freedom of choice different in kind from freedom of thought. Let us look at this a little more carefully. For me to know that I ought not to do A, for example, involves, if my analysis is correct, my acceptance of the judgment 'I ought not to do A.' Since 'I ought not to do A' entails the imperative 'Do not do A,' the acceptance of the former involves acceptance of the latter. Yet to choose to do A involves acceptance of the imperative 'Do A.' Therefore to choose to do what one knows one ought not to do involves the acceptance of contradictory imperatives. Is this possible? Every desire involves the acceptance of an imperative and certainly we can decide against acting on it. This is a matter of accepting both the imperative to do something and the imperative not to do it, but at different levels. The desire is a tentative acceptance with a reservation to explore the matter further; the decision has a finality about it. The former is tentative and with reservation because it springs from only a limited aspect of the situation; the latter is more definite in that it is in light of a more comprehensive view of the situation. The imperative arising from the more extensive view has precedent over one which follows from a more limited state of affairs. This is objectively so. To go against it is to choose the lesser good in preference to the greater, which is irrational. The problem is not whether one can represent to oneself the lesser good as the greater and thereby choose it. This would involve an error in valuation; if one should systematically make such errors one would not be counted rational. The question we are concerned with is whether a person can freely choose what he recognizes to be the lesser good, whether he can freely be irrational. I do not at all wish to deny that people do in fact do what they recognize they ought not to do, How else could we account for one's doing something while feeling guilty about it? The only question I am concerned with is whether a person *freely* decides to do what he does which he recognizes he ought not to do. It is obvious, I think, that such a decision cannot be a rational one; for a rational decision is one which is substantiated with good reasons (validating reasons not overridden by valid counter reasons). Obviously one cannot believe that there are good reasons (in this sense) for doing A and at the same time recognize that one ought not to do A. Thus the decision to do A when one knows one ought not to do A cannot be rational.

A rational decision is free. It is the acceptance of an imperative, the thinking that such and such is the thing to do in light of various relevant considerations. The thinking is directed and shaped in a noncausal way by semantic and logical relationships. But in what way is an irrational decision free? It is obviously not shaped and guided by semantic and logical relationships. If it were, it would be rational. It seems to me that something like this happens. Although it is freely formed as a cognition of a kind, a desire may cause physical action. However, for it to do so, insofar as one is a normal integrated person, its imperative must be accepted as the thing to do in the situation or at least as an "all-right" thing to do. In other words a desire has to become a decision. This frees it from being held in check by other thoughts about what is prescriptively required. It is given priority. If the decision is rational, it gains its position of priority from which it issues into action in a noncausal way. If the decision is irrational, the desire gains the kick-off position causally. A person finds himself with his mind made up. He is set to do such and such. He does not know how he reached the decision. It obviously was not guided and shaped by semantic and logical relationships in either a deliberative or an intuitive process. He cannot give reasons to justify the decision. Instead, he can give reasons why he should not do the thing in question. He recognizes that he ought not to do it; yet he finds himself set to do it. The "decision," if it may be called that, is the desire's gaining the position from which it can cause action—but the position was gained causally and thus the decision was not freely formed. We have previously seen how a desire, a perception, or a belief may be simply the effect of causal conditions or a free cognition. The same is true, I think, of decisions. It is only when decisions are rational that they are free.

This, however, raises the problem of responsibility. It might be asked how one can be held responsible for one's "decision" if it were causally produced. The answer, it seems to me, lies in the fact that although the decision was causally produced, it was so produced by virtue of one's not doing something one could have done. His failure to think the thing through to a rational decision, which he could have done, made it possible for the desire to gain the position from which it could produce action. If the person was in such a condition that he could not have reached a rational decision and thereby prevented the desire from producing action, we should not hold him responsible. What is at issue in determining responsibility is not whether the "decision" to act was rational and free but whether one was capable of a rational decision at the time. One might be capable of making a rational decision and yet through lack of sufficient effort let a desire take over in a causal manner. If so, one is acting as a slave to the desire; but one is responsible in that it is within one's power to be free.

We have to distinguish, then, between (1) making a correct rational decision, (2) making an incorrect rational decision, (3) reaching a decision by a desire's causally gaining a control position when a rational decision could have been made, and (4) reaching a decision by a desire's causally gaining control position when a rational decision could not have been made. One is responsible for decisions of types (1), (2), and (3) but not for (4). If a person is given to making incorrect rational decisions by virtue of systematically misevaluating situations, he may be said to be wicked. If he is given to causal decisions of type (3), he is said to be of morally weak character. If he is given to decisions of type (4), he is simply not a rational being and consequently is not responsible for his "decisions" and actions.

To admit all of this involves rejection of the naturalistic metaphysics; for it is the admission that a desire or decision is not simply organized matter, that it may not be simply an effect of natural causation, and that although it is in this sense a nonnatural event, it may be a causal agent in the executive order of nature. Furthermore, through the cognitive mediation of desire or decision, values have an influence on change and therefore should be taken account of in an explanatory account of human behavior. This is not to say that human behavior cannot be dealt with fruitfully for some purposes within a value-free framework. But if I am correct, such a linguistic framework is categorially inadequate for its subject-matter.

This much of the teleologist's case is, I think, on secure ground. If one must universalize a single category of causality, it would seem that the teleologist would have a better case than the naturalist; for we have found the latter to be inadequate in the area of the mental and there is reason to think that no such clear-cut inadequacy can be shown in any domain for the former. But certainly just because we have found one area where the teleologist seems to be right is no reason in itself for going any further with him. Consistency can be achieved by admitting naturalistic categories in the realm of the physico-chemical and perhaps even in the realm of the biological and by admitting teleological categories only in the realm of "freedom" or the mental. Just how far would we be warranted in going with the teleologist?

We should be reminded that in the area of the mental it seems that values are causally (in the teleological sense) effective only through cognitive mediation. An unknown obligation has no influence on what we do. If we are to consider value-requiredness as causally operative in any area other than those usually considered mental, we must, as it was pointed out earlier, do one of two things: either extend the domain of the mental to cover all areas in which we recognize teleological causality or consider value-requiredness in the areas concerned to be directly causally operative without the benefit of cognitive mediation. Although some great philosophers (e.g., Spinoza, Leibniz, Whitehead) have taken the first alternative, the second seems to me the more plausible course for the teleologist. It is not at all absurd to think of some values as effectual without being known and others as not. In fact, as it was remarked earlier, the teleologist might say that consciousness of values emerges precisely because it is required (in the value-sense) in order for certain types of values to be causally operative. It should be noted, however, that if values without cognitive mediation are causally operative, such causation is just as "deterministic" as naturalistic causation. Freedom is a function of cognitive mediation rather than of teleological causality.

## 7.4 Biological and physical phenomena and the teleological theory of change

Returning to the question of how far we should go with the teleologist, we have already said that there is nothing of an empirical nature in the realm of the biological or any other which would warrant the rejection of the naturalistic category of causality in favor of the teleological. It is not that kind of a problem. The only way to proceed is to consider how well a proposed category fits in with our general ways (categorial ways) of experiencing and thinking about a subject-matter. We have already seen that the category of natural causation simply does not fit our awareness of our mental experiences and our ways of talking about them. The question we now face is how well it fits our experiences of and thinking about biological phenomena.

Here the problem is difficult. The naturalistic category fits our scientific thought, but the teleological category fits our common-sense way of talking. So what we have to do is to evaluate the two categories as parts of philosophies₁ and not merely as philosophical₂ theories. This we did also in the area of the mental. There I said that the naturalistic category, although it is employed in scientific thought about the mental, is inadequate to its subject-matter. I feel fairly sure of this because of the way we must think about mental occurrences and human action in general if we are to get on at all with our intellectual and practical enterprises. This fact gives priority to the categories of freedom and value over those of science. In the area of the biological there is no such consideration to give priority to either the teleological or the naturalistic categories. It seems to me that the best that can be said for the teleological framework in this area as a philosophy₁ is that it seems very natural to the human mind. It is the way the "subject-matter" seems to prompt. I dare say the naturalistic framework of thought would never have emerged from or within our experiences of and thought about biological phenomena as such. It had its origin elsewhere and has been, as it were, forcibly applied here. There is little wonder there was such widespread protest in the nineteenth century to Darwin's attempt to account for biological phenomena within the framework of the naturalistic categories. It was widely felt that violence was done to the subject-matter. Even today after almost a hundred years of trying to think in this area within the naturalistic framework, it still seems awkward. The teleological categories are indulged in even by biologists themselves with the tacit understanding that it is only a manner of speaking. This natural and strong propensity of the human mind to think of biological phenomena in teleological terms and the apparent awkwardness and artificiality of the naturalistic framework may be counted in favor of the teleologist. Furthermore, it would in no way, so far as I see, hamper the work of the biological scientist to adopt the teleological category of causality as it is here interpreted. Therefore I am inclined to think that perhaps a fairly good case can be made for the teleological theory of change as a philosophy₁ in the biological realm.

But within the area of the purely physico-chemical the reverse seems to be the case. It would seem that the teleological framework would never have arisen from or within our experiences in this area. It arose or developed within our experience of human and other animal behavior and perhaps of biological phenomena and was then extended to the area of the purely physico-chemical. It has something of the same strangeness or artificiality in this sphere that the naturalistic categories have in the biological and the behavioral fields. In fact it seems that most people who have thought of the physical in teleological terms have felt compelled to posit minds or spirits in some form to make it at all intelligible. In other words, they have found it impossible to think of the *purely* physical in teleological terms. The same has been true of the biological, but to a lesser extent. An immanent teleological causality seems more intelligible there than in the purely physical. Of course some have thought of physical objects as having a "natural" place and as being moved toward it when misplaced and the like. Of course many have felt that values could not be causally operative at all without cognitive mediation, whether in the physical or biological domains. This is the one factor which has given rise to the god-belief. Operating within a teleological framework and with the assumption that values cannot be causally operative without cognitive mediation, one has either to resort to a pan-psychism of some form or to posit some one or several minds which shape or direct change for the realization of values. This is a parallel process to that of the scientist's positing unobservable physical entities and mechanisms in order to make the observable world intelligible within his naturalistic categories.

The apparent alien character of teleological categories in the physico-chemical realm and the parallel strangeness of naturalistic categories in the biological and the behavioral areas suggest that perhaps it is wrongheaded to urge a universal theory of change at all. Although the human mind seems to have a strong aversion to an ultimate dualism (or pluralism) of any kind, it may be that we simply cannot justify any monistic theory of change.

### 7.5 Religious experience and teleology

There is another area, even more treacherous than those already discussed, which needs to be considered. I refer to the domain with which religion concerns itself. Religious people, and perhaps everyone has his religious moments, wonder about the "meaningfulness" of human existence. They ask, does it make sense or is it an absurdity? Some affirm its meaningfulness; some, its absurdity. Both, however, ask the same question, namely, 'whether human existence is intelligible or makes sense,' which is formulated within the teleological framework. The only kind of answer they would consider relevant would be to the effect that human existence ought to-be, that it is prescriptively required either by the universe as a whole or by some part of it. To hold that each individual's existence and that of the race itself is prescriptively required gives the individual a sense of cosmic importance and a sense of significance to human life and history. Historical religions have always made this claim. This is the point of the Christian doctrine that every man is an object of divine love. To be loved, whether by man or God, gives one a "lift" precisely because love, if the cognitive theory of feeling and attitude advocated above is correct, is a mode of cognizing one as being of worth or of value, as being one who ought to-be. The fact of another's love gives assurance of one's worth. The fact of divine love gives one assurance that one's existence is something which is prescriptively required within the cosmic scheme of things.

The person who declares human existence to be an absurdity denies what the traditional religious person affirms. He finds a negative answer to the teleological question, 'why human existence and history.' He says that it does not make sense; it is an absurdity. Within his framework he is in the predicament of a natural scientist confronting undeniable physical events (for example, the strange happenings of flying bottles and bookcases in a house on Long Island in the early part of 1958) for which he has to conclude, perhaps, that there is no possible explanation within his framework of thought. Confronting such events, such a person would say, no doubt, that they did not make sense, that the whole situation was absurd.

There are those, of course, who refuse to ask the teleological question about human existence and history; for them both the traditional religious affirmation of the meaningfulness and worth of human existence (and the fulfillment character of history) and the pessimist's lament that it is all an absurdity are equally unintelligible. Neither answer is meaningful to them, because within their naturalistic framework of thought the question itself cannot be asked.

Yet the question seems to be humanly inescapable. The way human existence itself seems to force it upon us is prima facie evidence of the inadequacy of a framework of thought in terms of which it cannot be asked. And perhaps there are veridical religious experiences of the prescriptive requiredness of human existence.

It seems, then, that the teleological categorial scheme emerges and is more at home within a wider range of human experience than the naturalistic framework and that the former cannot be replaced by the latter. The only way metaphysical naturalism can be made at all plausible is to deny the cognitive character of all areas of experience other than that of sensory perception. Even then sensory experiences would defy the categories of naturalism. In any case, we have ample reasons, I think, for rejecting such a narrow empiricism. We must not only look to sensory perceptions and thought pertaining to them but also to our affective and conative experiences and thought pertaining to them in our attempt to formulate a correct philosophical view of the world as experienced by us. And of course we must not forget these experiences and thoughts themselves, for they are not only of or about reality but are also part of it.

# INDEX

Agent, problems of moral, 3-6
Aiken, Henry, 162-63
Approval(s), 57, 90-92, 96, 182-87, 196-98, 215-16; authority of, 161-67, 198-99; inconsistency of basic, 183-84; semantic correctness of, 183-87. *See also* Attitudes; Imperatives, basic rational
Argument(s), practical, 67, 118-19; statistical, 72-73; moral, 100, 101-2, 121-28; natural indicative, 116, 121; natural practical, 120-21, 129, 131-32, 152, 158-60, 173-74, 175, 193, 199; suppressed imperative premises of practical, 129, 135-51, 152, 153-60
Aristotle, 19, 26, 165
Attitude(s), how expressed by value-sentence, 87-92; have semantic dimension or content, 89-92, 98, 162, 168, 182-87; how we appraise moral, 92-96, 183-87, 195-98; authority of basic rational, 161-67, 198-99; cognitive claims of basic rational, 162, 180-87, 192, 195-98; the basic rational, 180-81. *See also* Approvals
Ayer, A. J., 41, 78-79, 83, 85

Baier, Kurt, 100, 102, 125-27
Believing, semantic dimension or content of, 89, 187-88
Bentham, Jeremy, 37, 46, 47, 58, 62-64, 149-50, 182
Broad, C. D., 11-12, 38-39, 72-73

Carnap, Rudolf, 22-23
Cartesianism, ethical, 65-69, 155
Causality, naturalistic concept of, 207-14; teleological concept of, 207-14, 220-21, 222-26; mechanistic concept of (*see* Causality, naturalistic concept of)
Change, theory of, 31; naturalistic concept of, 201-24; teleological concept of, 202-14, 222-26
Critic, problems of moral, 3-6

Darwin, Charles, 223
Decision, 154-60, 169, 215-21
Deliberation, 138-39, 143, 149, 161-62. *See also* Reasoning, practical; Reasoning, moral; Decision
Desire(s), 59, 136-38, 142, 168-80, 192-93, 215; language of, 135; semantic dimension of, 136-38, 171, 172, 173; primary, 137, 162, 168, 187; character of primary, 168-80; proper object of, 170; naturalist's position on, 171; inconsistency of, 172; semantic correctness of, 173-80
Dewey, John, 33, 37, 58-61, 73, 193
Disagreement, argument from the nature of ethical, 71-76, 78
Disapproval. *See* Approvals

Ethics, 6-10, 38, 46, 69, 151; philosophy of, vii, 3, 6-10, 33, 46, 53, 69, 100, 104; commendatory theory of, 13, 14 (*see also* Hare, R. M.); emotive theory of (*see* Naturalism, emotive)